# LIVESTOCK IN ORISSA

*The Socio-Economic Perspective*

# LIVESTOCK IN ORISSA

## *The Socio-Economic Perspective*

*Edited by*

M.P.G. KURUP

MANOHAR
2003

First published 2003



ISBN 81-7304-514-3

*Published by*

Ajay Kumar Jain for
Manohar Publishers & Distributors
4753/23 Ansari Road, Daryaganj
New Delhi 110 002

*Typeset at*

Digigrafics
New Delhi 110 049

*Printed at*

Lordson Publishers Pvt. Ltd.
Delhi 110 007

# Contents

# Abbreviations

| | |
|---|---|
| ADRI | Animal Disease Research Institute |
| ADSIS | Animal Disease Surveillance System |
| ADVO | Assistant District Veterinary Officer |
| AICRP | All India Coordinated Research Project |
| AH | Animal Husbandry |
| AH & D | Animal Husbandry and Dairy |
| AI | Artificial Insemination |
| ANP | Applied Nutrition Programme |
| ARD | Animal Resource Development |
| BIS | Bureau of Indian Standards |
| BQ | Black Quarter |
| C & WW | Child and Women Welfare |
| CB | Cross Breeding |
| CBR | Calf Born Rate |
| CD & PR | Community Development & Panchayati Raj |
| CDVO | Chief District Veterinary Officer |
| Cft | Cubic Foot |
| Cht | Chart |
| CILS | Clinical Investigation Laboratories |
| CLRI | Central Leather Research Institute |
| CMIE | Centre for Monitoring Indian Economy |
| CPRs | Common Property Resources |
| Cst. Prices | Constant Prices |
| Cur. Prices | Current Prices |
| DARD | Department of Animal Resource Development |
| DAH | Director Animal Husbandry |
| DAH & VS | Department of Animal Husbandry and Veterinary Services |
| DANIDA | Danish International Development Agency |
| DCS | Dairy Co-operative Society |
| DPAP | Draught Prone Area Project |
| DRDA | District Rural Development Agency |
| ET | Embryo Transfer |

| | |
|---|---|
| EWS | Economically and Socially Weaker Sections |
| F & ARD | Fisheries and Animal Resource Development |
| FED | Federation |
| FCM | Fat Correction Method |
| FMD | Foot and Mouth Disease |
| FSAI | Frozen Semen Artificial Insemination |
| FSB | Frozen Semen Bank |
| GGGMU | Greater Ganjam Gajapati Cooperative Milk Producer's Union |
| HS | Haemorrhagic Septicemia |
| HF | Holstein Friesian |
| IBD | Infectious Bursal Disease |
| ICAR | Indian Council of Agricultural Research |
| ICDP | Intensive Cattle Development Project |
| ICMR | Indian Council of Medical Research |
| IMRB | Indian Market Research Bureau |
| ILDP | Integrated Livestock Development Project |
| IRDP | Integrated Rural Development Programme |
| ISPO | Indo-Swiss Project Orissa |
| ISS | Integrated Sample Survey |
| ITDP | Integrated Tribal Development Project |
| ITDA | Integrated Tribal Development Authority |
| K.B. | Kalahandi Board |
| LLPD | Lakh Litres Per Day |
| Lmt | Lakh Metric Tonnes |
| LN2 | Liquid Nitrogen |
| LPD | Litres Per Day |
| LSR | Livestock Sector Review |
| MADA | Modified Area Development Agency |
| MBR | Methylene Blue Reduction |
| MFAL | Marginal Farmer & Agricultural Laabour |
| Mmt | Million Metric Tonnes |
| MOET | Multiple Ovulation Embryo Transfer |
| MTPD | Metric Tonnes Per Day |
| NABARD | National Bank for Agriculture and Rural Development |
| NBAGR | National Bureau of Animal Genetic Resources |
| NCAER | National Council of Applied Economic Research |
| NDDB | National Dairy Development Board |

| | |
|---|---|
| NDP | Net Domestic Product |
| NGO | Non Governmental Organisation |
| Nicnet | National Information Communication Network |
| NPRE | National Programme for Rinder Pest Eradication |
| NSDP | Net State Domestic Product |
| NSSO | National Sample Survey Organisation |
| NWDP | National Watershed Development Programme |
| NWDPRA | National Watershed Development Programme for Rural Areas |
| OAIC | Orissa Agro Industries Corporation |
| OBPI | Orissa Biological Products Institute |
| OBR | Out break Reporting System |
| OIE | Office International Epizootica |
| OLDS | Orissa Livestock Development Society |
| OMFED | Orissa State Co-operative Milk Producers' Federation |
| OMTDC | OMFED Training and Demonstration Centre |
| OPOLFED | Orissa Poultry Producers Co-operative Marketing Federation |
| OPPI | Organisation of Pharmaceutical Producers of India |
| ORG | Operation Research Group |
| OUAT | Orissa University of Agriculture and Technology |
| OVS | Orissa Veterinary Services |
| PFA | Prevention of Food Adulteration Act |
| P & C | Planning and Coordination |
| PPR | Pestes des Petit Ruminants |
| PRIYA | People, Rural Research and Youth Action |
| PRI | Panchayati Raj Institutions |
| RD | Ranikhet Disease |
| RIR | Rhode Island Red |
| SMP | Skimmed Milk Powder |
| SPCA | Society for Prevention of Cruelty to Animals |
| SLBF | State Livestock Breeding Farm |
| SDC | Swiss Agency for Development and Co-operation |
| SDVO | Sub Divisional Veterinary Officer |
| SFDA | Small Farmer Development Agency |

| | |
|---|---|
| SIDA | Swedish International Development Agency |
| SLBP | Special Livestock Breeding Programme |
| SNF | Solids Not Fat |
| TMDD | Technology Mission on Dairy Development |
| UGS | Utkal Gomangal Samiti |
| VOTI | Veterinary Officers Training Institute |
| WLH | White Leg Horn |
| WTO | World Trade Organisation |

# Preamble

*Livestock in Orissa: The Socio-Economic Perspective* is a modified edition of the 'Report of the Steering Committee for Livestock Sector Review: 1999'. The Steering Committee was appointed by the Government of Orissa in 1998. The purpose of bringing out this special edition of the Steering Committee Report is to offer a wider range of users, facts and perspectives related to livestock in Orissa, an analysis of the sector's impact on state economy, employment potential, rural income generation, livelihoods and gender issues. The state livestock sector review itself was a very comprehensive exercise over a two year period, involving over 25 of the senior livestock specialists in the state reviewing in detail each of the livestock species involved and a series of consultations with a variety of stake holders, over three hundred of them, across the sector: farmers, livestock professionals, scientists in livestock and allied fields, economists, sociologists, environmentalists, administrators and policy makers; all in an extremely well structured participatory format. The specialists and stake holders involved are acknowledged and their details exhibited in Table G.10 in Appendix to this publication.

The Livestock Review Exercise was undertaken by the Government of Orissa, primarily as an approach to a new livestock sector policy framework for the state: as a result the attempt was to focus on the larger picture on how best Orissa can navigate it's livestock sector policies over the coming decades, so that the sector can play its appointed role in the growing, modernising state economy. The approach to policy however is well grounded in analysis and the policy frame itself leads to the action plan for sector development, species wise. This edition preserves the spirit of the Steering Committee Report and ensures that the wealth of information and analysis it contains are not lost to the users of this book

This book owes its existence to the generosity of the Government of Orissa which enabled this special edition, particularly to Shri S.C. Hota, Agricultural Production Commissioner and Shri A.K.

Tripathy, Commissioner cum Secretary, FARD. The editor of this book had the privilege of being the coordinating consultant of the Livestock Review Exercise in the state and therefore brings with him the insight gained from the extensive consultations and specialist advices under the Review Exercise. The idea of bringing out a special edition of the Steering Committee Report originated with Mr. Jan Morrenhof, the Chief Project Adviser of the Indo-Swiss NRMPO and inputs for updating the data in the Steering Committee Report for this edition came from the State Department of Animal Husbandry, the OMFED and the Liaison Consultant Dr B.N. Mohanty.

The Livestock Sector Review and the publication of this book have been facilitated by the Indo-Swiss NRM Programme Orissa and funded by the Swiss Agency for Development and Cooperation (SDC) and Intercooperation.

Editor

MAP SHOWING DISTRICTS OF ORISSA AND THEIR CODE NUMBERS (GIS MAP)

*Map not official and not to scale*

| *District* | *Code No.* | *District* | *Code No.* |
|---|---|---|---|
| Angul | 9 | Kendrapara | 18 |
| Balasore | 4 | Keonjhar | 2 |
| Barghar | 5 | Khurda | 23 |
| Bhadrak | 12 | Koraput | 26 |
| Bolangir | 14 | Kandhamal | 21 |
| Boudh | 16 | Malkangiri | 25 |
| Cuttack | 17 | Mayurbhanj | 3 |
| Deogarh | 8 | Nuapada | 13 |
| Dhenkanal | 10 | Nawarangapur | 19 |
| Gajapati | 28 | Nayagarh | 22 |
| Ganjam | 25 | Puri | 30 |
| Jagatsinghpur | 24 | Rayagada | 27 |
| Jajpur | 11 | Sambalpur | 7 |
| Jharsaguda | 6 | Subarnapur | 15 |
| Kalahandi | 20 | Sundargarh | 1 |

# 1 Orissa: History and Attributes

## 1.1 Historical Background

Ancient Orissa[1] was the land of egalitarian republicans, dating back to the seventh century BC, with a social order and political structure considerably different from that of the northern plains of the Indian subcontinent. The word 'Orissa' is the anglicised version of Odiya, derived from Odra or Udra tribes, which once inhabited the central belt of what is now modern Orissa. It was the home of ancient Utkala and Kalinga Mahajanapadas (Republics), who played a prominent role in shaping the history of the region.[2] *Vedic Sutrakara Baudhayana* in sixth century BC, mentions Kalinga as the land beyond the Vedic Fold, untouched by the Brahminical influences and the caste system, unlike other parts of ancient India. Generously endowed with mineral resources, metallurgy and use of iron tools developed quite naturally in ancient Orissa. Kalinga had irrigated agriculture and extensive rice cultivation: a model, which spread along the southern coast to Andhra and Tamil Nadu. Historical evidence confirms that ancient Orissa had a flourishing maritime trade in Stone Age metals (iron, copper and tin), cotton textiles and food stuffs, with several of the South-East Asian countries, as early as the fourth century BC. The Kalinga Era was a watershed in the history of Orissa: conquest of Kalinga in 260 BC, was the turning point in the life of Ashoka the Great; and triggered the consequent spread of Buddhism far beyond the shores of India, to Sri Lanka, South-East Asia and even to China and Japan. Decline of Orissa started around the fifteenth century ad. and the region was marginalised over time to become a land of the poor. Revival and rejuvenation of Orissa

[1] References to ancient Orissa may well include parts of Jharkhand, Southern Bengal, Chhattisgarh and northern Andhra—all of which at various times were politically integrated into the different kingdoms of ancient and medieval Orissa.

[2] Historical References are based on *Bulletins of Indian Historical Review* (*ICHR*) and *Issues of Social Science Probings* (ed. R.S. Sharma) and *The Winds of Change: Buddhism and the Maritime Links of Early South Asia*, by Himanshu Ray.

started after Indian Independence, particularly after the formation of the new state of Orissa, in the Indian Union.

## 1.2 Attributes

Orissa now is the tenth largest state in the Indian Union, located along the eastern seaboard of peninsular India on the Bay of Bengal, between 17° 48'–22° 34' N latitude and 81° 24'–87° 29' E longitude, touching West Bengal on the north-eastern tip, with Jharkhand to the north, Chhattisgarh to the west and Andhra Pradesh to the south. Scheduled areas cover nearly 45 per cent of the geographical area, 36.70 per cent of the state's land mass is under forest cover, 50.74 per cent is the total cultivable area and 4.10 per cent,

TABLE 1.1: STATE PROFILE

| *Attribute* | *Measure* |
|---|---|
| Total Area: mln ha | 15.57 |
| Total Area: km$^2$ | 155707 |
| Share in Country Area % | 4.74 |
| Districts | 30 |
| Sub Divisions | 58 |
| CD Blocks | 314 |
| Tribal Blocks | 118 |
| Cities & Towns | 138 |
| *Gram Panchayats* | 5263 |
| Villages | 51349 |
| Population 2001: Total mln | 36.70 |
| Population: Urban mln / % | 5.40 / 14.97 |
| Population: Rural mln / % | 31.21 / 85.03 |
| Population Density per km$^2$ | 236 |
| Share in Country Population % | 3.57 |
| Sex Ratio (women: Men) | 0.97 |
| Schedule Castes % | *16.20 |
| Scheduled Tribes % | *22.21 |
| Overall Literacy % | 54.63 |
| Literacy Male % | 75.95 |
| Literacy Female % | 50.97 |
| Main Work Force % Ttl Popln. | *37.53 |
| Main Work Force ( Ur / Rl) % | *11 / 89 |
| Male Workers % Work Force | *73 |
| Female Workers % Work Force | *27 |

NOTE: *Figures relate to Census of India, 1991.
SOURCE: Census of India, 2001, Series 22, Orissa.

TABLE 1.2: WORK FORCE IN AGRICULTURE AND ALLIED SECTORS

| *Category* | *1991 nos mln / (%)* |
|---|---|
| Main Work Force | 11.88 (100) |
| Cultivators | 4.60 (38.7) |
| Agri. Labourers | 2.98 (25.1) |
| Livestock etc | 0.19 (1.6) |
| Others | 4.11 (34.6) |

SOURCE: Statistical Outline of Orissa, 1997.

permanent pastures. Human population in Orissa had been growing at about 20 per cent per decade over the two decades 1971-91, but has slowed down between 1991-2001 to 15.91 per cent. Some 85 per cent of the population live in rural areas (see Table 1.1) and depend primarily on agriculture for livelihood. Sex ratio: women per one thousand males in the state, declined from 981 in 1981 to 972 in 2001, consistent with the national trend. The overall literacy rate was 54.63 per cent in 2001, male 75.95 and female 50.97. *Some 37.53 per cent of the total population constitute the main work force in Orissa: within the gender groups, 54 per cent of all adult male and 21 per cent of all women constituted the main work force. Employment scenario in Orissa is dismal: employment opportunities in the organised sector made up of the government and public sector, central as well as state; quasi government; local bodies; and industries in the private sector, together absorbed only some 7.30 per cent of the total work force. And the remaining 92.70 per cent were left to fend for themselves: self employment or casual employment. Some 63.8 per cent of the workforce depends on agriculture for their livelihood, either as cultivators or agricultural labourers (see Table 1.2). Analysis of the employment structure based on the 2001 census enumeration is in progress and the indications are that major growth in employment during the 1990s will be in the services sector. Orissa is resource rich in minerals like Chromite 98.4 per cent, Bauxite 69.7 per cent, Iron Ore 26 per cent, Coal 23 per cent, and Graphite 38 per cent (per cent figures represent Orissa's share in all India availability of these minerals); China Clay; Fire Clay; Lime Stone; Quartz; precious and semi-precious stones; Copper; Nickel and Vanadium. The state also has abundant water resources. According to the Central Ground Water Board, Orissa has 23,300 mln cft of ground water, of which only 0.5 per cent has been harnessed so far. The state has many major rivers contributing to its irrigation potential. Total rainfall averages some 1482 mm, spread over the months of June through September, including the pre-monsoon showers in May, with an average 72 rainy days in a year. The major part of the precipitation: 1137 mm, however, comes down during the months of June, July and August (53 wet days). Monsoon in Orissa is notoriously capricious and is prone to brutal excesses in both directions.

### 1.3 Levels of Poverty

Orissa, even in 2002, is one of the least developed states in the Indian union, very low in industrialisation and with very high levels of poverty, in spite of rich endowments of natural resources like land, water, livestock, manpower and minerals. Planning Commission's recent estimates for Orissa show that Orissa is one of the two poorest states in the country, along with Bihar. Per capita Income growth in real terms was marginal over the past 15 years: from Rs.1314 in 1981 to Rs.1595 in 1996-7 (see Fig.1.1) at constant prices. Distribution of land in Orissa is highly inequitable and is to a large extent the *raison d'être* for the levels of poverty in the state. There were 3.94 million operational land holdings in Orissa in 1991, of which small and marginal holdings accounted for nearly 80 per cent and the remaining 20 per cent come under the categories semi-medium, medium and large (see Table 1.3).

Including the landless (1.57 mln), total households work out to some 5.79 mln. The small and marginal farmers together owned only some 47 per cent of the total operational land (see Table 1.4), while the remaining 53 per cent belonged to the semi-medium,

Table 1.3: Distribution of Land Holdings

| *Category* | *Holding Nos '000 1986 / 1991* | *% to Total Holdings 1986 / 1991* |
|---|---|---|
| Marginal | 1868 / 2118 | 52.09 / 53.65 |
| Small | 910 / 1035 | 25.38 / 26.22 |
| S. Medium | 583 / 594 | 16.26 / 15.04 |
| Medium | 204 / 186 | 5.69 / 4.71 |
| Large | 21 / 15 | 0.58 / 0.38 |
| All | 3586 / 3948 | 100 |

Source: Statistical Outline of Orissa, 1997.

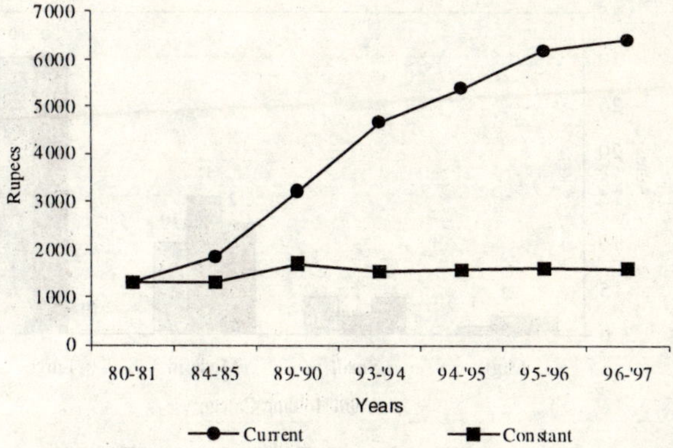


SOURCE: Economic Survey Orissa, 1998.

FIG. 1.1: PER CAPITA INCOME.

TABLE 1.4: DISTRIBUTION OF HH LAND HOLDING CATEGORY WISE 1991

| *Category* | *HH %* | *HH Nos* |
|---|---|---|
| Landless | 27.21 | 1574700 |
| Marginal | 43.45 | 2515500 |
| Small | 17.97 | 1034600 |
| S Med | 8.77 | 507500 |
| Medium | 2.48 | 143500 |
| Large | 0.22 | 12300 |
| Total | 100 | 5788200 |

SOURCE: Land & Livestock Holding Survey, NSSO.

TABLE 1.5: AREA OWNED DISTRIBUTION AND LAND HOLDING CATEGORY WISE

| *Category* | *Area in '000 Ha 1986 / 1991* | *% to Total Area 1986 / 1991* |
|---|---|---|
| Marginal | 919 / 1045 | 17.47 / 19.73 |
| Small | 1273 / 1426 | 24.20 / 26.93 |
| S. Medium | 1568 / 1561 | 29.80 / 29.47 |
| Medium | 1167 / 1012 | 22.18 / 19.11 |
| Large | 334 / 252 | 6.35 / 4.76 |
| All | 52.61 / 5296 | 100 |

SOURCE: Statistical Outline of Orissa, 1997.

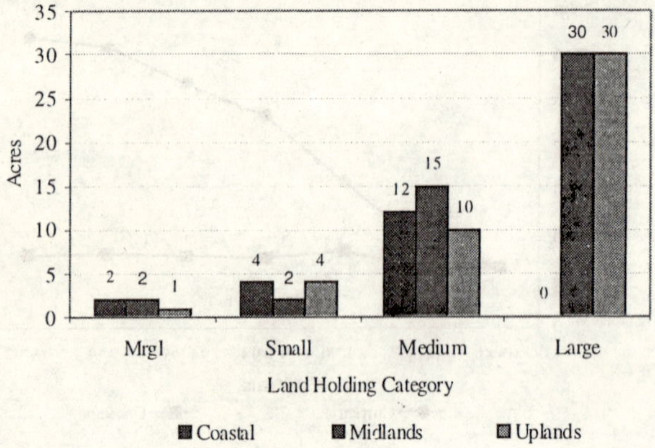


SOURCE: LSR Field Survey, 1999.

FIG. 1.2: INDIVIDUAL HOLDING SIZE IN ACRES.

medium and large farmers (see Table 1.5). Over the years there has been progressive shrinking of the holdings, reducing the average holding size: 1.34 ha in 1991 to 1.30 ha in 1996 see Fig. 1.2). Actual land holding size varies widely among the holding categories and the zones. The poverty ratio in the state was assessed as some 49 per cent in 1993-4, but with the modifications in the recall period for estimation of private consumption(expenditure in 2000, the ratios of poverty in all states have undergone drastic revision and for Orissa the ratio is has come down to around 30.

## 1.4 AGRICULTURE

Orissa can be classified according to altitude into three zones: low: 26 per cent; medium: 34 per cent; and high altitude: 40 per cent (Table 1.2 in Appendix). Agro-climatically, the state is divided into ten zones: see map on p. 23. The characteristics of the different agro-climatic zones are presented in Table 1.1 in the Appendix. Total cultivable land is 7.90 mln ha. In 1996 the net sown areas was some 6.21 mln ha and gross cropped area 9.67 mln ha (see Table 1.6). Gross irrigated area was 2.44 mln ha, some 25 per cent of the gross cropped area and 7.23 mln ha, 75 per cent, rain fed. The share of the different sources of irrigation was: major and medium irrigation projects: 60 per cent; minor irrigation projects (flow): 20 per cent; and lift irrigation projects: 20 per cent. Agriculture and animal

AGRO-CLIMATIC ZONES IN ORISSA (GIS MAP)

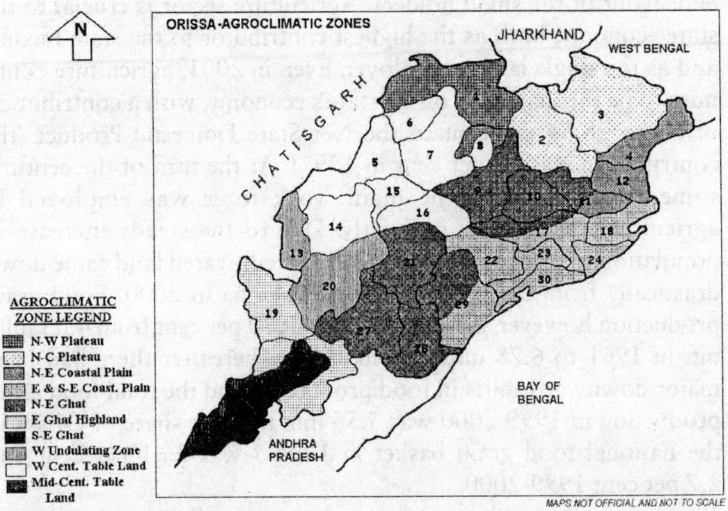


| *District* | *Code No.* | *District* | *Code No.* | *District* | *Code No.* |
|---|---|---|---|---|---|
| Angul | 9 | Cuttack | 17 | Jajpur | 11 |
| Balasore | 4 | Deogarh | 8 | Jharsaguda | 6 |
| Barghar | 5 | Dhenkanal | 10 | Kalahandi | 20 |
| Bhadrak | 12 | Gajapati | 28 | Kendrapara | 18 |
| Bolangir | 14 | Ganjam | 25 | Keonjhar | 2 |
| Boudh | 16 | Jagatsinghpur | 24 | Khurda | 23 |
| Koraput | 26 | Nayagarh | 22 | Kandhamal | 21 |
| Puri | 30 | Malkangiri | 25 | Rayagada | 27 |
| Mayurbhanj | 3 | Sambalpur | 7 | Nuapada | 13 |
| Subarnapur | 15 | Nawarangapur | 19 | Sundargarh | 1 |

SOURCE: Courtesy N.S.R. Sastry.

TABLE 1.6: AREA UNDER CULTIVATION

| *Crop* | *Area '000 ha* | *Output '000 mt* |
|---|---|---|
| Cereals | 4732 | 6370 |
| Oulses | 897 | 413 |
| Oil Seeds | 458 | 243 |
| Spices & Condiments | 184 | 214 |
| Fibre Crops | 64 | 335 |
| Vegetables | 744 | 6475 |
| Sugar Cane | 27 | 1594 |
| Tobacco | 9 | 7 |

SOURCE: Statistical Outline of Orissa, 1997.

husbandry in Orissa, as in the rest of India, is predominantly the endeavour of the small holders. Agriculture sector is crucial to the state economy, both as the highest contributor to the state income and as the single largest employer. Even in 2001, agriculture continues to be the main stay of the state's economy, with a contribution of about 28.54 per cent to the Net State Domestic Product (the contribution was 31 per cent in 1997). At the turn of the century, some 65 per cent of the main work force was employed in agriculture, directly or indirectly. Due to the steady increase in population, the per capita availability of cultivated land came down drastically from 0.39 ha in 1951 to 0.17 ha in 2000. Food grain production however, increased by about 70 per cent from 4.03 mln. mt. in 1961 to 6.78 mln. mt. in 1996. Thereafter there had been major downward shifts in food production and the total food grain production in 1999-2000 was 5.56 mln mt. The share of Orissa in the national food grain basket in 1994-5 was 3.61 per cent and 2.7 per cent 1999-2000.

## 1.5 Animal Husbandry

Next to agriculture, animal husbandry is the major source of supplementary income for rural households. Livestock production has always been an integral part of the rural livelihood systems in Orissa, all through the known history of the state. The predominant farming system in Orissa is the mixed crop-livestock farming system and over 90 per cent of all farms of all categories conform to this farming system. The livestock wealth of Orissa is impressive in numbers across all species (see Table 1.7), constituting a natural

Table 1.7: Livestock Population

| *Livestock Population* | *Numbers mln* |
|---|---|
| Cattle | 13.81 (59.17) |
| Buffalo | 1.38 (5.94) |
| Sheep | 1.76 (7.56) |
| Goat | 5.77 (24.73) |
| Pig | 0.60 (2.57) |
| Others | 0.00 (0.00) |
| Total Livestock | 23.33 (100) |
| Total Poultry | 18.43 (100) |

Note: Figures in ( ) are % to total LS.
Source: State Livestock Census, 2001.

resource base with immense livelihood implications, even though productivity levels are very low. Livestock holding in Orissa is equitable as over 80 per cent of all livestock are owned by the marginal/small holders and the landless. Some 80 per cent of all rural households own livestock of one species or the other, or a combination of some of them, cattle being the most popular and therefore the preponderant species. The main livestock products in the state are milk, meat, egg, bone, skin, hide, offal, manure (dung) and draught power. The output of major livestock products in the state in 2000 was: milk 0.85 mln mt; meat 43000 mt; eggs 822 mln; manure 19.04 mln mt and draught power 194 mln kWh.

# 2 Livestock in the Economy of Orissa

## 2.1 Livestock Wealth of Orissa

Livestock production in Orissa, like its agriculture, is the endeavour of the small holders. There are hardly any big players in the sector, except in poultry in recent years. Next to agriculture, livestock is the major source of supplementary income for rural households. Livestock production has always been an integral part of the rural livelihood systems in Orissa, all through the known history of the state. Over 80 per cent of all households own livestock of one species or the other. Livestock production takes place in millions of tiny and small holdings (3.68 mln) scattered throughout the length and breadth of the state, 80 per cent of them marginal, small or landless. There has been little or no change in the livestock production organisation in the state over the past five decades of planned development. Along with agriculture, livestock continues to be the prime livelihood of the vast majority of the rural households. In 1995 Orissa had a total livestock population of 24.27 mln, but by 2001

Table 2.1: Livestock and Poultry Population

| *Livestock* | *Nos mln 1995/2001* | *% Change* |
|---|---|---|
| Cattle | 14.77 / 13.81 | -6.49 |
| Buffalo | 1.65 / 1.38 | -16.36 |
| Sheep | 1.87 / 1.76 | -5.88 |
| Goat | 5.41 / 5.77 | +6.65 |
| Pig | 0.53 / 0.60 | +13.21 |
| Others | 0.00 / 0.00 | 0.00 |
| Total Livestock | 24.27 / 23.33 | -3.67 |
| *Poultry* | | |
| Fowl Indigenous | 12.49 / 13.45 | +7.69 |
| Fowl Improved | 2.70 / 4.11 | +52.22 |
| Duck | 0.72 / 0.65 | -9.72 |
| Others | 0.10 / 0.22 | +120 |
| Total Poultry | 16.01 / 18.43 | +15.12 |

Source: State Livestock Census, 1995 and 2001.

this has come down to 23.33 mln on account of the losses suffered during the devastating cyclone in October 1999. The impact of the cyclone on the populations of cattle, buffalo, sheep and duck, has brought about major decline in their numbers, while goat, pig and poultry have shown remarkable resilience and have not only made up the loss but also made impressive gains in their numbers (see Table 2.1). Improved fowls (commercial hybrids) increased by over 52 per cent in their numbers over the 1995 population, indicating energetic growth of the organised poultry industry in Orissa, between 1995-2001. Total estimated asset value of the livestock sector as on March 2002 is Rs.42.09 bln, at current prices: a decline in value by Rs.2.29 bln (5.16 per cent) from Rs.44.38 bln, in 1998. This decline is substantially on account of the killer cyclone. The species wise contribution to asset value and the unit value of each are presented in Table 2.1 in the Appendix. More than half the total asset value of the livestock sector in Orissa is on account of the adult male among cattle, clearly indicating the primacy of the working male in the livestock/farming systems in Orissa.

## 2.2 Stock Holding and Equity

Scattered holdings, very small numbers per holding and low productivity for all species are the hallmark of the traditional livestock production system in Orissa. Livestock holding in Orissa appears to be less iniquitous than land holding. Marginal farmers, small holders and landless, together own over 80 per cent of all livestock (except buffalo and pig) and over 90 per cent of the *desi* poultry (see Table 2.2 and Figs. 2.1, 2.2, 2.3 and 2.4) and they constitute the *core livestock production sector* in Orissa. Over 80 per cent of the milch animals including crossbred cows, are owned by

Table 2.2: Ownership of Livestock in Orissa (%)

| *Land Holding* | *Cattle* | *Buff.* | *Sheep & Goat* | *Pig* | *Poultry* |
|---|---|---|---|---|---|
| Landless | 8.62 | 0.00 | 25.08 | 0.00 | 44.66 |
| Marginal | 64.79 | 22.75 | 51.04 | 25.49 | 39.49 |
| Small | 17.73 | 28.57 | 11.37 | 31.37 | 8.01 |
| S. Medium | 5.83 | 14.29 | 8.26 | 31.37 | 4.53 |
| Medium | 2.64 | 33.33 | 3.43 | 11.76 | 2.49 |
| Large | 0.22 | 1.06 | 0.47 | 0.00 | 0.82 |

Source: See note 2 on page 29.

this core sector. Pigs and buffalo tend to concentrate in small and medium holdings. Gains from livestock production are for this reason, more equitably distributed than income from land. Investments in the development of livestock, is therefore the critical pathway to rural prosperity, in Orissa, as in all of India. The pattern of animal holding varies considerably among individuals, land holding categories and regions. Larger farmers tend to hold larger numbers, but not in proportion to their land holding size. Fowls account for over 95 per cent of total poultry. Among fowls, *desi*

LIVESTOCK HOLDING PATTERN

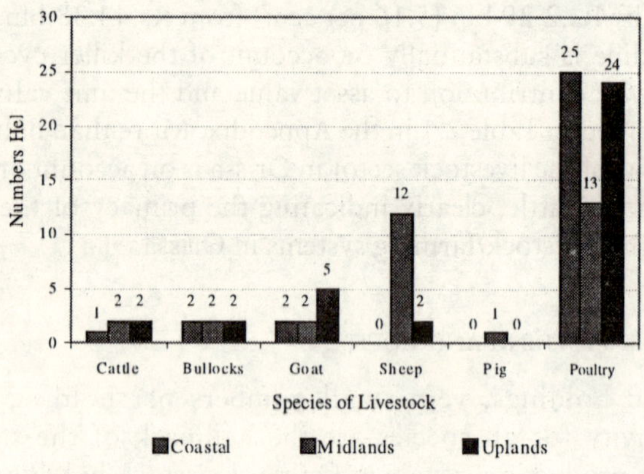


FIG. 2.1: INDIVIDUAL HOLDING (NOS).

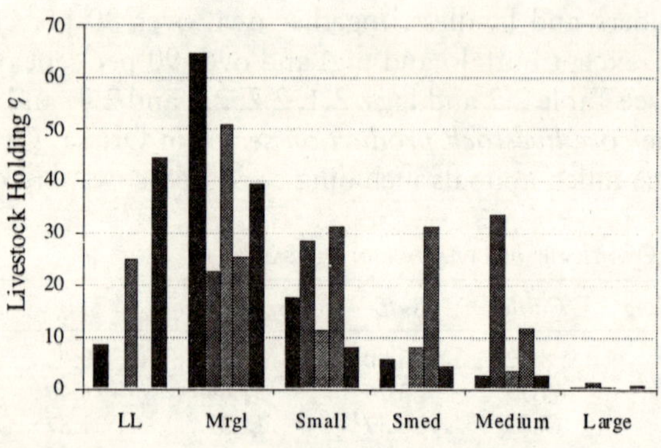


FIG. 2.2: LAND HOLDING CATEGORY WISE (%).

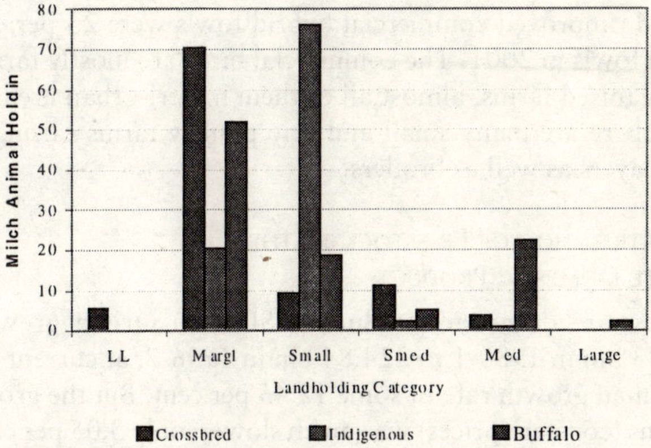


FIG. 2.3: MILCH ANIMAL HOLDING (%).

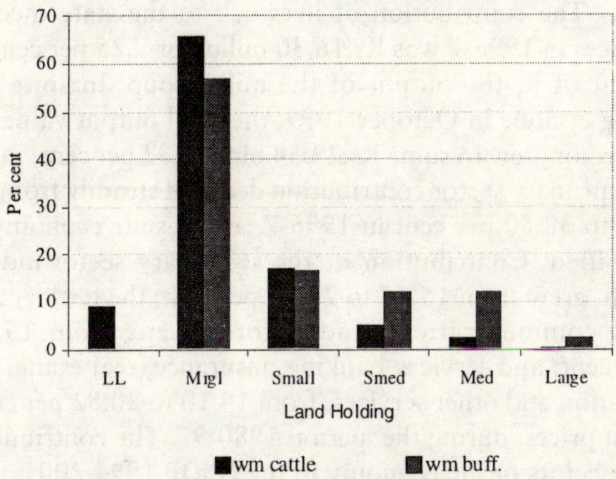


FIG. 2.4: WORK ANIMAL HOLDING (%).

NOTES: 1. Distribution, Land Holding Category wise, is based on *Land & Livestock Holding Survey* 1992, NSSO Report No. 408, 1997, and total numbers in each category on Orissa State Livestock Census 2001 for these charts as well as the Table above.

2. Individual Holding: are Modes in Frequency Distribution based on *Orissa LSR Field Survey* 1999.

fowls constitute 75 per cent of all fowls and they are all held in the backyard. Improved commercial hybrid fowls were 23 per cent of the total fowls in 2001. The commercial birds are mostly farmed in large organised farms, almost all of them in peri-urban areas, even though there are many small and tiny poultry farms raising commercial layers as well as broilers.

## 2.3 Contribution of Livestock to the State Domestic Product

The net state domestic product (NSDP) in Orissa grew from Rs. 34.43 bln in 1980-1 to 224.84 bln in 1996-7, at current prices, at an annual growth rate of some 12.45 per cent. But the growth in real terms (constant prices) was much slower: only 3.05 per cent per annum. Agriculture including livestock continues to be the main stay of the state economy with its contribution of about 31 per cent at current prices in 1996-7 (total primary sector at current prices: 38.50 per cent), highest among all sectors. The primary sector is made up of agriculture, livestock, forestry, fishery, mining and quarrying. The contribution of livestock to the state income at current prices in 1996-7 was Rs.16.30 billion or 7.25 per cent: over 65 per cent of it, the output of the milk group. In spite of the devastating cyclone in October 1999, the total output value of the livestock sector grew to some Rs.23.34 bln (+4.32 per cent) in 1999-2000. The primary sector contribution declined steadily from 52.33 in 1980-1 to 38.50 per cent in 1996-7, as the state economy grew and diversified. Contribution of the secondary sector-industrial production, grew from 15.45 to 21.32 per cent; the tertiary sector-transport, communication, trade, storage, etc. from 15.12 to 20.82 per cent; and services-banking, insurance, real estate, public administration and other services, from 14.10 to 20.82 per cent, all at constant prices, during the period 1980-97. The contribution of the major sectors of the economy to the NSDP 1994-2001 and the product wise values of livestock output 1999-2000, are presented in Table 2.2 and 2.3 respectively, in the Appendix.

## 2.4 Supply of Livestock Products

Livestock sector outputs are milk, meat, wool, eggs, poultry, draught power and manure. In addition there are co-products like skin, hide and by-products of animal origin. Milk production in Orissa grew by 166 per cent: from 0.32 mln mt in 1980 to some 0.85 mln mt in 1999-2000, at a simple average annual growth rate of 8.28 per cent, even though annual growth rates from one year to the next, fluctuate violently. The total milk production in 2000-1 was some 883520 mt, enabling a per capita availability of 67 g per day. Orissa however consumes substantial quantities of milk solids, mostly powders and infant foods, imported from other states in India (some 170000 mt liquid milk equivalent), raising the per capita consumption to 80 g per day. Meat production (not including poultry meat) grew by 126 per cent: from 16843 mt to 38380 mt (*Economic Survey* 2002), during the same period. The annual growth rate and the proportion of the various kinds of meat, varied from year to year. Some 70 per cent of the human population in Orissa are non-vegetarians. The per capita per non-vegetarian (approximately 25 mln) availability of meat in 2001 was 1.54 kg per year. Egg production in Orissa grew from 348 mln to some 933 mln, some 168 per cent, between 1980 and 2001. Per capita availability in 2001 was 26 eggs per year assuming that the entire population consume eggs: however the per capita consumption was 35 eggs per year, considering the supply of some 350 mln eggs annually imported from other states (344 mln eggs in 1997: *Report of the Poultry Group,* LSR Studies 1998). Broiler production in the state commenced in the late 1980s and has grown to some 16.5 mln broiler birds a year, by 2001. There is considerable export of broilers from the state to neighbouring states. In 1998 the LSR team reported export levels of some 3.6 mln, however no data is available for current levels of export. For purposes of calculation the current export is reckoned some 5 mln birds per year and consumption in the state 11 mln. *Desi* poultry meat production was 5696 mt in 1997 (DAH & VS statistics), a per capita availability of 237 g, per non-vegetarian. Meat production from broilers and culled birds from the commercial layer farms was some 10400 mt in 1997: 432 g per year per capita non-vegetarian and total poultry meat consumption per capita non-vegetarian 669 g per year. By 2002, however, because of the sizable increases in the supply of broiler and poultry meat on account of the increased commercial layer population, per capita consumption of poultry meat is reckoned as some 900 g per capita non-vegetarian.

## 2.5 Demand for Livestock Products and Elasticity

Orissa has one of the lowest per capita incomes among all states in the country. Private consumption expenditure on livestock products as well as cereals, is much lower in Orissa than the national average. Nutritional demand of milk in Orissa worked out on the basis of the ICMR norm of 220 g per cap per day, would be some 2.94 mln mt in 2001. The economic demand for milk in Orissa, is worked out using the annual growth rate of private consumption expenditure (4.2 per cent) and the expenditure elasticity of milk (1.45 per cent). Estimate of the nutritional demand of meat too is based on ICMR norms. The economic demand of meat, egg and fish as a group, as well as expenditure elasticity of demand for the group, were both worked out on the basis of private consumption expenditure data (fiftieth round NSSO 1993-4), for Orissa and all India (see Table 2.3). The projected demand for this group by 2006 is some 5.24 lkh mt. Private domestic consumption expenditure on meat, eggs and fish are higher than on milk in Orissa: while all India, the expenditure on milk had always been higher than on meat, egg and fish. Consumption of milk and meat in Orissa had grown with availability, but has not reached their per capita potential. All livestock products are both income and price elastic in Orissa. Demand for all livestock products is highly expenditure elastic in rural Orissa (see Table 2.4)

Table 2.3: Private Consumption Expenditure as % to Total HH Expenditure on Food Items

| *Item* | *Orissa* *Urban / Rural* | *India* *Urban / Rural* |
|---|---|---|
| LS Products | 9.9 / 6.5 | 13.20 / 12.80 |
| Milk | 4.9 / 2.4 | – |
| Meat | 5.0 / 4.1 | – |
| Cereals | 38.90 / 19.90 | 24.20 / 14.00 |

Source: National Informatics Network, NDDB.

Table 2.4: Expenditure Elasticity of Demand for Livestock Products: Orissa/India

| *Expenditure Elasticity* | *Milk* | *Meat, Egg and Fish* |
|---|---|---|
| Urban | 1.45 / 1.19 | 1.42 / 1.19 |
| Rural | 2.12 / 1.75 | 1.28 / 1.08 |

Source: National Informatics Network, NDDB.

TABLE 2.5: SUPPLY AND DEMAND OF LIVESTOCK PRODUCTS: ORISSA

| *Product* | *Supply 1996* | *Consumption / Yr 2001* | *Nutritional Demand 2006* | *Economic Demand 2006* |
|---|---|---|---|---|
| Milk | 1.02 mln mt* | 27.38 kg per capita | 3.02 mln mt | 1.52 mln mt |
| Meat (All) | 0.66 lmt | 2.62 kg per capita NV | 1.41 lmt | 2.07 lmt |
| Egg | 1166 mln** (0.58 lmt) | 32 nos (1.60 kg) per capita | – | 1500 mln (0.76 lmt) |

NOTES: * includes the equivalent of 1.7 lmt of milk imported from other states;
** includes 344 mln eggs imported from other states.

SOURCE: Nutritional Demand: Orissa LSR 1999; Economic Demand: National Informatics Network, NDDB.

(expenditure elasticity of demand: over 2) and rising incomes state wide (3.07 per cent per annum in real terms), therefore, will raise consumption levels of all livestock products, assuring healthy demand growth in the state (see Table 2.5).

## 2.6 PRICES OF LIVESTOCK PRODUCTS

Wholesale price indices for Orissa was not available and hence price analysis of livestock products (see Table 2.6) based on national indices were carried out for the sake of completeness of the macro economic analysis. Relative price of milk was lower during 1981-96 vis-à-vis prices of food articles, but marginally higher than prices of all commodities. Milk prices grew at a simple annual average of 8.4 per cent during this period, compared to 9.0 per cent for food articles and 8.3 per cent for all commodities. Relative prices of mutton were high all throughout the period 1981-96 and mutton prices grew sharply at 11.5 per cent per annum. Relative prices of

TABLE 2.6: INDEX NUMBERS PF WHOLESALE PRICES (BASE 1981-2 = 100)

| *Commodity* | *1982-3* | *1985-6* | *1990-1* | *1995-6* | *AGR* %* |
|---|---|---|---|---|---|
| All Commodities | 104.9 | 125.4 | 182.7 | 295.5 | 8.3 |
| Food Articles | 111.1 | 134.1 | 200.6 | 335.7 | 9.0 |
| Milk | 110.6 | 140.4 | 209.2 | 313.8 | 8.4 |
| Egg | 108.9 | 125.0 | 160.0 | 272.2 | 15.0 |
| Poultry Meat | 117.4 | 139.9 | 158.5 | 256.8 | 6.5 |
| Mutton | 107.8 | 142.3 | 219.0 | 436.3 | 11.5 |

NOTE: * Simple Annual Growth Rate.

SOURCE: AHS Series 6, Dept AH & D, GOI, 1997.

poultry meat were marginally higher than milk prices to begin with, but dropped below milk prices by 1985. Poultry meat prices grew at a modest rate of 6.5 per cent per annum-far slower than milk, food articles and all commodities, during the period. Though the relative prices of eggs were always lower than milk, food articles and all commodities during the entire period, egg prices grew at a much higher rate of 15 per cent annually. Retail prices of livestock products in the major markets in Orissa are exhibited in Table 2.4 in the Appendix.

## 2.7 Employment in Livestock Sector

Agriculture including animal husbandry continued to be the largest employer in Orissa even in 1998. Some 65 per cent of the main work force in Orissa (7.77 mln workers) was involved with livestock either as owners or as hired labourers, in 1991. Aneja et al. (1980) estimated that 130 man-days per year are required for the care and management of one milch animal, together for all activities including grazing and fodder collection. The LSR macro economic study (1998) reports an average of 110 man-days of employment per year, for livestock keeping families in Orissa. This in 1996 would add up to some 325 million man-days of total employment for the care and management of livestock in Orissa. Traditionally the chores related to care and management of livestock, in livestock owning households are shared between the men and women in the family: milking of milch animals, grazing of animals in commons or forests, movement of animals to markets and handling of animals for AI or health care are the chores for men; while women attend to fowls, pigs, goats, stall feeding of all animals and cleaning. The distribution and growth of rural employment, across different sectors all India, is presented in Table 2.5 in the Appendix. Information of a similar nature for Orissa is not available. On all India basis livestock sector accounted for 6.6 per cent of the total rural employment (principal employment) in 1987-8. While total rural employment grew at an annual rate of 1.75 per cent between 1975-88, employment in the livestock sector grew at the rate of 4.5 per cent per annum over the same period. The employment elasticity of output is 0.91 in the livestock sector as against 0.41 for the rest of agriculture.

## 2.8 Impact of the Livestock Sector on Rural Income

Traditionally livestock provide the much needed supplementary income to farmers all over India and Orissa is no exception. Next to crop production, animal husbandry is the most important income generating activity, supporting livelihood. Over 80 per cent of the rural households in Orissa keep livestock of one species or the other and earn incomes out of them. Orissa was included in a nation wide study on dairy systems, carried out by the National Council of Applied Economic Research (NCAER) in 1990. The stratified sample size in Orissa comprised 22 villages and 317 households, in the operation flood districts in the state. On the basis of the study, the NCAER reported that revenue from sale of milk alone accounted for over 40 per cent of the household income in the eastern region (see Table 2.7). Household incomes in Orissa, from the different species of livestock and their produces vary with the species farmed, but added up to more than 30 per cent of the total income. The averages represent income from the respective species, accruing to households keeping them (see Table 2.8). None of the species have performed to their full potential, as feed and management conditions

TABLE 2.7: ANNUAL HOUSEHOLD CASH INCOME BY DIFFERENT SOURCES (%)

| *Zones* | *Crops* | *Dairying* | *Others* |
|---|---|---|---|
| East Zone | 29.04 | 40.43 | 30.52 |
| North Zone | 48.65 | 31.57 | 19.79 |
| West Zone | 44.91 | 34.33 | 20.76 |
| South Zone | 65.24 | 20.91 | 13.86 |

NOTE: Figures relate to All Households in the Districts Studied.
SOURCE: NCAER, Impact Evaluation of Operation Flood, 1999.

TABLE 2.8: HOUSEHOLD INCOME FROM LIVESTOCK IN ORISSA, 2000

| *Species* | *No. of HH** | *Ave. Annual Income (Rs.)* |
|---|---|---|
| Bovines: Milk / Live Animals | 2.39 mln | 5150.00 |
| Sheep & Goat: Live Animals | 1.98 mln | 1515.00 |
| Pig: Live Animals | 0.23 mln | 1304.00 |
| Poultry Meat / Live Birds (Back Yard) | 2.24 mln | 1205.00 |
| *Desi* Eggs (Back Yard) | 2.24 mln | 482.00 |

NOTE: *Number of HHs Keeping the Respective Species of Livestock.
SOURCE: LSR 1999: Figures updated to 2000.

prevailing in the villages are poor and therefore there is immense scope for productivity enhancement and incremental incomes, for the farm households from their livestock.

## 2.9 Women in Livestock Sector

Labour input required in the traditional farming systems in the country for livestock keeping is that of low quality and often not skilled. 'More often than not, in such low productivity framework, livestock maintenance is relegated to those persons in the labour force whose opportunity cost is low' (NCAER). In most parts of India the bulk of the chores related to care and management of livestock, in livestock owning households, therefore fall on the shoulders of the family women and children. The NCAER study, as a general assessment reports that almost 90 per cent of all household chores related to family livestock are carried out by the women in the family. Hired labour is seldom employed in livestock production. The NCEAR study also reports that, in the eastern region, there appears to be considerable deviation from this national trend. For example, among the livestock keeping households, adult female labour hours/days, are as high as (see Table 2.9) 63 per cent of adult male hours/days, in the west zone; and as low as 13 per cent in the east zone. Female labour, in the east zone, participate the least in dairy related activities. The LSR field survey (April-May 1999) reported the general work sharing pattern within the family, in livestock owning households. Depending on the nature of the terrain

Table 2.9: Sharing of Household Chores for Livestock (%)

| *Daily Chores* | *Men* | *Women* | *Children* |
|---|---|---|---|
| Feeding | 40 | 60 | 8 *** |
| Watering | 39 | 61 | 0 |
| Grazing + | 72 | 13 | 15 |
| Cleaning | 11 | 68 | 6 *** |
| Milking | 72 | 28 | 4 *** |
| Sale of Milk | 82 | 18 | 10 *** |
| Attending Sick Animals* | 86 | 12 | 2 |
| Detection of Heat** | 45 | 55 | 0 |

Notes: * Occasional work, **No Special Time needed, ***Only in Uplands, + Animals sent for Grazing unattended.

Source: LSR Field Survey, 1999.

(coastal, midland, upland), there were considerable differences in husbandry practices and this was seen to influence work sharing among the family members. What was clear, however, was that unmindful of the location of the farm household, certain tasks related to the care and management of livestock were more gender specific than others. For example, feeding, watering and cleaning were predominantly chores for family women; grazing, sale of milk and attending to sick animals including taking them to the veterinary dispensary were men's tasks; while activities like milking and heat detection, even feeding and watering to an extent, are shared among men and women in varying proportions. Decision making on matters related to livestock are shared between the husband and wife in varying degrees, depending on the issue involved. Women's share in decision making in dairy related activities in the family, formed an important part of the ISPO gender study 'Role of Women in Animal Husbandry in Orissa', concluded in March 1999. The study concludes that women in Orissa are enormously influential in shaping decisions in their private family domain, on almost all matters related to livestock keeping, although these decisions are often expressed/ acted upon in public by the men in the family. What comes out loud and clear from this study is that women are the bedrock of stability in rural Oriya families; that all family decisions concerning family welfare (particularly those related to family livestock) are balanced in scope and content by the family women; and that targeting women as the development partner in all future animal husbandry development projects will be the key to project success. The patriarchal tradition in the rural society and the succession laws in Orissa, exclude women from inheriting land and this in turn denies them access to institutional credit. Social structure of the rural families discourage women from acquiring skills, as training for such skills require them to be away from home for days together. The patriarchal ambience of the institutional set up in the livestock sector is not conducive to sectoral development as it is unable to reach out to rural women and often ignores their rightful claim to knowledge acquisition and empowerment. A recent development in the livestock sector in Orissa, concerning empowerment and participation of women is the rapid growth in the number of all women managed dairy co-operative societies under the OMFED (330 by end 1998). The OMFED now has a separate, gender-sensitised group looking after empowerment of rural women. The gender study conceptualised the relative role of the genders in livestock development and management in Orissa, as follows:

CONCEPT DIAGRAM

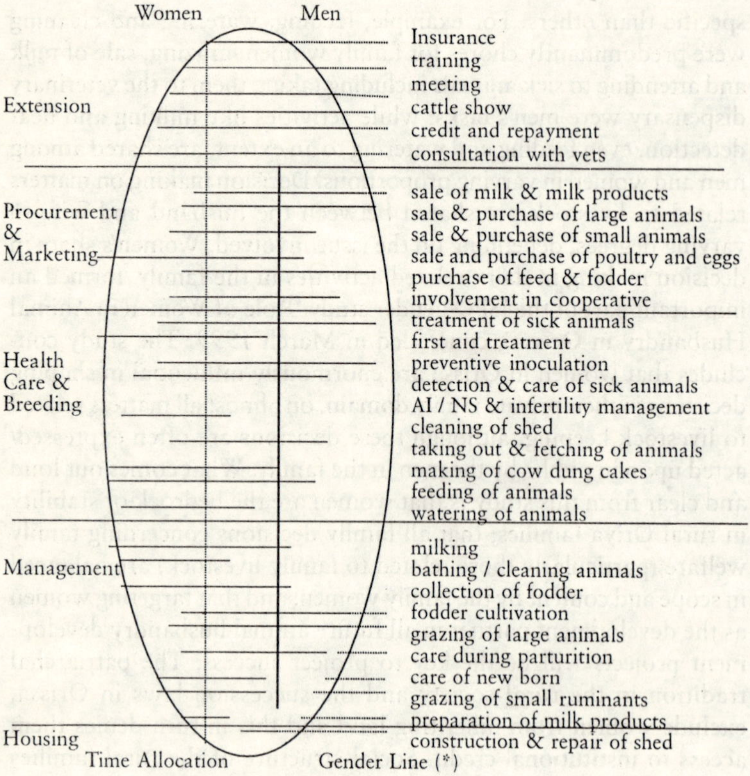


NOTES: (*) Weightage for Gender Roles

- Time spent
- Decision on allocation of (scarce) resources
- Choice between alternatives
- Extend of stake (importance attached to income)
- Knowledge and its transmission
- Risk taking
- Thinking and worrying

## 2.10 Credit in Livestock Sector

Credit in the livestock sector comes from both the traditional as well as the formal channels. Formal channels usually handle the credit associated with specific schemes of the government for assistance to the economically and socially weaker sections (EWS), who form the prime target group for credit. The formal credit institutions normally handle the government's scheme credit in rural Orissa and there are some 5476 of them (see Table 2.10). National Bank for Agriculture and Rural Development (NABARD) is the apex rural credit development institution for agriculture and rural development. Its main function is to refinance rural credit institutions like co-operative banks, commercial banks for rural projects and regional rural banks; and to promote integrated rural development. Animal husbandry sector is an allied activity along with fishery. Livestock is not NABARD's thrust area and NABARD refinances only some 20 per cent of the livestock schemes. During 1997-8, NABARD provided a total refinance assistance of some Rs.1283.19 mln to Orissa, of which livestock sector's share was 10.03 per cent (Rs.128.76 mln): Rs.44.85 mln for dairy development; Rs.20.14 mln for poultry; Rs.19.41 mln for sheep and goat and pig development; and Rs.44.36 mln for other AH activities. In spite of the large spread of credit institutions in rural Orissa, formal credit by and large still eludes the

Table 2.10: Rural Credit Institutions in Orissa 1996

| | |
|---|---|
| Primary Agricultural Credit Cooperative Societies | 2807 |
| Central Cooperative Bank Branches | 291 |
| Regional Rural Banks | 763 |
| Scheduled Commercial Bank Branches | 1615 |

Source: National Bank for Agriculture and Rural Development.

Table 2.11: Livestock Credit Need, Orissa, 1999-2002

| *Area of Credit* | *Credit Requirement Rs. mln* |
|---|---|
| Cattle & Buffalo Purchase | 1876.20 |
| Fodder Development | 232.40 |
| Poultry Development | 385.60 |
| Sheep, Goat & Pig Development | 398.00 |
| Purchase of Bullocks & Carts | 588.80 |
| Total | 3481.00 |

Source: NABARD, Bhubaneswar.

livestock holders. Formal credit channels are rigid and often insensitive, taking away all the advantages of the government's socially oriented credit schemes. In effect the cost of credit from these institutions are so high on account of the delays and the procedural wrangles involved, the rural credit seeker finds it no better than the high interest loans of the money lender. The most effective and well-entrenched credit institution in rural Orissa, serving the livestock sector, is the traditional money lender. Their influence among the rural population is still formidable and they serve almost half the credit needs of the rural livestock holders. This has been established by micro studies on rural credit in different parts of the country including the World Bank sponsored studies in rural Karnataka (1996). Flexibility, accessibility, informality and instant availability, are all factors in their favour, in spite of high interest rates and the not too pleasant recovery methods. Credit availability to the livestock sector in Orissa has not been estimated and there are no data available on the total credit disbursements in the sector, particularly from the non-formal sources. The only information available is the NABARD refinance assistance to the ground level credit institutions in 1997-8 exhibited above. NABARD projections of the credit need in the livestock sector in Orissa, during the ninth five year plan period, 1997-2002, indicate a total requirement of some Rs.3481.00 mln through formal financial institutions (see Table 2.11). The NABARD estimates deal mainly with the various scheme credit and the government's poverty alleviation schemes and do not cover the credit need from informal sources. As the general indications are that half the credit need of the livestock sector comes from informal sources, the informal credit need would also be in the region of Rs.3000 mln, for the period 1997-2002, adding up to a total credit need of some Rs.6000 mln between 1997-2002.

## 2.11 Subsidies in Livestock Sector

Under the current economic policy of the government, subsidy is not a favoured instrument in development planning. Livestock sector in India, has not attracted any direct subsidies except through the poverty alleviation programmes of the government, like IRDP. Agriculture (crop production) on the other hand, has all along been a prime candidate for subsidies, both direct and indirect. Even in the agriculture sector, policy change in the government has seen drastic reduction in subsidies in the recent times. Orissa government too has no schemes offering substantial subsidies to the livestock sector. Subsidies in agriculture in the central sector all India, was Rs.16000 (CMIE) in 2000-1 for food and fertilizer alone. There are in addition indirect subsidies for irrigation, power and a host of other inputs and services. The Central Government's policy not to tax agricultural income, tariff concessions for many of the inputs, low basic tax rates for agricultural land, all put together account for a total of over Rs.25000 crore as direct and indirect subsidies for agriculture, all India. Orissa too is a beneficiary for a proportionate share of this largesse. Livestock sector on the other hand, receives no direct subsidies except the free services of the government departments of Animal Husbandry and a small part of the subsidies (Rs.300 crore all India) available under IRDP. Many of the subsidies in agriculture, however, are in some measure beneficial to livestock production as well, like subsidies for irrigation, power, water, soil conservation, etc.

## 2.12 Livestock Insurance

Livestock Insurance Scheme was first introduced in 1974, through the four subsidiaries of the public sector insurance company General Insurance Corporation of India (GIC is now under liquidation and the four subsidiaries are independent companies: 2001). The scheme provides insurance cover to all species of livestock and poultry. The National Commission on Agriculture has recommended livestock insurance as an input to promote investments in high quality animals. Premium rates are flexible, special rates are available for livestock coming under the government's poverty alleviation programmes. Policies normally indemnify death of livestock and in special cases even cover permanent total disability (PTD). Sum assured is 100 per cent of the market value. Master policies and discounts provide attractive offers to groups and institutions for large scale insurance cover. Insurance sector made remarkable progress in rural insurance during the two decades 1980-2000. The entire rural insurance however is only 6 per cent of the total insurance business. Though livestock insurance is yet to contribute to business profit, the scheme had considerably impacted the growth and output of the livestock sector and can claim credit in good measure, for its contribution to the modernisation of the livestock and poultry industry in the country. Details of policies and premium rates are exhibited in Table 2.6 in the Appendix.

*From April 2002, the Insurance Companies (all four of them) have withdrawn all schemes mentioned above. Because of heavy claim ratio, premium rate now is 8 per cent of the sum assured for all animals Plus 5 per cent of it as surcharge. Government Scheme Animals however continue to be insured at the concessional premium rate of 2.25 per cent.*

# 3 Milch Animals in Orissa

## 3.1 Milk Production

Milk production in Orissa involves three species of milch animals: cattle, buffalo and goat. The contribution of goat to total milk production is very small and the producing households use goat milk mostly for home consumption. Goat milk is not usually traded: if sold at all, it is as mixed milk, in cow or buffalo milk. This chapter therefore would deal with cattle and buffalo, while goat is clubbed with sheep and is discussed under small ruminants in the chapter on 'Meat Animals'. Total milk production in Orissa in 1998-9 was 7.32 lmt, less than 1 per cent of the total national production of some 74.70 mmt, making Orissa seventeenth in rank for milk production, among all states in the Indian Union. Milk, on all India basis, is the second largest crop after rice, in terms of total quantity output (milk: 74.70 mmt; rice: 86.08 mmt, in 1998-9). In Orissa too milk is indeed the second largest crop, but amounts to less than 15 per cent of the total rice production in the state (milk: 7.32 lmt; rice: 5.39 mmt, 1998-9). The contribution of the different species of animals to total milk production in the state in 1998-9 (see Fig. 3.1) was local cattle: 3.17 lmt; cross bred cattle: 2.72 lakh mt (adult breedable female crossbreds are only 0.32 mln, 7.7 per cent of the total adult female, and they account for 37 per cent of the total milk production); buffalo: 1.41 lmt; and goat: 0.028 lmt. The total milk production in the state increased to 8.84 lmt by 2001 (see Fig. 3.2). Milk production in Orissa takes place in millions of small holdings scattered across the length and breadth of the state. The average holding size is 3-4 animals of all age groups together, cattle or buffalo or both. Milch animals constitute an integral component of the livelihood mechanism of the rural poor and over 80 per cent of the milch animals in the state are owned by marginal/small farmers and the landless. There are very few large cattle or buffalo holdings in the state.

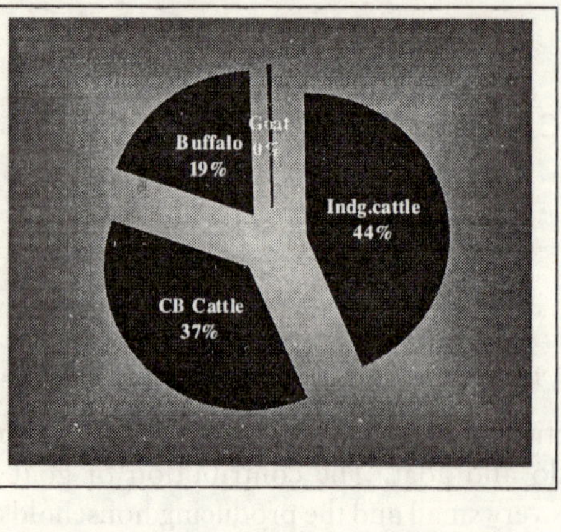


FIG. 3.1: SHARE OF DIFFERENT SPECIES IN MILK PRODUCTION.

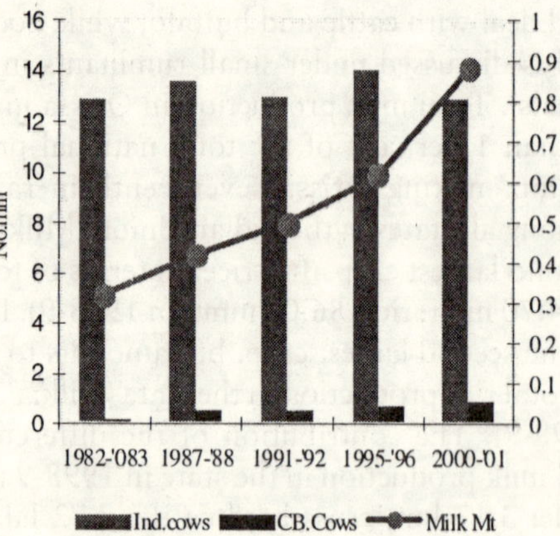


FIG. 3.2: INFLUENCE OF CB COWS ON MILK PRODUCTION.

## 3.2 PRODUCTIVITY ANALYSIS

Cattle and buffalo in Orissa are in general small (body weight: 180 kg cattle; 250 kg buffalo), nondescript and extremely low producing animals. Levels of their productivity, worked out on the basis of (i) officially declared production aggregates for each category for 1998-9 and (ii) the adult breedable female animals in each category (state livestock census 2001) are presented in the Table 3.1. Considerable differences exist in productivity levels of almost all

TABLE 3.1: BREEDABLE FEMALES WITH TOTAL MILK PRODUCTION

| *Animal Category* | *AB Female 2001 mln* | *Total Milk Production 2001 lmt* | *Milk Prodn per AB Female (/ Day g / /Year kg)* |
|---|---|---|---|
| Indg. Cattle | 3.82 Total | 3.17 | 227 g / 83 kg |
| Indg. Cattle | 1.72 in Milk | 3.17 | 505 g / 184 kg |
| CB Cattle | 0.32 Total | 2.72 | 2239 g / 850 kg |
| CB Cattle | 0.20 in Milk | 2.72 | 3726 g /1360 kg |
| Buffalo | 0.40 Total | 1.41 | 965 g / 352 kg |
| Buffalo | 0.21 in Milk | 1.41 | 1840 g / 671 kg |

SOURCE: LSR Estimates updated to 1998-9.

categories of milch animals between districts: Khurda, Puri, Bargarh, Cuttack (cattle), Sundargarh, Jajpur and Cuttack (buffalo), top in productivity. Milk production in the state district wise, along with average yield per animal and per capita availability of milk are presented in Table 3.1 in the Appendix. Performance recording of milch animals is not practiced as a tool for selection of breeding bulls in Orissa, except under the centrally sponsored progeny testing scheme for cross bred bulls. Limited data from the recording under the scheme indicate that a random sample of test daughters (cross-bred) averaged 1956.41 kg in 300 day first lactation (sample size 708 daughters, range 1800-2093 kg). See Table 3.2 in the Appendix.

## 3.3 CATTLE AND BUFFALO POPULATION: ANALYSIS AND DYNAMICS

Cattle are the preponderant species among all livestock and also the most popular: nearly all rural households own cattle (80 per cent) while some own both cattle and buffalo. Population density varies from district to district, average for the state is: cattle: 89, buffalo 9, per km$^2$, in 2001. Livestock census enumeration in the state is undertaken once in every five years, with the latest round of census in 2001. Population size of all species has increased over the years between 1956-2001: by over 50-360 per cent for different species; with pig, poultry and goat, registering the highest growth. Changes within the cattle and buffalo populations over the period 1966-2001 are exhibited in the Table 3.2.

Cattle population in Orissa has grown steadily over the period up to 1995, with significant changes in its composition, category wise. Cross bred cattle were enumerated separately only from the 1982

TABLE 3.2: CHANGES WITHIN THE CATTLE AND BUFFALO POPULATION

| *Years* | *Indigenous (nos)* | *Percent change* | *Crossbred (nos)* | *Percent change* | *Buffalo (nos)* | *Per cent change* |
|---|---|---|---|---|---|---|
| 1966 | 10,627747 | – | – | – | 12,68,837 | – |
| 1972 | 11,495602 | ( + ) 8.4 | N.A. | N.A. | 13,99,013 | (+) 1.02 |
| 1977 | 12,120767 | ( + ) 5.4 | N.A. | N.A. | 13,58,451 | (-) 2.89 |
| 1982 | 12,929788 | ( + ) 6.7 | 2,26,463 | N.A. | 13,33,208 | (-) 1.85 |
| 1991 | 13,013813 | ( + ) 0.64 | 5,63,344 | (+) 148.90 | 15,08,919 | (+) 13.17 |
| 1995 | 14,027605 | ( + ) 7.2 | 7,38,295 | (+) 31.05 | 16,52,100 | (+) 9.48 |
| 2001 | 12,898275 | (-) 8.105 | 9,12,164 | (+) 23.88 | 13,88,024 | (-) 15.98 |

census and has since grown rapidly up to 1995. Initial enthusiasm in adopting cross breeding is visible from the sharp drop in the growth of indigenous cattle (0.64 per cent) during the decade 1982-91 and the phenomenal growth in the numbers of crossbreds during the same period (149 per cent). Like wise, one can also sense the rapid disillusionment in cross breeding that set in during the next five year period 1991-5, with much slower growth in the number of cross-breds (31.05 per cent) and the reversion to indigenous cattle, which grew 7.2 per cent over 1991. Growth analysis of the cattle population between 1995 and 2001 is complicated by the impact of the 'super cyclone': in case of indigenous cattle and buffalo: the numbers have fallen back to 1982 level for cattle and to 1972 in case of buffalo. Even in the growth of crossbred cattle, the slowing down is largely on account of the loss of large numbers of crossbreds during the cyclone. Crossbred cattle account for only about 6.60 per cent (0.91 mln) of the total cattle population. The total adult female in the population is 4.14 mln (Indg: 3.82 mln and CB: 0.32) and working male 5.17 mln. Male outnumber the female among cattle (53 : 47), as farmers still breed cattle mainly for the production of work bullocks. Male crossbreds account for only some 28 to 30 per cent of the total crossbred population in all four census rounds since 1982, indicating a differential and poorer survival rate for the male, far below that of the female crossbreds. This is a reflection of the general farmer perception about crossbred male: useful neither for work nor for breeding. District wise distribution of cattle and buffalo 1995 and 2001; the livestock numbers over different census rounds and percentage change in case of each species 1956-2001; are presented in tables 3.3 and 3.4 respectively, in the Appendix.

Buffalo population is comparatively small, 1.39 million, constituting only some 6 per cent of the total livestock in Orissa. Among buffalo, growth had not been steady as in the case of cattle, but staggered and slow: -2.89 to -1.85 per cent quinquennial, until 1982. Somehow 1982 appears to be a water shed in the growth and development of buffalo as the decennial growth 1982-91 spurts from -1.85 per cent to (+) 13.17 per cent and further (+) 9.48 per cent in the next five years up to 1996. The buffalo numbers went down drastically again in 2001 by about 16 per cent, most likely on account of the impact of the 'super cyclone'. Male buffalo numbers had steadily declined over the years from 1972 up to 2001, and there was a sharp decline in numbers between 1995-2001 (10 per cent), again possibly on account of the cyclone. Buffaloes are primarily used as draught animals in Orissa—the male-female ratio in the population is 54 : 46. With the market pull for high fat milk generated by the milk collection programme of the OMFED, grading up of all local buffalo types with breeds like Murrah, has gained popularity. In 2001 improved buffaloes constituted less than 4 per cent of the total buffalo population. Households owning buffaloes only, are very few: less than 7 per cent of the total. The distribution pattern of the buffalo population in the state indicates the increasing popularity of buffalo as a milch animal, in the wake of the organised milk collection in the state. Current estimates (ISS 1998-9) show that some 22 per cent of the households, about 1.00 mln, keep buffaloes along with other animals, mostly cattle. The distribution of the cattle and buffalo populations and the number of households owning them districtwise (1995), are presented in Table 3.5 in the Appendix. National trends in cattle and buffalo population growth, is considerably different from what has happened in Orissa. The growth rate in the country for *desi* cattle was 0.11 per cent, for crossbred 5.92 per cent; and in case of buffalo 1.89 per cent (annual growth rate, inter censal—1987-92; source: *Basic Animal Husbandry Statistics*, 1997, AHS Series 6; Department of AH&D, GoI). Census tables for the 1997 round of livestock census are yet to be published by the GoI.

### 3.4 Breeds of Cattle and Buffalo in Orissa

By far the vast majority of cattle (90 per cent) and buffaloes (80 per cent), in Orissa, are nondescript. Orissa has no recognised breeds of cattle native to it and is populated with varying types of nondescript cattle. Parlakhemundi, a well known, recognised, draught breed of buffalo, is a native of Orissa. Some local strains of cattle and buffalo have acquired specific names and some amount of parochial loyalty. They all exist in small, circumscribed areas and in very small numbers. The average mature body weight of these animals: cattle: some 180 kg; buffalo 250-300 kg. The more important strains among cattle are: Binjharpuri, Ghumusari, Khariar and Mottu; and among buffalo Manda, Jirangi, Sambalpuri, Dhenkanal, Paradeep/ Kujang, Bheda, Parikuda/Chilika and Kalahandi. Most of these buffalo strains are draught varieties. None of these strains of cattle or buffalo are recognised by the ICAR / NBAGR and no detailed studies of these strains had ever been attempted. The natural breeding tracts and the main characteristics of these strains of cattle and buffalo are listed in Tables 3.6 and 3.7 in the Appendix for the sake of completeness of this analysis. Experts in the State Department of Animal Husbandry and OUAT, claim that buffalo strains in Orissa are possibly the 'swamp type' as studies by the OUAT, both by students for their Master's theses, as well as the university's finding under an ICAR research scheme on the subject, showed that local buffaloes from different parts of the state exhibited a karyotype of 2n = 48 chromosomes; where as Murrah buffaloes (riverine type) in the state had 2n = 50 chromosomes. Crosses of local buffaloes with Murrah exhibited 2n = 49 chromosomes. See Exhibit 3.8 in the Appendix. This is an area which needs immediate attention of the ICAR for a large scale study on the subject, as it may have some implications for the recommended breeding policy for buffaloes in the state-large scale grading up of local buffaloes with Murrah breed.

# 4 Draught Animals in Orissa

## 4.1 General Background

Cattle and Buffalo constitute the exclusive draught animal species in Orissa. Horse, pony, donkey and camel are not used as draught animals in the state. The overwhelming dependence on work animals for farm power in Orissa, is reflected in the composition of the cattle and buffalo populations in the state-male: female ratios in the populations are in favour of the male, 53 : 47 among cattle and 54: 46 for buffalo (livestock census 2001). At the turn of the century, Orissa is among the few remaining states in the Indian Union that is almost entirely dependent on work animals for farm power. Nationally, over the years since Independence, mechanical and electrical power sources have steadily replaced work animals from many of the farm operations like pumping, lift irrigation, haulage of goods and to an extent even from land operations like tilling and cultivation, severely circumscribing their role as a farm power source. In 1961 the contribution of work animals to the total energy requirements of the farming sector in the country was 71 per cent; by 1991 this has come down to 23 per cent[1] (see Fig. 4.1). The numbers of the male among cattle and buffalo, all India, had been steadily shrinking and the male: female ratio moving in favour of the female: 49.66 : 50.33 in cattle and 20.79 : 79.21 among buffalo, in 1992 (see Tables 4.1 and 4.2 in the Appendix). Work animal numbers in the country dropped sharply by some 12 million among cattle and by 2 million among buffalo, between 1977 and 1982. Relentless fragmentation of land holdings, reduction in size of holdings, inability of the tiny holdings to support draught animals, comparative cost advantages in hiring of tractors and power tillers for land operations, have all seriously undermined the draught animal economy in the country leading to a perceptible change in the

[1] Mittal and Srivastava, *Proceedings of the Workshop on Human and Draught Animal Power*, Harare, 1993 (FAO Rome).

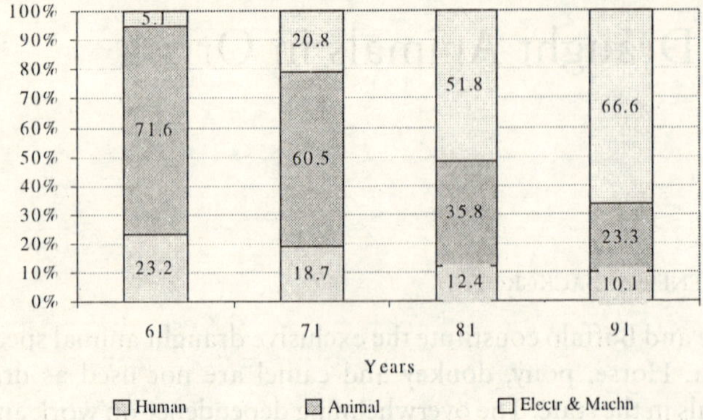


FIG. 4.1: CONTRIBUTION OF WORK ANIMALS TO FARMING SECTION

priority of the farming community in bovine breeding—from work animal production to milch animals, in most of the progressive states in India.

However, crop production in Orissa is almost entirely dependent on work animals for farm power and the primary objective of the farming community, in the breeding of cattle and buffalo consequently, continues to be the production of work animals. In Orissa too, increase in the number of land holdings due to fragmentation of land, renders small-holdings progressively unviable. Number of holdings increased from 3.41 mln to 3.94 (16 per cent), in the 20 years between 1971-91; the increase more pronounced among the 'under 2 ha' class (small and marginal holdings), from 2.60 mln to 3.16 mln, 22 per cent, during the same period. The average holding size consequently went down from 1.47 to 1.34 ha for all categories and from 0.96 to 0.78 ha, among the small and marginal holdings. These changes in land holding have on the long term, adversely impacted the draught animal economy in Orissa, have altered the work animal holding pattern, reducing the number of households owning work animals and the numbers owned per household. Draught animal economy in Orissa in general and the continued dependence of the farming sector on work animals for farm power, will therefore have considerable impact on the breeding policy for cattle and buffalo in the state.

## 4.2 Draught Animal population

Total male among cattle and buffalo were some 7.25 mln and 0.75 mln, respectively, in 2001 (see Table 4.1). Working male numbers grew steadily between 1956-95, while the working male numbers dropped sharply between 1995-2001, both among cattle (over 5 per cent) and buffalo (10 per cent). The density of work animals varies in the different agro-climatic zones: average for the state per 100 ha: 166; irrigated area 195; dry area 143; tribal and hilly area 137 (1996). This growth in working animal numbers had, however, not been even and the periods of uneven growth overlap the periods of sharp reduction in the working male numbers among cattle and buffalo in the rest of India (see Fig. 4.2).[2] The impact of the increase in the operational holdings on the draught animal holding pattern in Orissa or the economic challenge of the slow but steadily increasing onslaught of tractors and pump sets on draught animal economy has not been assessed in quantitative terms for want of authentic information. Such an analysis is perhaps possible, when the findings of the recent 'Farm Mechanisation Survey' of the State Department of Economics and Statistics, becomes available. In tandem with the overall 16 per cent increase in the number of holdings between 1971-91, there appears to have been a compensating increase in draught animal numbers in Orissa, maintaining the average draught animals at 1.55 per holding. Fragmentation of land holdings was more pronounced among the marginal and smallholdings, even more so among the marginal holdings. To interpret this paradox in rational economic terms is difficult as it has considerable social and behavioural overtones, virtually intangible. Yet the economic fallout

Table 4.1: Draught Animal Population

| *Year* | *Wrkg Male Indg. Cattle* | *% Change* | *Wrkg Male Buffalo* | *% Change* |
|---|---|---|---|---|
| 1966 | 43,96,954 | N.A. | 5,98,170 | N.A. |
| 1972 | 46,63,330 | (+) 6.06 | 6,30,348 | (+) 5.38 |
| 1977 | 48,68,676 | ( + ) 4.40 | 5,93,870 | (-) 5.79 |
| 1982 | 48,27,403 | (-) .85 | 5,60,564 | (-) 5.61 |
| 1991 | 48,39,446 | (+) 0.25 | 6,30,440 | (+) 12.47 |
| 1995 | 55,24,517 | (+) 14.16 | 6,37,118 | (+) 1.06 |
| 2001 | 52,28,519 | (-) 5.36 | 572338 | (-) 10.17 |

[2] Ibid.

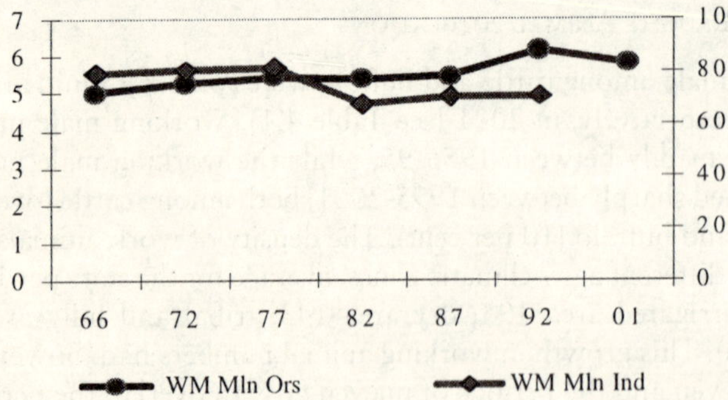


FIG. 4.2: WORKING MALES (BOVINE).

of this paradigm, are severe and adverse for the small and marginal farmers. Shrinking holdings from 0.96 ha to 0.78 ha, effective use of the bullocks limited only to some 120 days in a year, mounting costs for feeding and managing bullocks for all 365 days, access to alternative sources of farm power and yet the overriding compulsion to have absolute control over farm power, leave them no alternative, but to own draught animals. Absence of lease markets for draught animals, lack of custom hiring facilities for tractors and other farm machinery in Orissa villages, lack of enterprise and entrepreneurial skills among the richer, progressive farmers, are all manifestations of a primeval, primitive and insular rural society. Dynamic and enlightened rural leadership to help the farming community to break out of their primitive mindset is the prerequisite for the development of Orissa villages and the state's rural economy.

## 4.3 LAND UTILISATION IN ORISSA

The total geographical area of the state is some 155707 km$^2$ or 15.57 mln ha. The total cultivable land in the state is 7.90 mln ha, approximately half of its total land mass. The net sown area in 1996 was 6.21 mln ha and gross cropped area 9.67 mln ha: a cropping intensity of 1.56. The gross irrigated area was only some 2.44 mln ha, 39.29 per cent of the net sown area in 1996. While this is the current picture of the utilisation of land in the state, the scope for increasing the gross cropped area is enormous: both by increasing the net sown area to cover all the cultivable land (+20 per cent) and by increasing the gross cropped area through expanding irrigation facilities (+20 per cent). The total ground water resources of Orissa are some 23300 mln cft, according to the Central Ground Water Board and of this, only some 0.50 per cent has been tapped so far. The estimated, increased gross cropped area by 2020 is some 13.00 mln ha: an increase of roughly 35 per cent over the existing 9.67 mln ha. Farm power to crop the increased gross cropped area to an extent will come from draught animals, as the existing numbers are arithmetically adequate to cultivate over twice the existing gross cropped area. This, however, would be an oversimplification, as the spatial distribution of the millions of land holdings is likely to impose geographical limits on their expanded utilisation. Therefore, bulk of the additional energy/power load will most likely be met from electrical and mechanical sources.

### 4.4 Farm Power Need in Orissa

Power rating of the non-descript work bullocks, for the purposes of planning, is usually taken as 0.4 hp (0.33 hp weighted average)[3] of continued farm power over a six-hour work day. Work output in terms of area of land worked in one six-hour work day, by one pair of working male, is 0.33 ha, the national average for nondescript working male; or 19.80 ha in a crop year comprising 60 cropping days. Work animals in Orissa, both bullocks and male buffaloes are small in size, although the buffaloes are a shade larger than the bullocks, both in body size and body weight. Their average work rating is much lower than the average for nondescript bullocks in the rest of India. The draught animal group for the LSR project reported a work rating of 0.3 hp for the bullocks in Orissa and work output of only 0.5 acre (0.22 ha) over a four hour workday per pair or 13.2 ha per crop year of 60 cropping days. This has been confirmed by the findings of the LSR Field Survey, in April-May 1999. Cropping season in Orissa, as in most other states in the country, lasts 30 days in *kharif* and 30 days in *rabi*, a total of 60 days in a calendar year. Orissa does have some cropping in *zaid*, but the areas involved are very small and hence for the purpose of calculation of farm power need, it could be ignored. The gross cropped area in the state in 1996 was 9.67 mln ha. To cultivate

[3] Gyanendra Singh, *Impact of Draught Animal Power Use in Agriculture*, CIAE, 2000.

9.67 mln ha over 60 days of *kharif* and *rabi* seasons, in one crop year, the total work animal need would be some 0.75 mln pairs. The current work animal numbers in Orissa is nearly 3 mln pairs, or about four times the actual numbers required. The spatial distribution of the 3.94 mln operational land holdings spread throughout the length and breadth of the state makes rationalisation of the use of work animals some what difficult. The need for every farmer to keep a pair of working male, arises from his determination to hold absolute control over farm power to ensure timely cultivation, even though there are better and more economic ways of ensuring it. Even under the prevailing production organisation—production taking place in millions of tiny, widely scattered holdings—it is possible and also necessary, that farmers share their draught animals to their common advantage. The average holding size among the small and marginal farmers is only 0.78 ha, or just enough for a pair of working male to complete in 4 working days, per season.

While the most frequent work animal holding size is 2 per holding in all areas—coastal, midland and upland—in the state (LSR Field Survey April-May 1999), a large number of farmers make do with just one work animal and practice work sharing with other neighbouring farmers. This is particularly the case with those among the land less who own work animals. The land less agricultural labourers owning work animals offer team labour (man and animal) or the share-croppers among them share the work with other farmers. Among the land less, only some 6 per cent however, hold bullocks, invariably one bullock per holding. A unique work sharing arrangement locally known as 'Panchak', prevalent in the midlands, especially in Sundargarh and Bargarh districts, is a kind of unwritten agreement where five farmers come together to pool their human labour and work animals; and jointly carry out all the cropping operations in all their fields, during the season (LSR Field Survey April-May 1999). It is essentially a simple work sharing arrangement and as the name indicates is often among a group of five; but in many cases larger groups are involved. Such work sharing arrangements, while excellent as models, are the exceptions rather than the rule in the vast majority of operational holdings. Even after making allowances for all mitigating factors that might impede the rational sharing of work animals among a group of farmers, it should still be possible to use one pair of work animals for cultivating at least 3 ha of cultivable land (among small groups of farmers), during a 30 day cropping season; even though one pair is capable of cultivating some 7 ha during the same time frame. This would rationalise the work animal numbers needed, to a reasonable 1.50 mln pairs or half the present numbers.

Breeding better work animals with higher work output (a section of the small farmers and the land less however prefer the local small bullock as they are apprehensive of their ability to feed and manage a larger version); developing lease markets for work animals; and encouraging farmers to share work animals intra village or within a cluster of adjoining villages, are measures which can rapidly rationalise the work animals numbers and bring all round improvement in household economics, reducing pressure on feed and fodder and vastly improving the sustainability of all animal agriculture in Orissa. Gradual introduction of *partial mechanisation of farm operations*, along with these measures, will hasten this process to the advantage of the farming community as well as the state. For the limited purpose of this study, farm power need assessment is confined to land preparation and cultivation; but does not include other energy inputs required for agriculture, like lift irrigation or for pump sets. In terms of mechanical/ electrical power the draught animal power needed (0.75 mln pairs) of Orissa is equivalent to: 0.45 mln hp or 0.36 mln kW. Obviously, the 5.18 mln working male (2.59 pairs) in the state are now terribly under utilised; their average individual use for farm power would not exceed 25 days per animal in a year together for *kharif* and *rabi*; as the vast majority of farmers seldom use them maximally, by sharing them with others, to utilise their full potential.

### 4.5 Farm Mechanisation in Orissa

While discussing the farm power sector in Orissa, it is economically prudent to go beyond work animals and assess the process of mechanisation of farm operations in the state. The growth of the mechanisation process can be assessed from the numbers of tractors and pump sets in operation in the state. All India the population of draught animals declined steadily as the number of tractors and power tillers (as well as pump sets) grew and the period of the most spectacular fall in draught animal numbers (1972-82) also happens to be the period in which there is a spurt in the growth of tractors and power tillers. This however is not the case in Orissa: growth of agricultural machinery had all along been sluggish and the numbers of tractors and pump sets seem to have no influence on the draught animal population size. See Figs. 4.3 and 4.4. Growth in numbers of tractors, pump sets and other agricultural implements in Orissa between 1961-2001 are presented in the Table 4.2 below and Table 4.3 in the Appendix. Compared to many of the progressive states in the country, Orissa is lagging behind in the matter of farm mechanisation. The common picture that one encounters in other states, particularly in irrigated areas, is one of privately owned tractors available within the village for custom hiring, for operating the smaller holdings; and in many cases co-operatives or private entrepreneurs actually setting up service centres providing custom hiring facilities of agricultural machinery, and selling of other farm inputs like seeds, fertiliser and pesticides, as commercial ventures. This scenario is generally absent in Orissa villages. There are however exceptions: The NABARD and some of the co-operative banks in the state have made a beginning in 1995, in financing agro-service centres in selected districts, particularly Puri and Bargarh. The co-operative bank in Bargarh had so far financed six agro-service centres in the Bheden and Amba-bhona Blocks. Shri Harihar Naik,

TABLE 4.2: FARM MACHINERY AND IMPLEMENTS

| *Machinery and Implements* | *1961* | *1972* | *1982* | *1991* | *1994* | *1996* | *2001* |
|---|---|---|---|---|---|---|---|
| Tractors (nos.) | 194 | 1748 | 1188 | 8518 | 10041 | 12050 | 8670* |
| Pump Sets (nos.) (electric, including Tube Wells) | 140 | 404 | 5718 | 8500 | 14450 | 23000 | 297884 |
| Bullock Carts (no. lakh) | 5.12 | 5.87 | 7.07 | 7.97 | 9.47 | 10.50 | 6.89 |
| Sugar Cane Crushers (animal operated) nos. '000) | 12.80 | 18.43 | 1.00 | – | – | – | 10.86 |
| Sugar Cane Crushers (power operated) nos. '000 | 0.74 | 7.70 | 13.40 | 15.00 | 16.50 | 17.80 | NA |
| Ploughs (wooden) nos. lakh | 22.78 | 27.12 | 30.45 | 30.75 | 31.00 | 31.65 | 34.02 |
| Ploughs (iron) nos. lakh | 0.11 | 0.79 | 1.06 | 1.65 | 2.30 | 2.91 | 12.33 |

NOTE: *Tractors used for agricultural purposes, LS Census 2001.

SOURCE: OUAT Vision Towards 2020 AD, quoted in the Draught Animal Group Report 1998.

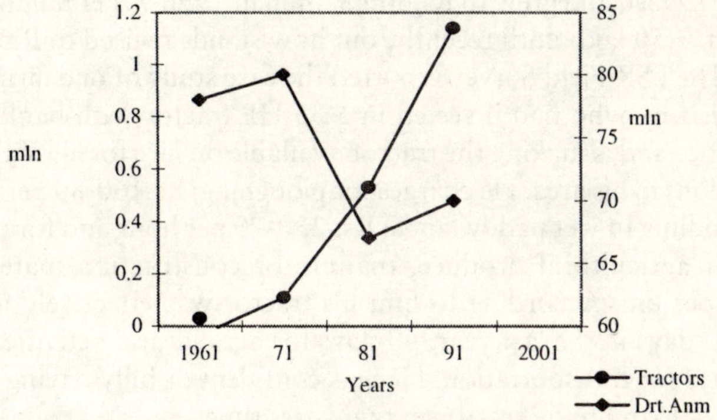


FIG. 4.3: DRAUGHT ANIMALS *VS* TRACTORS, INDIA.

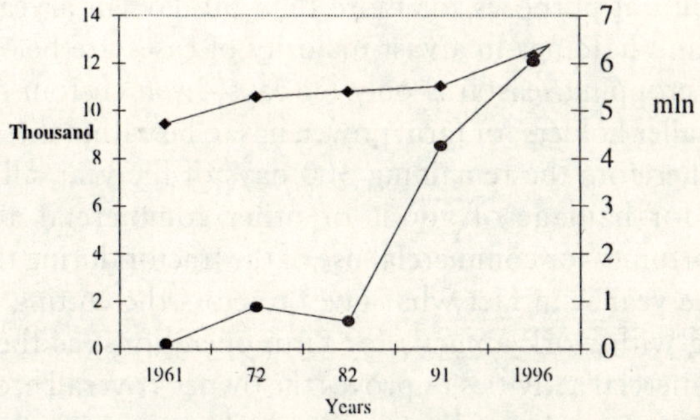


FIG. 4.4: DRAUGHT ANIMALS *VS* TRACTORS, ORISSA.

Sanjampalli, Amba-bhona Block and Shri Ravi Narayan Das in Bhankud, Bheden Block are two among the rural entrepreneurs owning full fledged agro-service centres, with tractors and all accessories, diesel pump sets and power sprayers. Both of them were financed by the SDCC: Shri Naik Rs. 343698 and Shri Das Rs. 381475. In 1998-9 Bargarh district had in all some 1990 tractors. Orissa Agro-Industries Corporation, with the assistance of the NABARD, is promoting a pilot scheme for establishing agro-service centres in selected villages. The scheme provides credit facilities for purchase of tractors, power tillers and other farm equipment for setting up agro-service centres. The ground level institutional credit with NABARD refinancing for farm mechanisation was Rs. 233.90

mln in 1995-6 and grew to Rs.609.87 mln in 1996-7. Per unit outlay was Rs. 3.50 lakh until recently, but now stands revised to Rs. 6.50 lakh. The LSR Field Survey reported the case study of one farmer in Puri district, who had invested in a 35 HP tractor with bank loan assistance and is making the tractor available on hire for agricultural operations in his area. He charges for ploughing: Rs.160-80 per hour, for puddling in wet paddy lands: Rs. 230-70 per hour and for transport of agricultural produce, manure or construction materials: Rs.70 per km. According to him his tractor was effectively in use for 270 days in the last year: 60 days for agricultural activities and 210 days for transportation. He was confident of fully paying back the bank loan on the tractor in two years time.

Privately owned tractors in Orissa as well as all over India, though owned by farmers and registered as farm machinery, cannot be used for agricultural purposes for more than 60 days in a year, as the owners' land holdings in a vast majority of cases are below 10 ha and total cropping season is only 60 days. Even custom hiring by him to smaller holders for farm power, has to be within the cropping season. Therefore the remaining 300 days of the year, all tractors are used for haulage of goods or other commercial activities. This opportunity for commercial use of the tractor during the major part of the year is in fact what gives tractors the cutting edge for competing with work animals for farm operations; as the income from commercial activities improves the owner's overall economics, often enabling cross subsidising hiring for farm operations by small holders within the village. From the farmers' point of view also hiring a tractor for cultivating his land in *kharif* and *rabi*, offers him a far better economic alternative; than having to own, feed and manage a pair of bullocks year round, just for using it for farming only on 60 days or even less (please see Box).

CASE STUDY SUMMARY: ORISSA LSR FIELD SURVEY, 1999

| | |
|---|---|
| Land holding size | 2 acres |
| Hire charges for tractor in *kharif* @ Rs.270 per hour for puddling | Rs. 540 |
| Hire charges for tractor in *rabi* @ Rs.180 per hour for ploughing | Rs. 360 |
| Total hire charges for tractor, in a year | Rs. 900 |
| Feeding and other costs for one pair of work bullocks per year | Rs. 7000 |

A 35 hp tractor normally can cultivate 2.50 ha of land in one 8 hour shift under Orissa conditions and often 5 ha in two shifts, depending upon the demand and urgency of the operation. The extent of land covered will vary considerably with the type of operation. Even though fuel consumption too vary depending on the operation, a standard operation like the use of a Fixed Time Tiller will entail a fuel consumption average of some 5 litres of diesel oil per hour or 40 litres per shift. All these calculations are based on subjective assessments and are exclusively to be used for the purpose of reckoning the over all tractor requirement of Orissa for partial mechanisation of farm operations. Farmers all over India hire tractors to till the land and for other basic land operations only. A number of activities are still work animal based, for example seed drilling and inter cultivation. And hence the mention of *partial mechanisation*. If Orissa goes in for partial mechanisation of land operations in agriculture, the 9.67 mln ha of gross cropped area would require only some 64500 tractors operating one shift over 60 cropping days or some 32250 tractors, if two shifts are operated. Therefore Orissa's total tractor requirement will be somewhere between 32250 and 64500 and petroleum fuel requirement for partial mechanisation some 154.80 mln litres of diesel oil. Orissa already has some 12050 tractors and if those among them that are rural based are made available for custom hiring to small holders, as much of it as possible on daily double shift, it would be an excellent pilot project in farm mechanisation. The pilot would cover some 20 per cent of the agricultural operations and can as well be a pilot for rationalising and reducing the bovine numbers.

### 4.6 Work Output of Draught Animals in Orissa

The total farm power need of Orissa for the 9.67 mln ha gross cropped area is some 0.75 mln pairs of work animals, or 0.45 mln hp, or 0.36 mln kW. By 2020 the gross cropped area is projected to grow to some 13.00 mln ha, an increase of some 35 per cent, requiring a corresponding increase in farm power to some 1.00 mln pairs of work animals, or 0.61 mln hp, or 0.54 mln kW. The currently existing work animal population is some 5.18 mln (2.59 mln pairs), with a potential power rating of 1.85 mln hp, or 1.38 mln kW. This potential is largely under utilised or in effect wasted, as its utilisation currently is only less than 30 per cent. The expanded gross cropped area in 2020, will surely have no dearth of farm power, even if the work animal population goes down by 50 per cent by then! Animal draught power is still very much in use for transport and haulage of goods in Orissa. There were over a million bullock carts in Orissa in 1996. Together for personal transport and inter/intra village transport of farm produce, the estimated use reported by the draught animal group is some 60 days in a year. This works out to the use of some 1.00 mln pairs of work animals to haul the 1.00 mln existing bullock carts for a total of some 60 days in a year; or 0.60 mln hp, or 0.45 mln kW for transport. Monetising this work output, the contribution of the work animals to the total output value of the state livestock sector in 2001 was some Rs.584 mln (please see Box for details).

DRAUGHT ANIMAL OUTPUT IN ORISSA

(i) *Farm Power*: on fuel equivalent basis (cost of 154.80 mln litres of diesel oil at 1996 price of Rs. 11 per litre) is Rs. 1703 mln.

(ii) *Farm Power*: on electrical power equivalent basis (cost of 0.36 mln kW used for 4 hours per day for one 60 day crop year or 86.4 mln kW hours @ Rs. 3 per kWh or unit) is Rs. 259.2, say Rs. 260 mln

(iii) *Transport*: on electrical power equivalent basis as fuel equivalent is difficult to work out(0.45 mln kW used over 4 hours a day over 60 working days or 108 mln kW h @ Rs. 3 per kWh or unit) is Rs. 324 mln.

(iv) Total contribution of draught animals for farm power and transport, to the output value of the livestock sector in Orissa is Rs. 584 mln in 1996.

### 4.7 DRAUGHT ANIMAL HUSBANDRY

All categories of farmers in Orissa own and keep draught animals, as farm power comes predominantly from draught animals-cattle as well as buffaloes. In 1996, each of the 3.94 million operational land holdings had an average of 1.55 draught animal, but the holding pattern differs from the average: among the land less category only 6 per cent keep draught animals; marginal and small farmers constitute over 80 per cent of the holdings and they account for only 49 per cent of the draught animals, 2 holdings among them ownig on average one pair (3.15 mln holdings owning 3.02 mln work animals). The 0.79 mln semi-medium, medium and large farmers have among them some 2.77 mln draught animals, 45 per cent of the total, but draught animal holding among them varies considerably, some of them owning two or more pairs while others own none. Draught animal holding among the higher categories of land holdings depends on the actual extent of land held by them, type of crop grown and ownership of, or access to, tractors. Among the marginal and small farmers, the husbandry practices are primitive, animals often have no shelter, are fed exclusively on crop residues, mostly paddy straw and sparse grazing for 300 days of the year when they are idle; and some 2 kg of rice bran/broken rice/horse gram husk, additional, when they work. The feeding and management cost per animal head for idle days comes to Rs. 1800 to 2000 and for the working seasons Rs. 780 to Rs. 1000 for 65 days and for the whole year some Rs. 3000-500, together for all home grown and bought in items. Crop residues fed are usually home grown and the concentrates fed, bought from local markets.

### 4.8 Draught Animals and Bovine Population Size

Draught animal numbers are inextricably linked to the bovine population size in the state. The primary objective of the farmer in Orissa in the breeding of bovine still continues to be production of work animals. The 5.80 mln work animals need annual replacement at the rate of some 15 per cent, as the productive life span of draught animals seldom exceed 6 years. This replacement requirement works out to supply of some 0.90 mln draught animals each year. With current levels of breeding efficiency of 0.6 calf per cow per year in Orissa, this level of replacement will require some 2.90 mln cows or some 60 per cent of the total adult breedable female among cattle and buffalo in the state, to be committed to bullock production annually; in fact almost all breeding female every year, in addition to limited imports from other states. *This limits the flexibility of the state breeding policy and the breeding options open to the state.* Reduction in the dependence of the state on draught animals for farm power, therefore, assumes enormous priority for the state government from the point of view of: balancing supply of the various animal products for consumption within the state and sustainability of animal agriculture in general. Cattle and buffalo account for over 90 per cent of the states livestock load on animal equivalent basis and already their numbers are far beyond the capacity of the state's land mass to sustain. It is abundantly clear that even without major mechanisation efforts, it is possible to rationalise the numbers of work animals and therefore, the overall size of the bovine population in the state, to half the present size, over a couple of decades, if astute policies are set in place, starting with the tenth five year plan and continued over the next 20 years, by the state government. These measures are detailed in the Box below.

MEASURES FOR RATIONALISING BOVINE POPULATION SIZE

(i) Encourage optimal sharing of work animals among farmers
(ii) Improve quality of work animals through grading up with Hariana Breed
(iii) Vigorously encourage lease markets for work animals and tractors
(iv) Promote Agro-Service Centres as commercial ventures in all major villages, enabling the farming communities custom hiring of tractors and power tillers.

TABLE 4.3. DISTRICT WISE ESTABLISHMENT OF AGRO-SERVICE CENTRES (ASC) 2001

| *Sl. No.* | *District* | *No. of Beneficiaries Selected* | *No. of Cases Sent to Bank* | *No. of Self-Finance Cases* | *No. of Cases Sanctioned by Bank* | *No. of Cases Procurement completed* |
|---|---|---|---|---|---|---|
| 1. | Balasore | 37 | 37 | 0 | 28 | 27 |
| 2. | Bhadrak | 28 | 27 | 1 | 21 | 18 |
| 3. | Cuttack | 62 | 61 | 1 | 53 | 54 |
| 4. | Dhenkanal | 10 | 10 | 8 | 8 | 6 |
| 5. | Gajapati | 10 | 10 | 0 | 6 | 6 |
| 6. | Ganjam | 88 | 80 | 0 | 38 | 33 |
| 7. | Jagatsinghpur | 60 | 59 | 1 | 50 | 48 |
| 8. | Jajpur | 54 | 48 | 2 | 32 | 22 |
| 9. | Kendrapara | 49 | 40 | 1 | 30 | 24 |
| 10. | Keonjhar | 10 | 10 | 0 | 9 | 8 |
| 11. | Khurda | 20 | 19 | 1 | 14 | 14 |
| 12. | Mayurbhanj | 10 | 9 | 0 | 6 | 4 |
| 13. | Nayagarh | 8 | 8 | 0 | 5 | 5 |
| 14. | Puri | 54 | 48 | 0 | 26 | 24 |
| | Total | 500 | 466 | 7 | 326 | 293 |

SOURCE: IPICOL, Orissa, 2002.

Post cyclone interventions in the affected areas in the state have already started to implement some of the Steering Committee recommendations above (see Box), to reduce dependence on draught animals and to modernize agriculture in general. Number of ASC in villages has since gone up considerably: 161 in 1999 and 293 established post cyclone and already functional in 2002. This has improved farmers' access to farm machinery and has helped them in such areas to rely increasingly on machines for farm operations as the better economic alternative. The growth of ASCs is continuing (see Table 4.3).

# 5 Meat Animals in Orissa

## 5.1. Meat Production in Orissa

Meat production in Orissa involves several species of livestock: goat, sheep, cattle and pig, in that order, according to their contribution to total production. There are also other species contributing to meat production: such as poultry and broiler rabbit (now gaining importance as a source of meat). Poultry meat production is dealt with separately under poultry. Output of rabbit meat is very small and is not reported. Total production of meat from ruminants and pig in 1998-9 was 38119 mt. Poultry meat, from *desi* birds in backyard units, culled birds from the commercial farms and broiler (consumed in Orissa), together contributed an additional 16096 mt of meat in 1998. Buffalo ceased to be a meat animal in Orissa in 1990 and meat output from buffalo is not officially reported since then. The Fig. 5.1 shows per cent contribution of different species of meat animals to total meat production in 1998-9. The specieswise meat production over the years 1980-99 is presented in Tables 5.1

Table 5.1: Number of animals slaughtered with their carcass yield

| *Species* | *No. Slaughtered 1994-5 / 1998-9* | *Carcass Yield kg 1994-5 / 1998-9* |
|---|---|---|
| Cattle | 22334 / 16649 | 102.70 / 101.50 |
| Sheep | 1193190 / 881421 | 10.08 / 9.74 |
| Goat | 1356182 / 2753255 | 9.12 / 8.95 |
| Pig | 85649 / 110580 | 29.81 / 28.95 |

Table 5.2: Skin / Hide of animals (slaughtered / fallen)

| *Source Hide / Skin* | *Cattle No. mln/ %* | *Buffalo No. mln/ %* | *Goat No. mln / %* | *Sheep No. mln / %* |
|---|---|---|---|---|
| Slaughter Animals | 10.90 / 5.57 | 8.10 / 10.55 | 68.99 / 68.40 | 27.82 / 62.04 |
| Fallen Animals | 10.80 / 5.51 | 7.60 / 9.90 | 6.41/ 6.45 | 3.58 / 7.98 |
| Total Population | 195.87 | 76.77 | 99.41 | 44.84 |

Source: CLRI Study, 1987; Note: Nos in million.

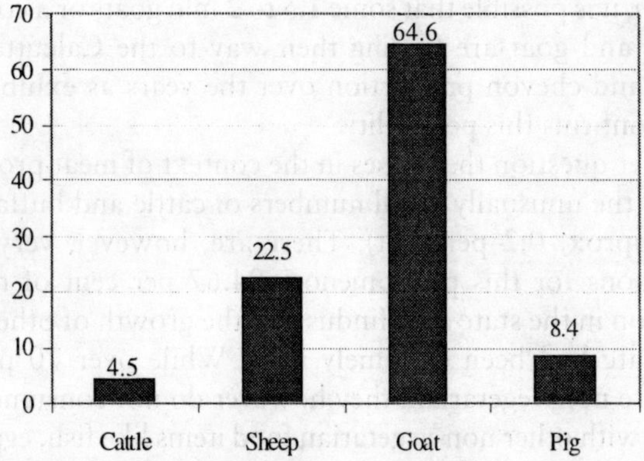


FIG. 5.1: CONTRIBUTION OF MEAT ANIMALS TO TOTAL MEAT PRODUCTION

in the Appendix. The number of animals slaughtered and the carcass yields for the different species, reported by the Integrated Sample Survey (ISS 1994-5 and 1998-9), Department of Animal Husbandry, Orissa, are presented in the Table 5.1. The number of animals from different species slaughtered, as reported by the ISS, raises many questions and to an extent even casts doubts on the accuracy of the reported data, the most glaring improbability being the numbers of goat reported as slaughtered. Total goat and sheep populations in 1995/9 were 5.41/5.77 mln and 1.87/1.72 mln respectively. The numbers slaughtered from each species were 25/48 per cent of the population in case of goat and 64/51 per cent in case of sheep, in the two years compared here. Chevon is comparatively more popular than mutton in Orissa and therefore, a sharply lower than normal slaughter percentage among goat needs explanation. A Central Leather Research Institute (CLRI) study (see Table 5.2) on slaughter by-products in 1986 indicates a slaughter per cent more or less similar for sheep and goat and a rather high annual turnover in the populations in both the species. While there could be questions about the absolute numbers, percentages reported by CLRI are closer to truth than any other set of data available in the country on this subject, if the sheep and goat populations are taken together. Therefore, the total slaughter among goat in Orissa should be somewhere around 3.2 / 3.5 mln annually, instead of 1.36 / 2.75 mln (in 1994-5 and 1998-9) as reported by the ISS. The explanation could be that with the market pull of the megalopolis of Calcutta next door, it is possible that some 1.5 to 2 mln goats or a combination of sheep and goat are finding their way to the Calcutta markets. Mutton and chevon production over the years as exhibited in the annex, confirms this possibility.

Another question that arises in the context of meat production in Orissa is the unusually small numbers of cattle and buffalo slaughtered (approx. 0.2 per cent). There are, however, very plausible explanations for this phenomenon. 94.67 per cent of the human population in the state are Hindus and the growth of other religions in the state had been extremely slow. While over 70 per cent of Oriyas are non-vegetarian, they however do not consume beef, but make do with other non-vegetarian food items like fish, egg, chicken, mutton and chevon. The national average for slaughter among cattle and buffaloes is some 5 per cent among cattle and 10 per cent among buffalo (CLRI 1987). The possibility therefore exists, that at least some half a million cattle and some buffaloes are taken across the border to Calcutta, for slaughter. This does alter the livestock sector output value, as trade in so many animals brings in a substantial income to the state. At the exhibited values per bovine in the asset value table in Annex, the additional income to the state on account of live cattle and buffalo trade for slaughter can be as high as some Rs. 750 mln.

### 5.2 Cattle and Buffalo as Meat Animals

Cattle and buffalo do contribute to meat production in Orissa, but are by no means the prime meat animals in the state. Less than 1 per cent of cattle and no buffaloes are slaughtered. Both cattle and buffalo provide meat as an adjunct to the milk system: mainly the old, infirm and malnourished animals constituting the meat stock. There are laws prohibiting the slaughter of cattle in Orissa, but these are reasonable laws unlike those in some of the northern and western states; and do distinguish between unproductive and productive animals in its application. While the number of cattle slaughtered in Orissa is very small, it appears that over half a million cattle and some buffaloes are taken across the border to Calcutta, as trade cattle for slaughter; as Calcutta is an insatiable market for beef. There are also contractors in Orissa and West Bengal arranging export of beef animals to Bangladesh through the many border crossings in West Bengal.

### 5.3 Small Ruminants: Goat and Sheep

Apart from cattle, the numerically most important species of livestock in Orissa is goat: 5.77 mln in numbers, 24.78 per cent of the total livestock population and with over 240 per cent growth in numbers during the period 1956-2001. Goats are distributed all over the state, but predominantly in the districts of Sundargarh, Mayurbhanj, Keonjhar, Balasore, Bolangir, Kalahandi, Phulbani, Ganjam, Jajpur, Angul, and Cuttack. Orissa has two important breeds of goat: Ganjam and Black Bengal, as well as some less important strains like Malkangiri and the Orissa Brown (see Table 5.3 in the Appendix). Goats contribute some 2500 mt of milk annually, most of it used for home consumption. The average body weight of the Ganjam goat is 20 kg and that of Black Bengal 15 kg. Meat yield from these breeds is estimated as 10 kg from Ganjam and 7.50 kg from Black Bengal. The total sheep population in Orissa is 1.72 mln (7.4 per cent of total livestock) distributed throughout the state, with major concentrations in Keonjhar, Mayurbhanj, Bolangir, Ganjam, Kalahandi, Cuttack and Koraput. The primary objective of sheep keeping is meat production, though they produce some wool as well. There are two recognised breeds of sheep in Orissa, Ganjam and Bolangir (see Table 5.4 in the Appendix). Adult body weight of the breeds average: Ganjam 25 kg; Bolangir 22 kg and meat yield 10-12 kg. Sheep and goat are farmed in Orissa primarily as meat animals. Orissa has several recognised breeds of sheep and goat native to the state. Sheep and goat are farmed predominantly by the land less and marginal farmers and to a lesser extent by the small farmers too (together some 80 per cent), as a means of livelihood. Medium and large farmers keep larger flocks for their own consumption and for commercial purposes. Some 0.60 million households keep sheep and 1.40 million keep goat, roughly 13 per cent and 30 per cent of all households, respectively. The distribution of sheep and goat in the state is presented in Table 5.5 in the Appendix. Also please see bar chart on page 28, Chapter 2, for individual flock holding size. Even though sheep and goat constitute the means of livelihood of over 40 per cent of its rural population, the GoO has not yet articulated an official policy for their breeding and development. Chevon and mutton are very popular meats (chevon more so) in Orissa and the market pull arising from this popularity had been instrumental in both rapid increases in their populations, as well as ever increasing meat prices. The discussion on the breeding and development of sheep and goat in this analysis is, therefore, based on the breeding precedents and development programmes implemented in the state over the years.

### 5.4 Development Activities under Poverty Alleviation Programme

With the launch of poverty alleviation and area development programmes: like Integrated Rural Development Programme (IRDP), Integrated Tribal Development Project (ITDP), Drought Prone Area Development Programme (DPAP), National Watershed Development Programme (NWDP) and other such programmes, a large number of productive assets in the form of sheep, goats and pigs were distributed to the beneficiaries (the resource poor farmers), on term loan and subsidy basis. These programmes, however, did not yield the desired results. During the eighth five year plan an Integrated Livestock Development Project in collaboration with Danish International Development Agency (DANIDA) was initiated (April 1993) in four blocks of Koraput district, covering 100 villages. The activities under the project involved introduction of Malpura rams for upgradation of local sheep to increase the body weight of lambs for meat purpose. Similarly Sirohi bucks too have been introduced for upgradation of the local goats. The details of the animals supplied are given in the Table 5.3. Efforts have been made by the ILDP to develop a flock of prolific sheep giving twin births and triplets. The seed stock is purchased from the farmers. Local farmers call this type of sheep 'Kuji' sheep. The purpose was to introduce prolificity in local crossbred populations developed by crossing with Malpura rams. It might reduce body weight of the crossbred. The crossbred of local x Malpura were found distinctly superior to local lambs, in body weight.

Table 5.3: Ram and Buck supplied in ILDP area

| *Name of Block* | *Ram* | *Buck* | *Total* |
|---|---|---|---|
| Jeypore | 33 | 6 | 39 |
| Koraput | 21 | 30 | 51 |
| Kundra | – | 10 | 10 |
| Laxmipur | 1 | 28 | 29 |

### 5.5 Piggery Development

Pigs are not popular meat animals in Orissa and consumption of pork is confined to tribal areas and among scheduled castes. The pig population grew from 0.53 mln in 1995 to 0.60 mln by 2001. Pork constitutes 8.4 per cent of the total meat produced in the state in 1998-9 (3202 mt), all of it consumed in the state. Some 223000 households, mostly tribal and scheduled, keep pigs as a means of livelihood. There is no processing or value addition of pork in Orissa.

In 1976-7 the state started a Special Livestock Breeding Programme (SLBP) as a centrally sponsored scheme for assisting the small, marginal farmers, land less agricultural labourers, Scheduled Tribes and Scheduled Castes. The objective was to help them to generate additional employment and income and thereby assist the target group in improving their socio-economic condition. The assistance was towards establishment of piggery units. The scheme was started in the districts of Keonjhar and Koraput and involved supply of three sows and one boar per unit, assistance to construct pigsty and assistance for concentrate feed. A sum of Rs.1200 was earmarked for each beneficiary initially, which was later increased to Rs. 3800. The scheme was renamed as Special Livestock Breeding Programme in the year 1985-6. The expenditure on the scheme and cost of establishment was shared equally between the Central Government and the State Government up to 1991-2. From the year 1992-3 the scheme was transferred to state sector and has been discontinued since then. During the tenure of the scheme from1976-92 some 2255 pig units were organised in Rayagada and 1814 pig units in Keonjhar district. At present the state department of AH &VS supplies the breeding stock (boar and sow) to pig farmers covered under various poverty alleviation schemes at the following cost:

| | | |
|---|---|---|
| Up to 15 kg body weight (male /female) | Rs. 500 | per animal |
| 16 to 30 kg body weight | Rs. 1000 | per animal |
| Beyond 30 kg weight | Rs. 30 | per kg of additional weight |

The technical know how on matters related to construction of house, breeding, feeding, management and health cover is provided by the Additional Veterinary Surgeon of the area as an when needed. Two non-governmental organisations one at Hadagarh in Keonjhar and the other at Tangi in Cuttack district are operating small demonstration units and provide training to farmers.

### 5.6 Slaughter of Animals and Meat Handling System

The slaughter and carcass handling system in the state are, to put it mildly, 'primitive'. There are no modern slaughterhouses with mechanical carcass handling system for hygienic meat production. There are however 93 registered slaughterhouses available in the state for cattle, sheep and goat. These are listed in Table 5.7 in the Appendix. Pigs in Orissa are slaughtered in the open air by special communities and are marketed in the towns and other urban agglomerations by vendors. In addition, there are many private butcher houses mostly located at street corners or private houses and many animals are slaughtered there. Though there are codes and standard practices prescribed by the Bureau of Indian Standards, these are not followed. Inspection of meat is cursory, often done by unqualified municipal staff. Almost all slaughterhouses in the state are owned by the local self-governments: city corporations, municipalities and *gram panchayats*. Slaughter laws are archaic and are seldom enforced. Slaughterhouses are more often than not, located in some unseemly corner of the town or village and can under no circumstances be considered food factories as they do not even have the bare minimum sanitation and hygiene standards. They are virtually high-risk joints from the public health point of view and need immediate policy attention of the GoO. When animals are slaughtered in modern slaughterhouses various by-products, viz., skin, hooves, horns, non-edible offal, blood, etc., are available and can be gainfully utilised. The utilisation of by-products of the slaughterhouse is negligible in the state expect skin and hides, which are collected by agents and are sent to the tanneries after primary salting. Skin is the most important by-product, which is used in the leather industry. Nearly 2.8 million pieces of sheep and goat skins are available in the state per annum. Ganjam sheep and goat produce excellent skins and the Bengal goats produce high quality and glossy skins, which are used for shoe uppers and fetch good prices.

# 6 Poultry in Orissa

## 6.1 Poultry Population

Poultry in Orissa is made up of two major species: fowl and duck; along with small numbers of others like guinea fowls, geese, turkey and quail. Poultry population in the state including all species of birds in 2001 was 18.43 mln (see Table 6.1) and the density of the population was 118 birds per km$^2$. Poultry numbers grew some 300 per cent between 1951 and 2001 (see Table 6.1 in the Appendix). Even in 2001 *desi* fowls accounted for 77 per cent of all fowl in the state. Between 1961-95 ducks registered the fastest growth among all poultry: 391 per cent (see Fig 6.1), but the duck population suffered severe losses during the 'killer cyclone' in 1999 reducing their numbers by some 10 per cent, by 2001. Egg production in Orissa was 73.3 mln in 1951 and increased to 933 mln by 2001. Consequently the availability of eggs per capita rose from 5 to 26 per head. Per capita consumption of egg in the state, however, is much higher, 35 per year in 2001 and to meet the shortfall in demand, nearly a million eggs are imported every day from neighbouring states. In comparison, total egg production all India was around 32.03 bln and availability per capita 37 in 1997-8. While the

Table 6.1: Poultry Population in 2001

| *Poultry: Type / Species* | *No. mln / %* |
|---|---|
| Total Poultry | 18.43 / 100 |
| Total Fowl | 17.56 / 95.28 |
| Total Duck | 0.65 / 3.51 |
| Total Others | 0.22 / 1.21 |
| Fowl *Desi* | 13.45 / 76.59* |
| Fowl Improved | 4.11 / 23.41* |
| Fowls: Layers | 4.68 / 26.65* |
| Fowl Layers *Desi* | 3.48 / 74.36* |
| Fowl Layers Improved | 1.20 / 25.64* |
| Duck Layers | 0.20 / 30.77* |

Note: *Per cent to total within the category.

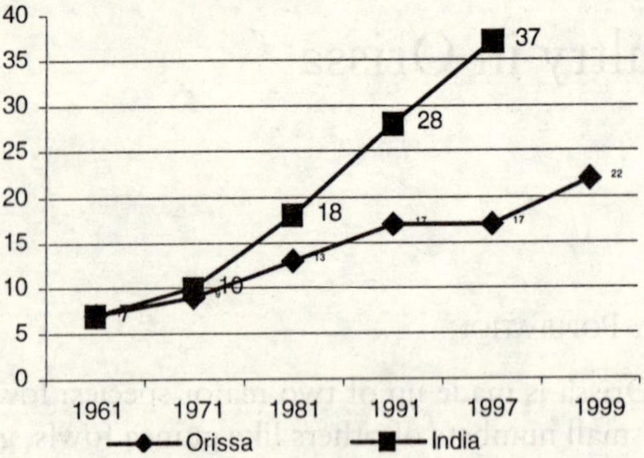


FIG. 6.1: GROWTH OF POULTRY POPULATION.

poultry population in the state is around 5 per cent of the all India population, egg production in Orissa is only some 2.6 per cent of all India production. As in all other livestock sub-sectors, this again confirms the lower levels of productivity in the state, in comparison to the rest of India. Lower productivity of the commercial flocks (157 in Orissa as against 277 eggs per layer, all India) and the smaller proportion of improved birds to total fowl in Orissa (less than 25 per cent), are obviously the reasons.

The average egg production in Orissa is about 102 eggs per layer for *desi* fowls and 157 eggs (236 per layer per year in large commercial farms) for improved fowl (see Tables 6.2 and 6.3 in the Appendix). According to the integrated sample survey 1998-9 the highest egg production in the state is in the district of Ganjam (25 per cent), followed by Khurda (9 per cent) and Mayurbhanj (8.7 per cent). Though *desi* birds account for some 74 per cent total layers among fowl in Orissa, their contribution to egg production is only about 57 per cent of the production in the state. The total number of eggs produced by *desi* birds was 268 mln in 1981 and increased to 431 mln eggs in 1998-9, an increase of 38 per cent. Until about 1960, almost the entire demand for eggs and poultry meat in Orissa was met by the backyard poultry system. Over the last four decades, this scenario has completely changed and supply of egg and poultry meat to urban areas now is almost entirely from the highly specialised hybrid layers and broilers, in the commercial farms. There are now in Orissa some 1500 organised poultry farms both large and small, with commercial hybrid layers, contributing 41 per cent of the total eggs produced in the state. The *desi* birds have given way to the more efficient commercial birds in meeting the demand of the large urban demand centres, but continue to prosper as an integral part of the smallholder livelihood system in rural Orissa. Ducks contribute annually 19.42 mln eggs (1998). Poultry meat production in Orissa is made up of the table birds coming from the back yard poultry units, culled birds from the commercial layer farms and the fast growing broiler industry. Broiler production in the state took off in the late 1980s and is now producing annually some 12 mln broilers, some 8.4 mln consumed in the state and 3.6 mln exported to other states. Total poultry meat production in the state was some 16096 mt in 1997: 5696 mt (35 per cent) from the backyard units and 10400 mt from culled birds and broilers consumed in the state. Per capita consumption of poultry meat in Orissa was 669 gm in 1997.

## 6.2 Production Organisation

Mayurbhanj has the highest concentration of poultry among all districts and accounts for nearly 12 per cent of the total population, followed by Ganjam with 8 per cent; the other districts with large population of poultry are Sundargarh, Keonjhar and Khurda. But the population of improved fowls was highest in Khurda, Ganjam, Cuttack, Balasore and Bolangir (2001). As everywhere else in India, poultry production in Orissa is organised in two widely different streams: (i) the traditional backyard poultry system and (ii) the growing modern, high-tech commercial poultry industry.

(i) *Backyard Poultry System* of the nearly 18 mln fowls in Orissa, over 74 per cent are *desi* birds. These birds are entirely raised in the backyards (2.14 mln: 45.42 per cent of all households), spread across all categories of holdings. A vast majority of these birds (over 90 per cent), however, are owned by the land less and marginal farmers, Scheduled Tribes and Scheduled Castes, and are managed in a most unorganised manner, considerably undermining the system's potential to contribute to household income, as well as family nutrition. The holding pattern varies widely, from as low as two to as high as thirty birds, with the most frequent holding size (mode) around twenty birds. All aspects of production and marketing—table birds and *desi* eggs—are entirely in the hands of the smallholder producers (landless, marginal and small) and through the traditional channels. Level of productivity of the birds is: 102 eggs per bird per year and less than a kg of meat per bird. Shrinking area for foraging (shrinking land holdings), lack of skills in almost all aspects of feeding and management, lack of genetic inputs to improve the *desi* stock, heavy losses due to diseases, losses from predators; and general lack of any skill transfer and extension support, are some of the factors contributing to the sub-optimal exploitation of the system for livelihood protection and livelihood generation. Smallholder backyard poultry production requires no land, uses minimal labour and capital, no overheads or out of pocket expenses and the system makes no demands on the meagre resources of the households. It is a production system that can be afforded by the poorest of poor and represents a significant part of tribal and rural economy in Orissa. Backyard units maintained by the resource poor are not considered useful for commercial bulk production, but constitute a gainful source of employment and supplementary income for the rural poor and contribute quality inputs to family nutrition.

*Desi* fowl is the most popular bird with the small holders and account for over 90 per cent of the backyard poultry. *Desi* eggs and *desi* chicken for the table, from the backyard units are very popular in Orissa and enjoy a *niche market* (almost 33 per cent of eggs and 35 per cent of poultry meat consumed in Orissa) with considerable scope for expansion. Most of the *desi* fowl found in the state are non descript. They are all coloured birds, vary greatly in their plumage, comb type, body confirmation and other anatomical attributes. They are, however, good brooders, excellent foragers and efficient mothers. Although mediocre in growth and productivity they are well adapted to local climatic and geographical conditions. And there is considerable genetic variability among them in their production traits and therefore it should not be difficult to improve their growth rate and natural attributes for endurance and survival, by selection. Ducks are very much relevant to the Orissa farming systems in the districts of Mayurbhanj, Kalahandi, Bolangir, Balasore, Sundargarh, Bargarh, Bhadrak, Keonjhar and Nawarangpur; even though ducks are distributed all over the state. Next to fowl, ducks are the most popular species in the backyard units. Total duck population in Orissa is only some 0.64 mln (3.51 per cent of total poultry) and they are mostly desi birds with no specific breed characterisation, except for strains along the Chilika lake borders, where a strain of ducks are referred to as the Chilika duck.

(ii) *Organised Poultry Industry in Orissa.* The commercial stream of the poultry industry is entirely in the hands of private entrepreneurs. They practice a highly intensive system of poultry production, utilising genetically superior hybrid layers and broilers. Average egg production from these birds was 236 per layer per year in 1998-9. Egg production in 1981 from the improved birds was 74 million eggs, which increased to 286 million eggs in 1997, an increase of over 285 per cent. Culled hens and cockerels were the contribution of the commercial layer farms to poultry meat output until 1980. The state now produces about one million broilers every month (12 mln annual, 3.8 per cent of the national broiler production) and some 3.6 mln (30 per cent in 1997) of the broiler produced in the state are exported to other states. The per capita availability of poultry meat was 128 gm in 1956 and increased to 669 gm in 1997.

According to a survey conducted by the department of AH & VS, Orissa in 1995-6, there were over 1650 poultry farms of varying sizes, in the state (see Table 6.4 in the Appendix). Only some 110 out of these are large commercial farms. In the small and medium size poultry farms the flock size varies between 1000 and 5000 layers, while the large farms usually have from 30000 to 100000 layers. The broiler industry in Orissa is growing at the rate of 15 per cent per annum, slower than the national growth rate, though. The layer industry is growing at 6 per cent per annum. There does not appear to be any enabling government policy to promote the growth and development of the commercial poultry industry in the state. For example, power tariff currently charged for poultry establishment is at par with the commercial consumer rates and is considered an unfair imposition, impeding the growth of the poultry industry. Organised poultry farming in Orissa strangely is a low key activity, considerably smaller than in neighbouring Andhra Pradesh, in spite of Orissa's nearness to the megalopolis of Calcutta and the tremendous market pull it offers.

## 6.3 Production Inputs, Services and Government Interventions

Both the state and the central governments have played a vital role in ushering in modern poultry farming in the state. Modern poultry farming in Orissa started with the establishment of a poultry-breeding farm at Angul in 1947, with 50 exotic birds. The strength of the farm was increased in successive five year plans and reached some 21000 birds by 1992. This farm has played a significant role in popularisation of commercial strains of poultry through training, demonstration and supply of nucleus stock to all other poultry farms established in the public sector, including the Central Poultry Breeding Farm, Bhubaneswar. In addition to the Angul farm, there are seven other poultry farms under the state department of animal husbandry. These are the district poultry farms at Bhanjanagar, Bolangir and Keonjhar (see Table 5.6 in the Appendix), two regional poultry farms at Semiliguda and Sundaragarh, and a special poultry farm at Chipilima. The poultry farm at Bhubaneswar was transferred to Orissa Poultry Federation (OPOLFED) in 1990. Production and supply of day old chicks has been the major function of these farms.

Other interventions under the five year plans include setting up of 27 ANP centres in Orissa, three Intensive Poultry Development Projects and a co-operative service society to provide institutional finance for marketing of eggs and supply of poultry feed to farmers. Poultry development programmes were taken up under the SFDA and MFAL projects in the districts of Dhenkanal, Ganjam, Bolangir, Cuttack and Keonjhar. Tribal development projects for poultry in tribal areas were started in Parlakhemundi, Gunupur and Keonjhar. Several programmes on development of poultry were attempted under DPAP and Dry Land Farming Project in Kalahandi, Kandhamal and Mayurbhanj districts; and under Tribal Welfare schemes in Jalada and Jhirpani in Sundargarh district and in Koraput. These were all tiny schemes, essentially for setting up tiny poultry units with commercial birds or their grades. These schemes were thoroughly incongruous to the context and a glaring mismatch to what the backyard poultry farmers actually needed (see box on p. 77). Almost all of them lacked the critical mass to kick-start a development wave among the poultry farmers. All of them without exception were infructuous and vanished without a trace at the expiry of their respective tenures.

There were also attempts under the plan schemes to upgrade the quality of the *desi* hens through exchange of *desi* cocks with purebred exotic cocks, supply of hatching eggs of White Leg Horn (WLH) and Rhode Island Red (RIR), along with some extension support. These programmes were massive in scale but were ill matched to the rural context (see box), were disjointed in application (over time and space) and like all short-lived schemes, were not sustained over

> What is most essential from the point of view of the backyard poultry farmers, but was beyond the focus of any of the plethora of schemes attempted under the several five year plans, was Disease Control—*arrangements in villages for poultry vaccination: training in poultry vaccination and supply of vaccines against the most prevalent poultry diseases.*
>
> Ranikhet disease alone wipes out whole flocks of newly hatched chicks year after year and is the single major impediment to progress in backyard poultry farming. Massive vaccinations against poultry diseases on a sustained basis is possible only when the skill for vaccination exists in the villages itself, farmers have access to vaccination when they need it and vaccinations become germane to backyard poultry farming.
>
> The backyard poultry units need a brooding hen with good mothering instincts, as home hatching of eggs for production of table birds is the primary objective of the backyard farmer. *Crosses and grades of exotic breeds of poultry therefore are of no use to him.* Development of the *desi* birds for faster weight gain under foraging conditions, is the direction that the state should follow in poultry breeding. There are many good desi breeds of poultry in India, selection among them and grading up of nondescript birds with them, has enormous scope. Disease control and regular vaccinations, innovative techniques for feed supplementation and skills in candling of eggs for better hatching output and optimum use of *desi* eggs, are the skills required right in the village for the backyard system. The ILDP, Koraput, Orissa and ILDP, Pudukottai in Tamil Nadu, have set the example in skill training and empowering village communities. Perhaps their experience will enable the Department of Animal Husbandry in Orissa to skill-train community link workers for all villages in Orissa, where backyard poultry farming is practised by large numbers of farmers.

time. The scheme failed to create any impact on the poultry farming system or on the quality of the *desi* stock. During the fourth plan period, a centre of the All India Coordinated Research Project of the ICAR on poultry was established in the OUAT, for research on development of economically viable commercial broiler stocks and to study the combining ability of the broiler stocks available in the country. The AICRP developed a sturdy coloured broiler strain well accepted by the small holder broiler producers. During the two years 1997-9 the OUAT project supplied some 244576 day-old commercial broiler chicks to poultry farmers. The project also was able to supply some 4000 pure bred parent stock annually to state poultry farms at Chiplima and Koraput, who in turn were able to supply an additional 400000 day-old chicks to farmers in their respective regions.

The private sector commercial poultry movement in India, has now reached the proportions of a thriving industry, highly skilled and equally well managed, comparable to the poultry industry anywhere in the world. They have developed their own support systems and breeding infrastructure and do not need the government's support for development, except enabling policies. It appears that the state department of animal husbandry has not yet woken up to this reality and is still involved with programmes directed to the promotion of the commercial poultry sector in the state. The time has come for the state to focus entirely on the development of the backyard poultry sector in the state and to direct all public funds for poultry development, to the support of the backyard sector. Conventional schemes followed so far, is not the need of the hour, but innovative ways to enhance the productivity of the backyard units. It is also necessary to provide breeding inputs to the backyard poultry system in the state. There are many specific and good breeds among the *desi* poultry in India. The economic traits among the *desi* fowls (growth rate and egg production) have enormous selection differential and can, therefore, respond rapidly to selection within their populations. This should form the subject of a detailed standalone study, followed by a master plan for backyard poultry development.

# 7 Animal Health in Orissa

## 7.1 Animal Disease Profile

Orissa has almost all the animal diseases known to mankind, even those already eradicated by many countries of the world. That Orissa is part of the tropics is often used as an excuse to justify the continued prevalence of these diseases. In reality, India as a country and Orissa as a state within it, have never seriously attempted to control and eradicate animal diseases (with the single exception of NPRE), but have always spent the lion's share of the public funds available to the livestock sector, on curative veterinary care. There have of course been disease control programmes and annual vaccinations, but they were all unsystematic, not of the scale required and applied sporadically all over the state. Like in all other states in the country, livestock in Orissa is ravaged by recurring epidemics, causing phenomenal production losses and lingering morbidity, costing the state dear in terms of money and lost opportunities in global trade. No estimates have been made of the losses due to animal diseases in Orissa, but in proportion to its livestock wealth, Orissa's share of the national losses works out to Rs. 2500 mln per year; or 15 per cent of the annual output value of the state livestock sector at 1998 prices. The profile of major animal diseases specieswise, recorded in 13 districts in the state between 1956 and 1997 and compiled by the Animal Disease Research Institute (ADRI), is given in Table 7.1 in the Appendix, to illustrate the general epidemiological situation. This however is not an exhaustive epidemiological profile of the state livestock sector. The animal disease profile in Orissa in 2001-2 is given in the Table 7.1.

A more comprehensive enumeration of the animal and poultry diseases prevalent in Orissa, specieswise, appear in Tables 7.1 and 7.2 in the Appendix. The listing, however, is not in the order of importance. The emerging diseases of livestock, comparatively new entrants to India and Orissa, are Bovine Malignant Catarrh, Infectious Bovine Rhinotracheaitis, Chlamydiosis among the bovines and Chlamydiosis and Blue Tongue in sheep.

TABLE 7.1 ANIMAL DISEASE PROFILE ORISSA, 2001-2

| *Disease* | *Outbreak* | *Attack* | *Death* |
|---|---|---|---|
| CCPP | 2 | 188 | 20 |
| TB | – | 182 | 6 |
| Bebesiosis | 30 | 1938 | 186 |
| Theileriosis | 32 | 147 | 8 |
| Trypanosomiasis | 4 | 127 | 2 |
| Brucellosis | 4 | 195 | – |
| PPR | 21 | 4223 | 693 |
| Anthrax | 12 | 169 | 76 |
| Rabies | 9 | 428 | 428 |
| CPD | 4 | 77 | – |
| FMD | 34 | 2239 | 2 |
| HS | 24 | 202 | 90 |
| BQ | 17 | 166 | 104 |
| Goat pox | 1 | 815 | 50 |
| Goat mange | 3 | 2360 | 180 |
| Sheep mange | 2 | 1025 | 43 |
| Swine Fever | 1 | 350 | 350 |
| Infectious Bursal Disease | 4 | 77042 | 27399 |
| Chronic Respiratory Disease | 2 | 21291 | 8361 |
| RD | 5 | 4343 | 996 |
| Others | | | |
| Coccidiosis | 6 | 52817 | 9503 |
| Infectious Choryza | 1 | 185 | 32 |
| Enteritis (Duck) | 1 | 1596 | 5 |
| Pediculosis | 2 | 6990 | 19 |

SOURCE: Report of Animal Disease Surveillance, ADRI.

The Department of Animal Resource Development is the agency of the state government responsible for animal health care and disease prevention. The department was carved out of the development department of the then Orissa province in 1946 and set up as an independent Department of Animal Husbandry and Veterinary Services, under a Director, with headquarters at Cuttack. When India entered the planned era of development in 1951, with the launch of the first five year plan, there were no participatory bodies or people's organisations capable of carrying development to every nook and corner of the state. The government, therefore, had no alternative but to resort to direct action for development and use the already existing department for the purpose. With each successive plan the department grew and expanded; and now has ended up as a behemoth, unwieldy and unviable, with some 6224 institutions under it,

5083 technical and professional men and women working for it and spending almost 95 per cent of the annual budget on its establishment alone, leaving just 5 per cent for development expenses, including drugs and consumables for veterinary hospitals and dispensaries.

## 7.2 Diseases of Bovine

Diseases of cattle and buffaloes commonly encountered in Orissa are listed in Table 7.1 in the Appendix. Rinderpest was one of the most devastating diseases of cattle and buffaloes and was widely prevalent in the state during the fifties, sixties and seventies. The disease profile from 1951-91 (see Fig. 7.1) indicates that there has been a significant drop in the number of seizures and deaths from 1961 onwards until 1990. The systematic and coordinated approach to disease control and eradication under the National Project for Rinderpest Eradication has rid the country of Rinderpest in a comparatively short span of time (1992-8). India is now free of Rinderpest. Orissa falls in zone 'B' (central and eastern states) of NPRE and discontinued vaccination against Rinderpest in 1995. India has been declared provisionally free of Rinderpest on 1 March 1998, by the OIE. Vaccination against Rinderpest is now administered only to small ruminants on account of the prevalence of PPR and in the border areas with Pakistan. Foot and Mouth Disease is now the major disease problem facing livestock production in Orissa, as in much of the Indian sub continent. Three of the classical serotypes of the FMD virus O, A ($A_{22}$) and Asia$_1$ have been reported

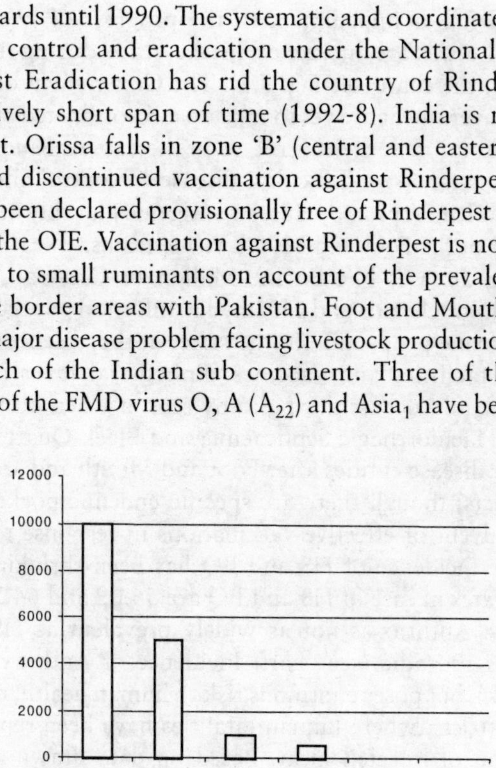


Fig. 7.1: Incidents of Rinderpest.

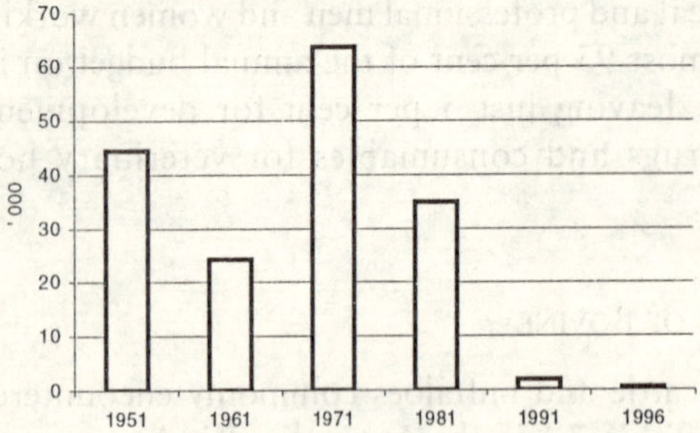


FIG. 7.2: INCIDENTS OF FOOT AND MOUTH DISEASE.

from various parts of the state. The disease affects all ruminants and pigs as well; and loss of production and morbidity caused by the disease is a major impediment to the progress of livestock production. The disease incidence in the state during 1951-96 is presented in the chart (see Fig. 7.2). The Government of India and the State Government are yet to take up a co-ordinated approach to Foot and Mouth Disease control, as in the case of Rinderpest. But then, FMD is far more difficult a disease to control and eradicate compared to Rinderpest, because of antigenic plurality and unstable antigenicity of the Foot and Mouth virus strains.

Emerging diseases like Bovine Malignant Catarrah, Infectious Bovine Rhinotracheaitis and Chlamydial infection pose considerable threat to bovine production in the state, in the absence of suitable diagnostic facilities and vaccines. Ephemeral fever is of lesser consequence and occurs during rainy season when biting flies are abundant. Haemorrhagic Septicaemia and Black Quarter continue to be major disease entities after Foot and Mouth and are prevalent in all districts, though there are specific endemic pockets as well. With the advent of effective vaccinations in response to outbreak reports, the incidence of HS and BQ has been shrinking steadily. Mortality rates in case of HS and BQ are 56.09 and 64.32 per cent respectively. Anthrax is not as widely prevalent as HS and BQ; incidence is sporadic (see chart: Incidence of Anthrax: grey and death: black), but poses enormous risk to human health, particularly in tribal districts, where human fatalities have been reported after consumption of infected meat. Based on data drawn at ten year intervals from 1951-96, bar chart (see Fig. 7.3) presents the incidence and death due to Anthrax.

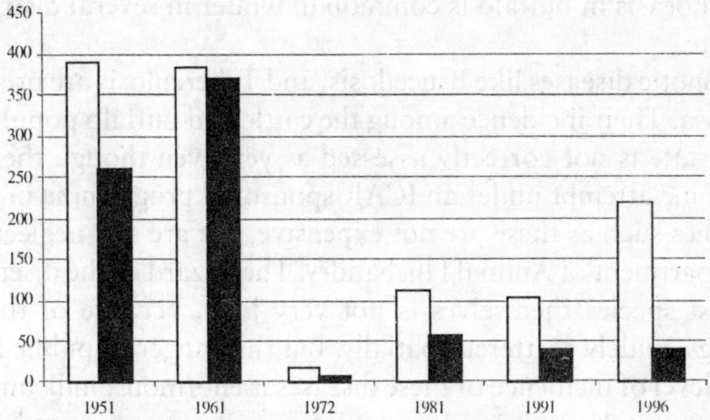


FIG. 7.3: INCIDENTS AND DEATH DUE TO ANTHRAX.

Rabies is an important zoonotic disease prevalent all over the state and both human and animals populations all over Orissa are at considerable risk. Though good anti rabic vaccines are available in the country now, prophylactic vaccination of stray dogs is hardly practiced at all. Prophylactic vaccination for pets against Rabies is not mandatory in this country. Even professionals often exposed to Rabies and at constant risk, like veterinarians, policemen and municipal workers are not protected. In the coastal districts water logging and flooding of low lying areas are routine annual features in Orissa and this exposes the animals of the area to fluke infestation. Fasciolasis and Amphistomiasis are endemic in such places. Parasitic infestation in cattle and buffaloes is heavy and the economic loss due to parasites is enormous due mainly to morbidity and even death in many cases. Diseases of skin and ecto parasitic infestation, though not fatal, often cause considerable morbidity. Blood Protista like Babesia and Theileria are prevalent and affect the highly productive cross bred cows, taking severe toll of life each year. Ecto parasites are responsible for transmission of Theileriosis and Babesiosis. Effective vaccines against Theileriosis are availble in India commercially, but the veterinary profession in Orissa have not made use of these vaccines to protect the valuable crossbred cows. '*Raksha Vac T*' produced and marketed by the public sector company Indian Immunologicals, is so effective that a single injection often protects a cross bred cow for many years. Sporotrichosis in cattle has also been encountered in many districts like Ganjam, Puri, and Cuttack. Stephanofilariasis is endemic in most of the coastal districts. Filarial

Ottorrhoeasis in buffalo is common in winter in several districts of the state.

Zoonotic diseases like Brucellosis, and Tuberculosis are prevalent in Orissa. Their incidence among the cattle and buffalo populations in the state is not correctly assessed as yet, even though there has been some attempt under an ICAR sponsored programme in 1963-8. Studies such as these are not expensive, but are still neglected by the Department of Animal Husbandry. The hazard of the diseases to the host species themselves is not very high, because of the tiny holdings, widely scattered spatially. But the danger to public health at any level of incidence of these diseases is enormous: milk and beef have become the major sources of infection to human population.

### 7.3 Diseases of Small Ruminants

A comprehensive list of the diseases of sheep and goat is presented in Appendix 7.1. Parasitic infestation, both ecto and endo parasites, is very common and is the major hindrance to the development of small ruminant economy in Orissa. Mange in goats is particularly fatal. Liver Fluke infestation and Strongylosis are common in sheep. Parasitic Gastroenteritis is quite common both in sheep and goats. Sheep and goat pox and Pestes des Petit Ruminants (PPR) have been great killers of small ruminants in the state. The virulent form of contagious pustular dermatitis in sheep and goat in several parts of Orissa cause large scale mortality although the disease is usually considered relatively benign. Chlamydial Pneumonia, Caprine Pleuropneumonia and Pneumonia due to various other causes, are major contributing factors to mortality among sheep and goats. Pasteurellosis and Entrotoxaemia are not uncommon.

### 7.4 Diseases of Pig

Swine fever, Ascariasis and Piglet Anaemia are considered economically the most important of all diseases among pigs. Foot and Mouth Disease in pigs is a major source of infection to other susceptible species in the vicinity, as pigs are amplifiers of the virus population and void enormous loads of the virus to their environs. India did not even have an oil adjuvant Foot and Mouth vaccine for prophylaxis among pigs until recently. Even though oil adjuvant vaccines are now in the market, vaccination of pigs against FMD is seldom practised in Orissa (see Appendix 7.1, for a comprehensive list of the pig diseases in Orissa).

### 7.5 Diseases of Equine

With the dwindling equine population in the state, hardly any importance is now attached to equine diseases. However, there are nomadic tribes, which often move with packs of ponies. The recent incidence of Trypanosomiasis among bovines in district Nawapara is believed to be through infected ponies among the tribal herds.

### 7.6 Diseases of Poultry

Poultry has a large number of diseases affecting them, most of them of viral origin and some of unknown etiology. The most important diseases of poultry in the state however are Infectious Bursal disease (Gumboro disease), Ranikhet disease, Avian Encephalomyelitis affecting chicks, Fowl Pox, infectious coryza, infectious Bronchitis, infectious Laryngio-tracheitis, Egg Drop Syndrome, Hydro-Peri-cardium-syndrome, Colibacillosis, Fowl Cholera, Salmonellosis and Aspergillosis. All these diseases have been encountered from time to time in the state and cause a great deal of loss to poultry farmers, particularly in broiler production. Extensive use of Ranikhet disease vaccine have controlled incidence of RD to a great extent in the organised poultry industry. But the major impediment to the development of the backyard poultry sector is the annual losses they suffer from RD. The state has not yet been able to set in place a system for satisfying the *massive vaccination need* of the backyard units, even though the ILDP in Koraput has already set up an effective model in the project villages.

### 7.7 Epidemiological Surveillance

The animal disease surveillance cell of the central department of AH & D has epidemiological units in all states including Orissa (ADRI). These units collect data on incidence of diseases and send data summaries to the central department. Guidelines for development of an animal disease surveillance system (ADSIS) were prepared by the central department in collaboration with national informatic centre, with plans to link all districts in all states through the *nicnet*. These systems are yet to become operational in Orissa. The conventional OBR system is still in place and all information for this analysis has come from it. However, experience shows that most epizootics get entry into the state or occur due to: (i) migration of livestock from one area to other including inter-state movements; (ii) spread due to improper disposal of carcasses; (iii) distress sale of animals and birds during out breaks; (iv) introduction of new varieties, specially in case of poultry, without zoosanitary controls; (v) land in certain areas prone to flooding and water logging; (vi) preponderance of arthropods vectors during rainy season; and (vii) *absence of a vigilance system with checks and controls. This is an area with major policy implication for the state.*

### 7.8 Disease Control and Prevention

Prevention and control of animal diseases in Orissa is not a priority for the state government: the bulk of the public funds available to the state department of animal husbandry is spent on curative veterinary care. Curative veterinary care generates only 'private good' to the owners of the animals cured, while prevention and control of diseases generates enormous 'public good', to the advantage of the state and the nation as a whole. The emphasis on public funded curative veterinary care over the 50 years of planned development, 1951-2001, has resulted in a vast veterinary network statewide rendering what the governments like to call 'free service' to the livestock owners—the poor quality and obsolescence notwithstanding. The state and central plan budgets annually include provision for vaccinating animals against all major diseases. However, the vaccinations are distributed all over the state, as a share of the plan budget due for each district. Several schemes, some of them centrally sponsored, are continuing in the state, particularly for Foot and Mouth: but they were all unsystematic, not of the scale required and applied sporadically all over the state. The Fig.7.4 presents the futility of such an exercise in disease control, for example, the total vaccinations against Foot and Mouth Disease in 1992 in the state was only some 289323, spread over the entire state and the animal population at risk was over 21.83 mln, statewide-vaccination coverage of just 1.33 per cent of the animals at risk. *Protection against foot and mouth disease should be based on herd immunity, involving all susceptible species in the area, and not by individual*

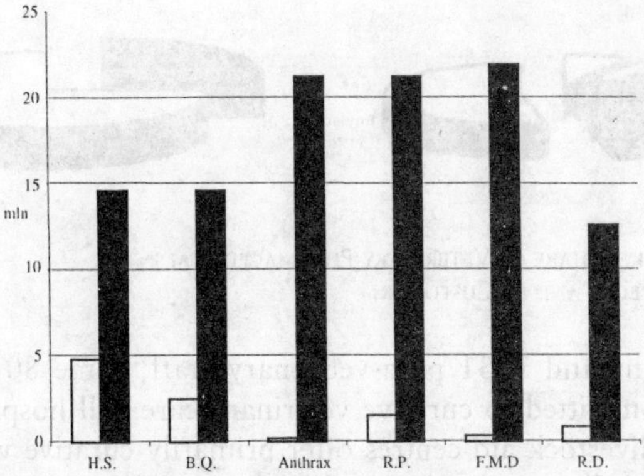


FIG. 7.4: ANIMALS AND BIRDS AT RISK AND NUMBER VACCINATED.

NOTE: This bar chart includes all species at risk and the nos vaccinated grey: vaccinations & dark: total numbers at risk.

*vaccinations, as targeted by the subsidised centrally sponsored scheme (Crossbred cows only' etc.)*. The vaccinations, therefore, could confer no immunity to the vaccinated animals and was an infructuous exercise.

This is the general experience with all vaccinations against all diseases, reducing vaccinations to a mere ritual. Application of the same amount of money perhaps on a planned disease control programme—based on a control plan, area specific and supported by a sound epidemiological surveillance system, can result in actual control of the disease targeted, with cost-benefit ratios, of a very high order. A classical example for this is the NPRE, which in a short span of just six years, rid India of Rinderpest.

## 7.9 ANIMAL HEALTH SERVICES

Livestock health care services in the state are primarily the responsibility of the State Department of Animal Husbandry & Veterinary Services. The department for this purpose has set up a state wide network of Veterinary Hospitals, Veterinary Dispensaries and Livestock Aid Centres: 541 Veterinary Hospitals and Dispensaries (2000-1). These veterinary institutions look after on an average some 28000 bovine; 14000 sheep, goat and pig; and some 34000 poultry per centre (arithmetical average, not actual coverage). The department for this purpose employs some 799 qualified

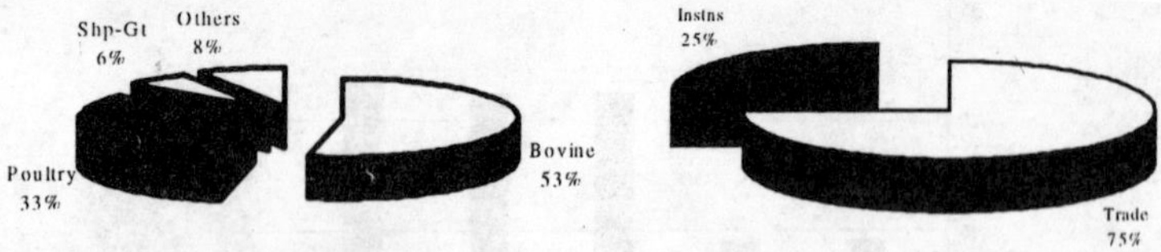


FIG. 7.5 MARKET SHARE OF VETERINARY PHARMACEUTICALS: BY SPECIES AND BY CUSTOMER.

veterinarians and 3031 para-veterinary staff, some 80 per cent of them committed to curative veterinary care. All hospitals, dispensaries, livestock aid centres offer primarily curative veterinary care, free to all animals presented to the institution. However, for many years now the free service has only been a mind set, as all these institutions receive only marginal supply of medicines, reagents and consumable, on account of stringent budgetary insufficiency. Almost 95 per cent of the department's annual budget from all sources (state plan, central plan and state non-plan) is spent on establishment: salaries, allowances, travel and transport, leaving only 5 per cent for medicines and consumable. The farmer receives only a prescription from the institution and he has to procure the medicines and consumable from the retail trade at his own cost. Where the professionals posted at these centres have to attend a case at the farmer's doorstep, the farmer has to bear the transport cost, cost of drugs and the practitioner's fee as well. And to compound and confound the issue, the institutions and their equipment are mostly obsolete and the service inappropriate.

Turnover of the veterinary pharmaceutical industry in India in 1997 was some Rs. 5000 mln. The market share of veterinary pharmaceuticals by species and by customer are presented in Fig. 7.5 and the market share, product groupwise in the Fig. 7.6 (Source: trade sources quoting ORG, Baroda, study carried out for the Organisation of Pharmaceutical Producers of India, OPPI, 1997). Institutional sale, mostly that of the state departments of animal husbandry, was only 25 per cent. Products like feed additives account for 22 per cent of the market and most of it was institutional. Therefore, the share of veterinary drugs and pharmaceuticals, all categories included, for all states put together, was less than 5 per cent of the total trade, equivalent to Rs. 250 mln annually or barely Rs.10 million per state. This in Orissa, works out to *Re. 0.88 per*

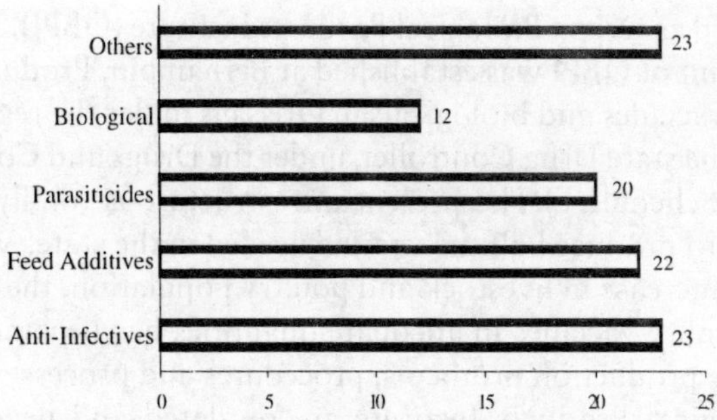


FIG. 7.6: MARKET SHARE OF PRODUCT GROUP.

*case treated for the nearly 12 mln cases in 1997.* This by no stretch of imagination can be called free service. The specialist team under the LSR exercise in their report assessed the purchase of vaccines from sources other than the OBPI at some Rs. 3 million per year. Similarly, the institutional purchase of medicines is placed by them at Rs.15 million annually. The prescription sale of veterinary medicines in the state is estimated as around Rs. 90 million and poultry feed supplements, etc., as Rs. 30 million.

The presence of private veterinary practitioners is confined to urban areas. Private practice, though not alluring, is currently gaining momentum due to the commercial exploitation of livestock, by producer households. Crossbred cattle has contributed to the potential for private practice as the producers can afford high quality service. However, the overcrowding of the practice market by government sponsored free service, leaves no space for free markets to emerge. Studies carried out by the Indian Institute of Management, Ahmedabad, recently, reveal that farmers across all categories, in the three study states, have overwhelmingly opted for paid, but good quality veterinary service, rather than the free services offered by the governments. It is therefore high time that the GoO seriously consider promotion of private veterinary practice starting with the tenth plan, instead of setting up more government owned veterinary hospitals and dispensaries.

## 7.10 VETERINARY BIOLOGICAL AGENTS

The Orissa Biological Product Institute is one of the oldest in the country. Its forerunner, the Orissa Serum Institute was established in 1946 at Cuttack. In 1961 the Institute was shifted to Bhubaneswar and renamed as Orissa Biological Products Institute (OBPI). In 1992 a satellite unit of OBPI was established at Berhampur. Production of veterinary vaccines and biologicals in Orissa is under the regulatory control of the state Drug Controller, under the Drugs and Cosmetics Act 1940 (Schedule-F).The present infrastructure is totally inadequate even to produce half the vaccine needed in the state. With the large-scale increase in livestock and poultry population, the need to produce quality vaccines in adequate quantities has become acute. The vaccine production protocols, procedures and processes, at the state Biological Products Institute are outdated and need to be updated. A fair degree of obsolescence has set in, as over the years there has hardly been any modernisation. Vaccines produced in the institute do not follow the mandatory quality control procedures and are of uncertain quality. No vaccines are produced in private sector in Orissa. The state purchases several vaccines to meet the requirement, from other states and from the trade. The vaccines produced in the OBPI and those procured from other states are exhibited in Table 7.2. All these vaccines are now available in the market (all of better quality and potency). It will be a far better option for the government both in terms of quality and costs, to buy these vaccines from the commercial manufacturers then continuing to run the OBPI.

TABLE 7.2: VACCINES PRODUCED AT OBPI AND PROCURED FROM OTHER SOURCE

| *Sl. No.* | *Vaccines produced in the OBPI* | *Sl. No.* | *Vaccines procured from other states* |
|---|---|---|---|
| 1. | H.S. alum adjuvant vaccine | 1. | Ranikhet disease (Lasota Strain) vaccine |
| 2. | Black Quarter vaccine | 2. | Freeze dried anti Rabies vaccine |
| 3. | Freeze dried Ranikhet disease vaccine, $R_2B$ | 3. | Gumboro disease vaccine |
| 4. | FD RD (F strain vaccine) | 4. | Swine fever vaccine |
| 5. | Anthrax spore vaccine | 5. | Sheep pox vaccine |
| 6. | Enterotoximia vaccine | 6. | Caprine pleuro pneumonia vaccine |
| 7. | H.S. oil adjuvant vaccine | 7. | Distemper and cannine hepatitis vaccine |
| 8. | Anti Rabies vaccine (Flury LEP, etc.) | 8. | Leptospira vaccine |
| 9. | FD Fowl Pox vaccine | 9. | Parvo virus vaccine |
| | | 10. | Foot and mouth vaccine |
| | | 11. | Faline leukopenia vaccine and |
| | | 12. | H.S. and B.Q. combined vaccine. |

SOURCE: OBPI Bhubaneswar, quoted by the LSR specialist team for Animal Health, 1998.

# 8 Feed and Fodder in Orissa

All livestock production in Orissa, across all species (except the organised poultry industry) depend on crop residues, crop by products and grazing in the common property resources (CPRs) in the state. The crop residues commonly available are straws, stalks, stovers, tops and crop thrush; crop by products like bran's, husk, chunni, cotton seed, expeller cakes and solvent extraction meals. Grazing accounts for less than 30 per cent of the total dry matter intake of the large ruminants and almost 100 per cent in case of small ruminants, in Orissa. Common property resources in the state are: permanent pastures, current and other fallows, land under miscellaneous tree crops and groves, cultivable wastes and forests (see Tables 8.1 and 8.2). The major resources of feed and fodder in

TABLE 8.1: DRY MATTER INTAKE: SOURCES

| *Sl. No.* | *Source* | *Per cent* |
|---|---|---|
| 1. | Dry Fodder | 63.00 |
| 2. | Grazing | 28.00 |
| 3. | Cult. Gr. Fodder | 0.50 |
| 4. | Crop By-products | 7.00 |
| 5. | Grains | 1.50 |
| | Total | 100 |

TABLE 8.2: COMMON PROPERTY RESOURCES IN ORISSA

| *Type* | *Area '000 ha / %** |
|---|---|
| Forests | 5722 / 37.1 |
| Miscl. Trees, Groves etc. | 715 / 4.6 |
| Per. Pastures & Grazg. Land | 514 / 3.3 |
| Cultivable Waste | 435 / 2.8 |
| Current Fallows | 210 / 1.3 |
| Other Fallows | 354 / 2.3 |
| Total | 7950 / 51.4 |

NOTE: * % to total geographical area.
SOURCE: Statistical Outline of Orissa, 1997.

the state are agricultural crop residues, cultivated green fodder, and edible herbage from cropped lands, crop tops and grasses from the fallows, field borders, road margins and grazing lands. The quantity of fodder consumed through grazing varies from region to region, season to season; and the extent of forest areas, grazing lands and their proximity to habitation. Collection of fodder leaves and local grasses is a normal practice in the hilly areas. The proportion of livestock maintained on grazing alone is very small in the agriculturally developed, irrigated areas. Feed and fodder *availability* estimated by the feed and fodder team of the LSR Project represents only what is produced in Orissa. Estimates of feed and fodder *requirements* by the team are based on nutritional norms prescribed as standards. Estimates of *actual consumption* of feeds and fodder are based on responses received from farmers during a field survey (March-April 1999) carried out under the Livestock Sector Review Project.

## 8.1 Crop Residues

Crop residues constitute the major source of fodder for livestock in the state. The most important among them in the state is paddy straw. Other crop residues are stalks and stover from maize, sorghum, pearl millet; residues of pulse crops: green gram, black gram, horse gram and sugar cane tops. Paddy straw production in Orissa during 1995-6 was some 8.09 mln mt. This quantity of paddy straw, however, is not fully available for bovine feeding, but has other demands on it for thatching of houses, packaging in industries and as raw material for paper mills. In the northern part of Orissa wheat straw is produced, but it is not generally fed to ruminants. As crop residues normally accrue in proportion to grain output, estimation of their availability, is based on crop production data for 1995-6. Grain to crop residue ratios used, are based on norms developed by S.K. Ranjhan (1991) and N.S.R. Sastry (1994). For calculating the quantities of fodder available through grazing, the total area under grazing is taken into account. Total crop residues available in Orissa in 1995-6 (a normal year) was some 16.50 mln mt. Cropwise details of straw/stover production are presented in Table 8.1 in the Appendix. The total crop residue output in Orissa in 1999-2000, however, was only about half of the 1995-6 supply (8.95 mln mt), most likely on account of the impact of the 'killer cyclone' in October 1999.

## 8.2 Green Fodder

Reliable estimates of green fodder production are not available. Green fodder comes mainly from the common property resources like permanent pastures, areas under miscellaneous tree crops, current and other fallows and forests. Bio-mass production in the CPRs has dwindled over the years due to over grazing and poor management; and has now reached almost the point of no return. Purposive cultivation of green fodder in Orissa is extremely small because of the generally poor quality of the milch stock and the pressure on land for human food production. Cultivation of improved fodder crops is, however, gaining popularity and in 1997-8 the department of AH supplied 150 mt of fodder seeds to interested growers. The state AH Department has seven fodder seed production farms. Besides producing quality seeds, many improved pasture grasses and legumes have been screened and multiplied for distribution to the farmers, by these farms. A centrally sponsored scheme is also under implementation in 15 districts of the state. The funding is on 50 : 50 share basis between state and centre. The main objective of the scheme is to augment the production of fuel wood and fodder by involving the local people in planning, implementation and management of the project. The outlay for the year 1999-2000 was Rs.60 mln. During 1999-2000 an area of 4,000 ha has been covered. Area under green fodder production exhibited is on the basis of information available in the published literature, the availability of cultivated fodder is calculated taking average production of 28 mt per ha per year. Total availability of green fodder in 1995-6 is presented in the Table 8.3.

Table 8.3: Availability of Green Fodder

| *Source* | *Area 100 ha* | *Prod. '000 mt* |
|---|---|---|
| Cultivated | 39.32 | 451.45 |
| Grazing | 2007 | 15824.5 |
| Total | 2046.32 | 16285.95 |

## 8.3 Concentrate Feeds

The most common agricultural by-products used as animal feed, available in significant quantities in the state are: rice bran, de-oiled rice bran, wheat bran, pulse chunni, oil cakes, solvent extraction meals and grain grit. Grain is not generally fed to cattle and buffaloes but is essential ingredient of poultry and to a certain extent in pig feeds. It is believed that some 2-10 per cent of the food grains produced in the state (depending upon type: fine/coarse, etc) are also available for animal feed production, most of which is fed to poultry and high yielding dairy animals. Balanced commercial cattle feed formulations now include up to 10 per cent grains, special rations for milk production, even higher proportions. Crop byproducts and grains produced in Orissa, coming into the animal feed chain are: 0.53 mln mt and 0.14 mln mt, respectively. Crop by-product/grain wise availability, produced in the state, is given in Tables 8.2 and 8.3 in the Appendix. The extraction rate used for cake/meal/bran/chunnies have also been exhibited for ready reference.

## 8.4 Feed and Fodder Requirements

Estimates of feed and fodder requirements are based on livestock and poultry population, production data available in the ISS 1994-5, Department of AH and the production data available in 'Agricultural Situation in the State' 1996-7. Estimaties of the nutrient requirements of livestock, are based on nutrient norms prescribed by S.K. Ranjhan (1991). The other assumptions used as basis for this calculation are: (a) sheep and goat population get all their feed requirement from grazing; and (b) pigs get 98 per cent of their feed requirement through scavenging. Total requirement on these norms and assumptions works out to: feed concentrates 9.12 mln mt; green fodder 39.50 mln mt; and dry fodder 41.75 mln mt. Species wise details of feed and fodder requirements are presented in Table 8.4 in the Appendix.

## 8.5 Balancing Feed and Fodder Demand and Supply

Nutritional demand and available supply of fodder and feeds grown in the state as reported by the LSR feed and fodder study do not match, leaving wide deficits in supply. This theoretical demand-supply position for feed and fodder in Orissa has not changed substantially over the past 50 years; and yet all species of domestic livestock grew 65 to 366 per cent over the period (see population figures in Chapter 2) and their output more than doubled: milk

TABLE 8.4: REQUIREMENT AND AVAILABILITY OF FEED STUFF

| *Feed Stuff* | *Availablity* | *Requirements* | *Deficit* |
|---|---|---|---|
| Dry Fodder | 16501.55 | 41753.21 | 25251.66 / 60.47 |
| Green Fodder | 16285.95 | 39496.09 | 23210.14 / 58.76 |
| Concentrates | 661.67 | 9115.57 | 8453.39 / 92.74 |

NOTE: Quantities in '000 mt. SOURCE: LSR F&F team estimates.

100 per cent, meat 100 per cent, eggs over 800 per cent and poultry meat 200 per cent, all in spite of the deficits (staggering) portrayed by these estimates. This clearly indicates that theoretical estimates are often misleading and unreliable. *Nutritional demand* and *effective demand* for feed and fodder are considerably different from (see Table 8.4 and Fig. 8.1) each other, as the effective demand is what is actually consumed for livestock production in the state and depends entirely on the feeding practices followed by the farmers. *Shortages exist and feeding is not optimal, but farmers make do with what is practical and economically sustainable.* The farming community balances the demand-supply gaps by following a discriminatory feeding regime within their herds, the high yielding animals receive larger quantities and better quality feed stuffs; older and unproductive animals receive the poorest quality and subsistence rations; work animals are raised on dry fodder only, with concentrate supplements during the working season. Home grown/bought out crop residues and grazing on CPRs, are the universal treatments for all animals.

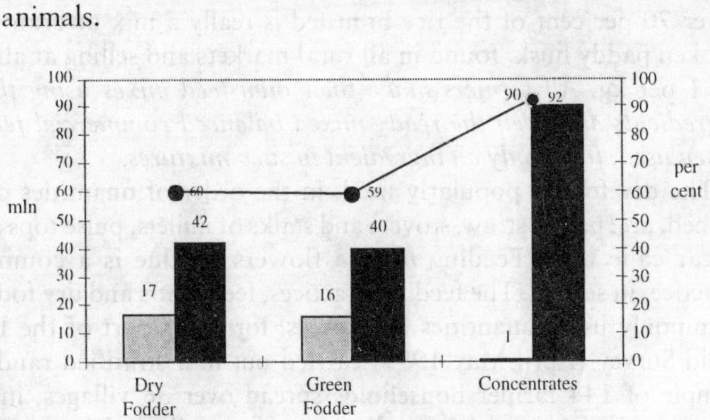


CHART LEGEND: BLACK: DEMAND; GREY: SUPPLY; LINE: DEFICITS.

FIG.8.1: DEMAND, SUPPLY AND DEFICIT OF FEED STUFF.

## 8.6 Feeding Practice in Producer HH and Common Feed Stuffs used

Feeding practices for large ruminants in villages follow more or less the same logic in almost all agro-climatic regions in the state. Small ruminants survive entirely on grazing. The feeding practices are all predominantly based on dry fodder, the most popular roughage being paddy straw, either home produced or bought from neighbours. Calves, growing stock and dry animals normally do not receive any concentrate feed and survive almost entirely on grazing and limited rations of dry fodder. All animals are sent out for grazing in nearby common property resources, often the village commons, the fallows, forests where nearby; and returned home in the evening. In some areas non-milking animals are not brought back home in the evenings but only at the end of the season. Concentrate feeds are fed only to milking animals and to the work animals during the work season and on days of heavy work of haulage and transport. There are milch animals reared in all the towns and cities in many households, as well as commercial milch animals, almost entirely stall fed on straws and with concentrate supplementation. The most popular concentrate feed ingredients used by Orissa farmers are: rice bran, chokker (wheat bran), dal chuni (a mix of husk, bran and small quantities of broken grains of different pulses, a by-product of grain and flour trade), rice polish, de-oiled rice bran, balanced concentrate feeds, grains grits, crushed paddy, maize and oil cakes. Over 70 per cent of the rice bran fed is really a mix of bran and broken paddy husk, found in all rural markets and selling at about Re.1 per kg. *All farmers make their own feed mixes using these ingredients and even the ready mixed balanced commercial feeds, when used, form only an ingredient in such mixtures.*

The dry fodder popularly used, in the order of quantities consumed, are: paddy straw, stovers and stalks of millets, pulse tops and sugar cane tops. Feeding *mahua* flowers residue is a common practice, in season. The feeding practices, feed stuffs and dry fodder commonly used, quantities and prices, formed a part of the LSR Field Survey (April-May 1999) carried out in a stratified random sample of 144 farmer households spread over 36 villages, in 12 districts. Information on feeding practices followed by farmers (modes in frequency distribution) gathered during the field survey are presented in the Table 8.5 and form the basis for the feed consumption analysis. All productive animals do not get the listed

TABLE 8.5: FEEDING PRACTICE BY DIFFERENT TYPES OF FARMERS

| | *Landless* | *Marginal* | *Small* | *Semi-Medium* | *Medium* | *Large* |
|---|---|---|---|---|---|---|
| Feed Type | Coastal | Midlands | Uplands | Coastal | Midlands | Uplands |
| Rice Bran | 2.00 | 2.00 | 0.50 | 2.00 | 5.00 | 2.00 |
| Rice Polish | 0.00 | 0.00 | 0.50 | 0.00 | 0.00 | 0.50 |
| Wheat Bran | 1.00 | 1.50 | 0.00 | 2.00 | 2.00 | 0.00 |
| Horse Gram Chuni | 0.20 | 0.25 | 0.00 | 0.00 | 0.00 | 0.00 |
| Mung / Urad Chuni | 1.00 | 0.00 | 0.00 | 0.00 | 0.00 | 0.00 |
| Crushed Paddy | 0.50 | 0.00 | 0.50 | 1.00 | 0.00 | 0.50 |
| Maize | 0.50 | 0.50 | 0.00 | 0.00 | 0.00 | 0.00 |
| Oilseed Cakes (GN/ TIL) | 0.50 | 0.50 | 0.00 | 0.50 | 0.00 | 0.50 |
| Balanced Cattle Feed | 0.00 | 0.00 | 3.00 | 0.00 | 2.00 | 2.00 |

NOTE: Quantities used per animal per day when fed, but not all at a the same time.

quantities of all the feed ingredients listed, but only a mix of some of them totalling to 2 kg per day. Feeding of concentrates is limited to milking animals and to draught animals on days when they work. With rare exceptions of crossbred animals, milch animals usually get concentrate feed for some 100 days in a year and draught animals 60 days in a year.

## 8.7 ANIMAL FEED CONSUMPTION IN ORISSA AND THE EFFECTIVE DEMAND-SUPPLY BALANCE

Dry fodder, mostly grown within the state, forms the staple for large ruminant production in Orissa. There is no evidence of large scale cross border trade in straws or other kinds of dry fodder. The supply of dry fodders available (see Fig.8.2) within the state, 8.96 mln mt, works out to some 2.37 kg per day per adult bovine unit, in the state. The large and small ruminants share the natural green fodder available in the state, particularly grazing. The supply estimate of 16.28 mln mt of green fodder therefore works out to an average share of some 4.32 kg per adult bovine unit per day and 0.70 kg per adult sheep and goat. Orissa is a state with many rivers and has an annual rainfall of some 1450 mm spread over some 4 months of the year (72 wet days). Natural bio-mass production in the state during the wet season, therefore, would be a major source of fodder for the ruminants in the state. A large quantity of natural, rain fed herbage, will therefore be available for chance grazing or cutting, during the wet months, for some 130 days. This will provide an additional

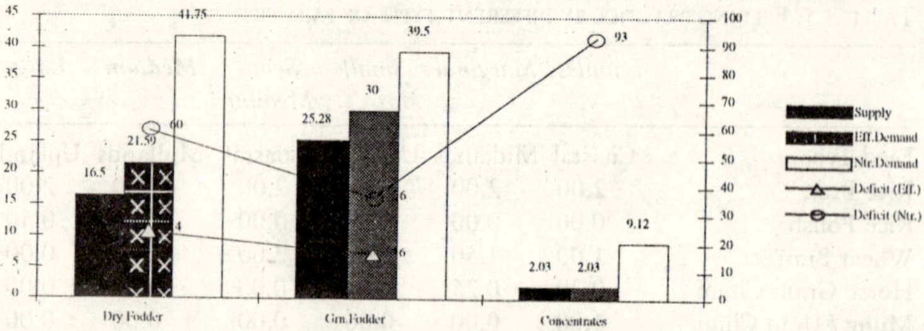


FIG. 8.2: SUPPLY / EFFECTIVE DEMAND AND SUPPLY / NUTRITIONAL DEMAND: FEED AND FODDER.

supply of some 9 mln mt of herbage over 130 days in the wet season or a per capita additional supply of some 3.50 kg green per day per bovine unit and a per capita availability of some 0.60 kg per day for sheep and goat. Based on the information presented in Tables 8.5 and 8.6 in the Appendix, the total concentrate feed consumption in the state for bovine feeding is estimated as some 2.12 mln mt per year, comprising all types of brans (rice bran, wheat bran, dal chuni): 1.60 mln mt; oil cakes: 0.22 mln mt; food grains (crushed paddy and maize): 0.22 mln mt; and branded balanced cattle feed 0.08 mln mt.

A comprehensive summary of the total availability of all animal feed stuffs in Orissa, along with their contribution to the dry matter intake of the animals, is presented in Table 8.6 in Appendix. Concentrate feed ingredients consumed in the state, 2.12 mln mt, both state grown and imported from out side the state, constitute the *effective demand* and therefore the *economic demand* for those commodities. Some 1.80 mln mt of these commodities are handled through the trade channels, wholesale as well as retail and the rest represent quantities home grown and directly consumed.

## 8.8 ANIMAL FEED INDUSTRY IN ORISSA

The compounded livestock feed industry in Orissa has grown rapidly in the past decade. There are 4 feed plants under the department of AH, 3 owned by the OAIC, 2 by the OPOLFED, 2 under the UGS, 1 belonging to the OMFED and 44 feed compounding plants in the private sector, together manufacturing some 80000 mt of balanced cattle and poultry feed annually in Orissa. The largest and the most sophisticated feed plants in Orissa belong to the OMFED and the

UGS, have a rated capacity of 100 mt of balanced feed pellets per day each and are located in Radhakishorepur and Patha respectively, in Cuttack district. The overall capacity utilisation of these plants is extremely poor in the government and co-operative sector and was less than 20 per cent in 1997. Feed plants in the private sector are all small plants with the exception of one or two with 50 mtpd capacity, but their capacity uitilisation is much higher, 50 per cent in 1997. A list of the feed milling plants in Orissa, their location and capacity is presented in Table 8.7 in the Appendix. Animal feed production is entirely under private sector, except the small feed plants run by the government departments and corporations. Although the government has a regulatory function, it has not been used to ensure quality standards in the feed industry. Consequently a number of the commercial brands marketed in the state are sub-standard.

# 9 Breeding of Livestock in Orissa

## 9.1 Planned Breeding Operations for Cattle and Buffalo

Livestock production is germane to the farming systems in Orissa—it is the major source of supplementary income, besides providing food security, protective foods; and the draught power extensively used in agricultural operations and rural transportation in the state. In spite of such critical contributions to family welfare, the subsistence farming systems prevalent in Orissa, apparently took the livestock sector for granted, contributing virtually nothing for developing the livestock system. Under interventions by the state government as a part of the planned development of the livestock sector, grading of indigenous cows with Hariana bulls by natural service, was started in early 1930s, to improve the productivity of the indigenous cattle for milk as well as work. The first AI centre was started at Cuttack Veterinary Hospital with Hariana and Red Sindhi bulls in 1949. Under the first five-year plan starting with 1951, six key village scheme units, each with six sub-centres and covering 3000 adult breedable female cattle each, were started in six of the blocks in the state. It had breeding facilities both through natural service and AI. The bulls used were of Hariana and Red Sindhi breeds. During the second plan 8 more such key village blocks were added—out of these, 2 were with natural service facilities, in the blocks at Kishorenagar and Bari in Jajpur district. Under the third plan, the key village scheme in Koraput was identified as Hill Cattle Development Scheme (1964). Fourth five-year plan introduced Intensive Cattle Development Projects (ICDP) in Cuttack and Puri districts (then undivided). Each ICDP had 100 AI centres grouped under 4 regional centres, covering in all around one lakh breedable female bovine, per project. During the fifth five-year plan two mini ICDP's were added, each with 50 AI centres, in Ganjam and Koraput districts. The semen bank at Cuttack was established under the fourth five-year plan exclusively for the ICDP areas. Frozen semen was introduced in the state in the year 1979 and by 1992 had replaced liquid semen in all AI centres throughout the state. Presently two frozen semen stations are functional in the state, one at Cuttack and the other in Bhawanipatna. Frozen semen of pure Jersey, crossbred Jersey, Hariana, Red Sindhi and Murrah buffalo are produced at these two semen production stations. These stations together produced, in the year 2000-1, some 0.14 mln doses of frozen semen. There were several special schemes both under the central and state plans, which were specifically for cattle and buffalo development, or which had a component for cattle and buffalo, under the various five-year plans, operating in the state between 1951 and 2001. For the sake of completeness of the sector analysis, the major ones among them are enumerated and exhibited in Table 3.9 in the Appendix.

## 9.2 Breeding Services in Orissa

Breeding services in Orissa, for cattle and buffalo are provided by three agencies: (i) State Department of Animal Husbandry; (ii) The Co-operative Milk Federation through its affiliated milk unions, and (iii) Utkal Gomangal Samiti (natural service).

Department of Animal Husbandry is the major provider of breeding services for cattle and buffalo in the state. Over the years between 1951 and 2001, the department established a vast, state-wide network of veterinary and animal husbandry institutions (see Table 9.1), including infrastructure for production of frozen semen and liquid nitrogen, distribution, storage and supply of semen and liquid nitrogen, production and testing of bulls; and field AI centres to deliver artificial insemination services, throughout the state. Institutions under the state department of animal husbandry are discussed in detail in Chapter 10 on 'Institutional Set Up and Infra-

Table 9.1: Breeding Support Institutions

| *Institutions* | *Nos* |
|---|---|
| Sperm Stations | 2 |
| Frozen Semen Banks | 5 |
| Liquid Nitrogen Plants | 12 |
| Cattle Breeding Farms | 12 |
| Training Institutions | 2 |
| Progeny Testing Scheme | 1 |
| Embryo Transfer Technology | 1 |
| AI Centres (DAH & VS) | 1788 |

structure'. The locations of all breeding support institutions except the field AI centres are exhibited in Table 3.10 in the Appendix. Artificial insemination services in the state started in the year 1949, with liquid semen. Frozen semen was introduced in the state in 1978 and over a fifteen-year period, by 1992, complete switch over to frozen semen for AI was achieved throughout the state. There are now, under the DAH & VS, 1788 AI outlets located at veterinary hospitals, Livestock Aid Centres and AI centres. In 1997-8 some 0.67 million inseminations were performed. In 1998, 40 years after the introduction of AI in Orissa, less than 5 per cent of the total breedable female cattle and not even 0.5 per cent of the female buffaloes, are bred by AI. The growth of AI services in the state over the years is exhibited in Table 3.11 in the Appendix.

Frozen semen production in Orissa is carried out in the two sperm stations, set up at Cuttack and Bhawanipatna. With financial grants from the Technology Mission on Dairy Development (TMDD) during 1997-8, both stations were expanded and modernised. The assistance from the TMDD was Rs.10.36 mln for Cuttack and Rs.5.38 mln for Bhawanipatna. The details related to these stations are presented in Table 3.12 in the Appendix. The semen production stations do not supply semen doses from the same bull to the same area for more than three years in order to avoid inbreeding among the cattle and buffalo populations. For storage and re-distribution of frozen semen, five semen banks have also been established at strategic locations. For the production of liquid nitrogen, the department has 12 small liquid nitrogen plants, with varying capacities ranging between 6 litres to 10 litres per hour. The total production of liquid nitrogen in 1997 was 0.36 million litres, against the demand of 0.40 million litres. The short fall in liquid nitrogen supply from the captive plants was made up by purchase of $LN_2$ from industrial gas manufacturers in the state. Production of breeding bulls is the responsibility of the twelve livestock breeding farms/bull mother farms of the department. The breeds maintained at these farms are pure Jersey, Hariana, Red Sindhi, Crossbred Jersey and Murrah buffalo. There are also two central cattle breeding farms of the GoI, Department of AH & D, in Orissa, one at Chipilima for Red Sindhi and Sindhi x Jersey crosses; and the other at Similiguda for pure Jersey. The performance of these farms and their contribution to the breeding efforts are discussed in Chapter 10 on 'Institutional Set Up and Infrastructure'. To train the AI personnel, the department has facilities at two locations in the state, at Cuttack and Bhawanipatna, with classrooms and hostel facilities. Training programmes for different categories of AI personnel are conducted in these two training centres. A progeny testing program for selection of AI bulls is being implemented since 1989 with the support of GoI. So far three batches of bulls have been covered under the scheme. Only one batch has completed the progeny test and three bulls have been found acceptable. Embryo Transfer Technology both for cattle and buffaloes, was introduced in the state as early as 1989, when an ET field centre under the Science and Technology Mission of the Department of Biotechnology, GoI, was established at Kalyani, under the OMFED. The central cattle breeding farm at Similiguda was equipped with ET facilities by the central department of AH & D, in the early 1990s. The state DAH & VS's ET centre was established in Cuttack, in 1994-5, with the objective of producing superior bulls for breeding, as well as for producing genetically elite bull mothers.

*OMFED and its AI Network.* The Orissa Co-operative Milk Federation and its affiliated unions started AI facility in the dairy cooperative societies in 1981 with frozen semen, primarily as a production support service for their producer members. Some 309 AI outlets (48 mobile cluster practices and 267 DCS based) were functional under the OMFED in 2002. Trained AI workers, all employees of the societies, provide the service at the DCS. The federation purchases frozen semen and liquid nitrogen from outside the state. The AI workers are selected from amongst the employees for each society and they undergo a training of six weeks in artificial insemination and veterinary first aid, at the federation's training centre OMTDC in Kalyani. In 2001-2 the Federation carried out some 100548 AIs in the DCS villages. The growth of AI between 1985-98 in OMFED's cooperative network is exhibited in Table 3.13 in the Appendix.

*The Utkal Gomangal Samiti.* The Orissa Cattle Breeding Association was formed in the year 1936, which was subsequently renamed as the Utkal Gomangal Samiti, with the main objective of upgrading indigenous cattle and buffalo through natural service. The Samiti's activities supplement the efforts of the department where artificial insemination facility has not reached so far. To support the natural breeding programs, bull rearing and fodder cultivation activities are also taken up by the Samiti. The Utkal Gomangal Samiti receives grants in aid from the government to meet expenditure on bull subsidy, rearing cost of bull calves, cultivation of fodder and the Samiti's establishment cost. In 1998-9 the grant provision was Rs. 1.00 mln under state plan and Rs. 2.20 mln under state non-plan. The Samiti have set up four bull rearing units at Patha, Sagadi, Angul, and Bhogara, where selected Hariana, Red Sindhi, Crossbred and Murrah buffalo bull calves are reared, after procuring them from individuals, state farms or central government farms. The Samiti provides a grant of Rs. 100 per month to the custodian of the bull. Between 1987-8, the Samiti has distributed some 1781 cattle bulls and 646 buffalo bulls. In addition OMFED distributed some 469 bulls during the same period and 146 bulls by the National Watershed Development Programme between 1996-8. Year wise details of natural service bull distribution is presented in Table 3.14 in the Appendix.

### 9.3 Artificial Insemination in Orissa: Performance Analysis

*Conception Rates and Calves Born.* Artificial Insemination of cattle started in Orissa as early as 1949, with the establishment of the first AI centre in the Cuttack veterinary hospital. This was followed by the launch of planned programmes for breeding of bovine, starting with the key village scheme in 1951. AI became popular by 1954 and large numbers of cattle were by then bred by AI. By 1998 the Department of AH & VS was carrying out some 0.67 mln AI in a year. The progressive growth of AI in the state from 1954 onwards, till 1998, is presented in Table 9.2 in the Appendix. The department routinely carries out pregnancy diagnosis of the inseminated animals, but only of a small sample of them and exhibit in their official reports a calf born rate (CBR) based on the pregnancy diagnosis. This CBR varies widely in the different years within a range between 27 per cent in some years to 59 per cent in others: but mostly centres around 40 per cent. Arithmetically the state records show the total calves born to 7.50 mln AI over the years 1954-5, as some 3.06 mln (some 40 per cent). The CBR unfortunately is too subjective an estimate and is therefore quite unreliable. The attempt here is an exercise to derive by analysis and triangulation, an approximation of the quality and achievements of the AI service in the state over the years. The

TABLE 9.2: ARTIFICIAL INSEMINATION AND CALF BORN (CB)

| *Years* | *AI (CB) nos. in lakh* | *CB nos. in lakh* |
|---|---|---|
| 1990-1 | 0.65 | Cens. 1991: 5.63 |
| 1991-2 | 3.03 | |
| 1992-3 | 2.82 | |
| 1993-4 | 2.94 | |
| 1994-5 | 2.84 | Cens. 1995: 7.38 |
| Total | 12.28 | Incremental: 1.75 |

total number of artificial inseminations performed in Orissa over the 40 years 1954-5, was some 7.55 mln together with exotic semen, crossbred semen and semen of indigenous bulls, both cattle and buffalo. There is no information available on the DAH & VS records, on the breedwise use of semen for AI for any of the 40 years between 1954-95, except for the period after 1985. In the absence of a system of identification of AI born calves by tattooing or ear tags, the only identifiable calves born to AI by virtue of their distinctive appearance, are the crossbred calves. Full information on AI with exotic and crossbred semen (which leads to birth of crossbred calves) are available only for the period 1990-5 (see Table 9.2). The incremental number of crossbred calves born, are derived from the state livestock census data for the 1982, 1991 and 1995 rounds. Total AI resulting in crossbred calves during 1990-5 (AI with exotic and crossbred bull semen) adds up to 12.28 lakh. Incremental number of crossbred calves born between 1991 and 1995, according to census tables are 174951, some 14.25 per cent, say 15 per cent of the total AI with exotic and crossbred semen, during the same period. This is a measure of the quality of AI in Orissa all through the 40 years 1954-95, as '1990-5' perhaps is the best period among the 40 years because: (i) all semen used was good quality frozen semen, (ii) AI in Orissa had by then had over 35 years of experience, and (iii) almost half the cows inseminated during the period were better than average crossbred cows. In the absence of breed wise details of semen used for AI for the entire period, it is impossible to make any assessment of the quality of the AI services in the state, except the test analysis of the crossbred calves born between 1990-5. The truth about the AI services in Orissa will emerge only if the DAH & VS makes a genuine effort to compute a reasonable table of breedwise semen use for actual AI over the years. Till then, the conclusion based on the interpretation of the test analysis, can only be that the over all success (conception rate) of AI performed between 1954-95, in Orissa, is somewhere between 10 and 20 per cent.

*Coverage of Breedable Female and Decline of AI Services*: The Department of Animal Husbandry and the OMFED together carried out some 0.74 mln artificial inseminations in 1997-8, in Orissa, when the total breedable female cattle and buffalo together was some 4.46 mln. With AI resulting in less than 20 per cent conception rate, necessitating some 5 AIs per conception, this works out to an AI coverage of some 0.15 mln breeding animals (simple arithmetical derivative), almost entirely cattle, less than 4 per cent of the breedable population. AI in buffalo was only some 8829 in 1997-8. Buffalo in Orissa is at present virtually out of the ambit of AI. In actual practice, however, farmers tend to desert the AI service and go for natural mating, if AI does not result in pregnancy after one or two attempts (farmers' response: LSR field study). The number of cows actually receiving AI service each year, could therefore be much larger than the simple arithmetic derivation of 4 per cent; in all probability it could be twice as much or even be up to 10 per cent, say half a million. Over the past five years, the AI system in Orissa has taken a severe beating, number of delivery outlets (AI centres) have gone down from 2091 in 1998 to 1510 (*Economic Survey* 2001), AIs carried out have fallen from 0.67 mln in 1995 to 0.23 mln in 2001 (see Fig. 9.1) and frozen semen production from 0.87 mln in 1996 to a mere 0.14 mln in 2001. The decline had started in 1998 and had been steady: AI 1997-8 0.67 mln, 1998-9 0.60 mln, 1999-2000 0.48 mln and 2000-1 0.23 mln. The devastation during the 'killer cyclone', diversion of public funds to relief and

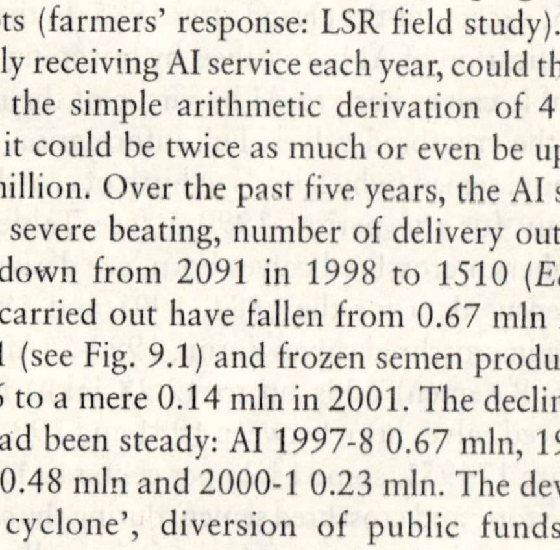


FIG 9.1: COWS RECEVING ARITICIAL INSEMINATION.

rehabilitation post cyclone, severe malnutrition of the livestock in the post cyclone rural Orissa, are all possible reasons for this decline.

### 9.4 Breeding Policy for Cattle and Buffalo in Orissa

Artificial insemination of cattle started in Orissa as early as 1949, but spread of AI to the different parts of the state took off only from the first five-year plan period onwards. Even though the programmes for genetic upgradation of cattle and buffaloes in the state of Orissa had been going on for many years, the state government announced a formal breeding policy only in 1982. Even in the absence of a comprehensive breeding policy frame till 1982, the breeding programme for cattle in the state had been directed towards the production of dual purpose animals: oriented towards the dual objectives of increasing of milk production and for developing draught animals for farm power, through grading up of the local cattle with the Hariana breed. The growth in milk production in the state, nevertheless was extremely sluggish, as the coverage of the breeding animals under the breeding programme was only marginal. Buffaloes were largely ignored by the organised breeding programmes and were left alone to be taken care of by the farmers owning them. Recognising the need for scientific and technological interventions in the breeding of the large ruminants, the Directorate of Animal Husbandry and Veterinary Services, constituted an expert committee to examine the policies and options available to the government for interventions. The department organised a cattle-breeding conference in December 1981 to consider the recommendations of the experts committee.

A detailed cattle and buffalo breeding policy, balancing the twofold objectives of increasing milk production and breeding of improved draught animals was formulated, on the basis of the discussions in the conference and was notified in March 1982. The policy covered the different regions of the state specifically, taking into account the already existing type of animals and preference of farmers, of the region. Orissa has no indigenous breeds of cattle native to the state. Therefore for cattle, Hariana was the breed of choice as the donor for grading up of the nondescript cattle in general as well as for production of improved draught animals. The dairy animal for Orissa was defined by the policy as the '50 per cent cross between the exotic Jersey breed with Hariana/Red Sindhi as the indigenous half'. In the big industrial cities of the state and their neighbourhood, the department was to try a crossbred mix with 25 per cent Friesian and 25 per cent Jersey as the exotic component. Hariana bulls and half bred bulls (50 per cent Jersey x Hariana) produced in the state livestock breeding farms were to be used for the breeding programme. Jersey bulls were to be provided by the exotic cattle-breeding farm at Chipilima. Distribution of semen from the Jersey/half bred (Jersey x Hariana) AI bulls was to be on the basis of the notified breeding policy for each region. The half bred bull semen was also to be supplied in all regions, even if such areas fall under Hariana upgrading tract. In the case of buffaloes too, Orissa did not have any recognisable indigenous breeds except Parlakhemundi, found in substantial numbers in Parlakhemundi and Gunupur subdivisions of Ganjam and Koraput districts. In these areas the policy was selective breeding within the breed with the objective of improving its desirable characteristics: draught ability and milk production. In the rest of the state, based on past experience, Murrah breed was chosen as the donor breed for grading up the local nondescript buffaloes. For over fifteen years from 1982 till 1998, this breeding policy was in force (at least in theory, as AI coverage of breeding populations were less than 5 per cent all along). Fresh guidelines were issued by the GoO in October 1998, vide its order no.17808 dated 15.10.98, for the breeding policy and the AI programme in the state. The detailed guidelines are exhibited as 3.15 in the Appendix. The gist of the guidelines dealing with breeding policy itself are reproduced below:

(a) Crossbreeding of 50 % indigenous cows, with pure HF semen should be adopted to limit exotic inheritance at 50 %.
(b) Effort should be made to upgrade the local indigenous stock through AI or natural breeding with Hariana and concentrating such draught power regeneration oriented breeding programmes in specific areas of Cuttack, Jaipur, Nayagarh and Kandhamal districts.
(c) Jersey, the milch breed of choice, should be made available throughout the state for crossbreeding programme, with maximum 50 % exotic inheritance.
(d) Since the Red Sindhi breed is not markedly beneficial either for milch or for draught purpose and does not have specific mention in the breeding policy, the department should retreat using this breed for up-grading purpose.
(e) Wherever advanced farmers are serious about raising the exotic level to 62 %, they may be encouraged to do so.

## 9.5 Progeny Testing Scheme

The State Department of Animal Husbandry started a field AI based (Contemporary Comparison) progeny testing programme for selection of crossbred AI bulls in 1987-8, as a centrally sponsored scheme (see Table 9.3). Some 120 AI centres grouped into 12 clusters of 10 AI centres in each, mostly in the key village and ICDP areas in Puri and Cuttack districts, formed the test area. So far three batches, with ten bulls in each batch, have completed test matings and the first batch has completed the test over a ten year period. The department reports that the test has enabled them to select three bulls as proven, out of the first batch. The technical programme for the test was the standard programme recommended by the department of AH & D, GoI, for all participants in the centrally sponsored scheme. This consisted of milk recording of the first lactation of identified test daughters at 30 day intervals and 10 recordings per daughter. The summary of records of the first batch test daughters averaged 1956 kg of milk in 300 days.

TABLE 9.3: PROGENY TESTING ATTRIBUTES

| *Recorded Traits* | *Performance Record Data* | *Deviation* |
|---|---|---|
| Number of test bulls in the Batch | 10 | – |
| Number of Daughters Recorded | 708 | – |
| Average 300 Day Lactation Yield | 1956.41 kg | +/- 32.21 kg |
| Average Fat per cent | 4.80 per cent | – |
| Average SNF per cent | 8.73 per cent | – |
| Age at Puberty | 901 days | +/- 16.74 days |
| Age at Conception | 960.65 days | +/- 18.59 days |
| Age at Girst Calving | 1242.33 days | +/- 18.21 days |
| Body Weight at First Calving | 285.03 kg | – |

SOURCE: B.K. Prusty quoted in the Report of the Milk Group, 1998.

## 9.6 Analysis of the Existing Breeding Policy for Cattle and Buffalo

Cattle and buffalo in Orissa are nondescript, low producing animals and there are no recognised descript breeds of cattle or buffalo in the state, except for some parochial strains among cattle and buffaloes. The current policy of the state government, for breeding of cattle and buffalo, is broadly in agreement with the national policy recommended by the GoI. The National Policy for cattle is cross-

TABLE 9.4: FROZEN SEMEN PRODUCTION AT CUTTACK AND BHAWANIPATNA FSB

| *Type of Bulls* | *No. of Bulls* | *Frozen Semen* | *Production Doses %* |
|---|---|---|---|
| Cattle | | | |
| Jersey | 26 | 288755 | (42) |
| Crossbred | 26 | 219807 | (32) |
| Red Sindhi | 13 | 145860 | (21) |
| Hariana | 6 | 37155 | (05) |
| Total | 71 | 691577 | (100) |
| Buffalo: Murrah | 5 | 1550 | |

SOURCE: FSBs Cuttack and Bhawanipatna, 1998.

breeding of the nondescript *desi* cattle with *exotic* breeds to produce *inter se mating* populations of *half breds*, constantly maintaining blood levels of the exotic and Indian parents, half and half, in the resultant populations. The approved strategy for this is *inter se mating* of the half breds, with intense selection of the half-bred bulls used. The recommended exotic breeds for crossbreeding are *Jersey* and *Holstein*. In Orissa the stated breeding policy seeks to address the state's compulsions: extremely poor levels of management and feeding; heavy dependence of crop sector on animal draught power; and the dire need for enhancing productivity of the milch animals in order to enhance farm incomes. The strategy to grade up the nondescript cattle with Hariana breed is most appropriate, both from the point of view of generally correcting the body size of the local cattle, as well as for draught animal production. The state department has been using pure Jersey semen for the crossbreeding programme in the state right from the beginning. But for the *inter se mating* of the adult breedable crossbred female, the state had not been able to arrange for adequate crossbred semen, nor are the crossbred bulls used, proven bulls. Adult crossbred female population in Orissa in 1998 was estimated as 0.40 mln and the animals breeding annually some 0.20 mln. The requirement of crossbred semen for breeding them *inter se* would be some 0.50 mln; while the total crossbred semen produced in the state is only some 0.22 mln. In addition OMFED has used some 70313 doses of crossbred semen imported from outside the state in 1997-8, making the total crossbred semen available some 0.29 mln doses (see Table 9.4), leaving a short supply of some 0.21 mln doses.

Breeding the crossbred female *inter se* with selected *half bred bulls* is the guiding principle of the breeding policy and failure to do so is wrought with serious negative consequences, both short and long term. Over the past four decades, the state's efforts in genetic upgradation, through crossbreeding of the nondescript *desi* cattle with exotic breeds, have paid marginal dividends and the results are poor: replacement of only some 7.25 per cent of the breedable female among *desi* cattle with crossbred cows. All discussions on the breeding policy for cattle and buffalo in Orissa are to an extent academic: the breeding policy has little relevance to the farming community in the state, as over 95 per cent of the state's breedable cows and buffaloes are beyond the reach of the AI service of both the departments and the OMFED. With 5 per cent coverage of breeding animals and five AIs on an average per conception, the breeding policy and the organised breeding programme in the state has failed to a great extent to function as a development tool.

There is currently in Orissa considerable bias in favour of Jersey as the donor breed. The world over Holstein is the most popular breed among cattle for milk production. The comparative advantages of Holstein over Jersey have not been conclusively studied under Orissa conditions. The farmers' acceptance or rejection of Holstein crossbred could have been conclusively determined, had the department tried Holstein in equal measure as well for crossbreeding in the state, giving the farmers an opportunity to judge for themselves first hand. There are many living examples of Holstein crossbreds, of almost all configurations, thriving in many milk sheds in India, under conditions far more adverse than can be attributed to any region in Orissa. The closest to home examples are the milk sheds in West Bengal (Chagda, Krisnagar) and Andhra Pradesh (Chittoor district). All milk sheds in Maharashtra, particularly Pune, Akluj, Ahmednagar, Sholapur, Kolhapur, have chosen Holstein as the donor for crossbreeding of cattle. Holstein predominates in the whole of Punjab and Hariana and even in the harshest districts of Gujarat (Mehsana, Banaskanta and Sabarkanta), as well as many other states in the country (see Table 3.16 in the Appendix). In the past Holstein crossbreeding has been considered suitable for trying out in urban and peri-urban areas. Urban areas are not and should not, be the arena for large ruminant farming, as there are major environmental consequences. The state policies should encourage removal of cattle and buffaloes from urban areas, for the benefit of both man and animals alike.

The policy for the breeding of buffalo through grading up of the local buffaloes towards Murrah, using pure bred Murrah bulls progressively on the base populations, is most appropriate. The provision in the existing policy to develop the Parlakhemundi buffalo through selective breeding, is untenable from the user point of view. User preference in the Parlakhemundi tract also is overwhelmingly in favour of grading up with Murrah. There however is need for caution: if the local buffaloes in Orissa are indeed the swamp type (2n = 48), as established by the OUAT, then use of riverine type buffaloes to grade them up might, on the long term, have adverse consequences for the buffalo population in the state. Even if there are no major adverse consequences in the short term, there is need for thorough investigation of the long term consequences, as reliable data on the subject are scanty. This issue however can be settled quickly, if the National Bureau of Animal Genetic Resources is asked to study the matter and advise the Orissa government, suitably. There are similar reports on the existence of swamp type buffaloes from other states as well: Kerala, Assam and Manipur.

The current programme for field progeny testing in Orissa needs modification and perhaps, standardisation in tune with other successful such programmes in India. The test is essentially based on *contemporary comparison of daughters* of the test bulls and should conform to strict frames of time and generations—all contemporaries (test daughters of all bulls in the same batch, in statistically relevant numbers) being born, performing and recorded, within the span of the same period to qualify as contemporaries. It is also necessary that all records are comparable and must be expressed as 'Standard Lactation, 4 per cent FCM' and corrected for 305 day performance. For this, every recorded sample must be fat tested and the fat records too taken into consideration for computing the standard lactation. Currently the progeny testing programme in Orissa has no arrangements for fat testing of recorded samples.

## 9.7 Recommended Breeding Policy for Livestock in Orissa

### (A) BREEDING POLICY FOR CATTLE

Cattle in Orissa are small and very low in production, both in terms of milk as well as draught power. The state is currently at the bottom of the list for milk production among all states in the country, and has the lowest per capita availability of milk—65 g. per head per day. Crop production in Orissa is still heavily dependent on draught animals for farm power and this is likely to continue for the next two to three decades. Therefore the primary breeding objectives for cattle in the state should be twofold: (i) breeding of improved milch animals, and (ii) breeding of improved draught animals. A basic prerequisite for achieving both these objectives is a foundation animal with better body size and body weight: an increase from the present average of 180-200 kg to 300-350 kg as the first step. This goal common to the two objectives can be achieved by vigorously following the existing breeding policy for *grading up* of the Orissa cattle with the Hariana breed as the donor not only in the presently identified areas, *but in all districts all over the state as a Policy Universal.* This programme of *grading up* should continue for a period of the next 25 years, over five generations of progenies. The *grading up* with Hariana should be through a massive AI coverage, bringing under it as many of the breeding female among local cattle; and supplemented by natural service with Hariana bulls, where AI is not feasible. The outcome of this *grading up* will be a large population of graded Orissa cattle, closer in many attributes to the Hariana breed, providing:

(i) Excellent draught animals with better body size and higher work output, for farm power;
(ii) Excellent foundation stock of female, with larger body size, better genetic architecture for milk production, as the base population for crossbreeding with exotic breeds.

*Policy for Milch Animal Production.* The policy for milch animal production will be *crossbreeding* of the local nondescript cattle with exotic breeds to produce *inter se mating* populations of half breds, maintaining the genetic contribution of the two parental types constantly half and half, ensuring endurance and survivability from the Indian Mother and high milk production qualities from the exotic sire. For *inter se mating* of the half breds, genetically evaluated *$F_1$ crossbred bulls* (exotic x Hariana) will be produced in identified breeding farms, using multiple ovulation embryo transfer technology (MOET) for building up an open nucleus breeding system (ONBS). Selection of crossbred bulls from the crossbred populations in Orissa *will not start earlier than the fifth generation* of inter se mated progenies under this policy. All $F_1$ crossbred bulls used for *inter se mating* will simultaneously be progeny tested through field AI contemporary comparison. AI will be the primary tool for crossbreeding. The exotic breed used as donor for crossbreeding *should progressively be Holstein* and Jersey should be phased out gradually from category A and B districts over the next 25 year period; *while Jersey will continue in category C areas*. Table 9.1 in the Appendix on breeding policy orchestration specifies the strategy for the change over and the areas for the progressive introduction of the Holstein.

(B) BREEDING POLICY FOR BUFFALO

The breeding policy for buffalo will be grading up of the buffaloes in the state with selected Murrah bulls in all districts, including the Parlakhemundi areas—a 'Policy Universal' for the entire state. The grading up programme will continue for 25 years, over five generations of progenies under the policy. Selection of bulls from among the progenies in the field in Orissa will not start earlier than the fifth generation of the progenies. *The grading up programme will primarily be based on extensive AI coverage of the breeding buffalo female*, supported by natural service by selected Murrah bulls positioned in the villages where AI is not feasible. The AI coverage of buffalo at present is scanty—just 8000 AI in 1997-8. Rapid genetic improvement of the buffalo population is possible only if AI covers increasing proportions of the breeding female among buffalo year after year, as AI is the only tool that can carry genetic inputs into populations *en masse*. Buffalo bulls for the grading up programme and for natural service, should be selected from among the sons of the registered bull mothers in the field recording programme in Haryana/Punjab, until such time as the selection of bulls start from among the progenies in the field in Orissa. All Murrah bulls used for AI in Orissa will be progeny tested through AI contemporary comparison. The outcome of the breeding policy implementation will be: (i) a large population of high yielding buffalo female in the state; (ii) regular supply of large numbers of superior male buffalo work animals, and (iii) a generous supply of high quality meat animals for use in the state or for export to other states.

(C) GOAT BREEDING PROGRAMMES

There are two identified and characterised breeds of goats in Orissa—Ganjam and Black Bengal, which constitute the bulk of the goat population in the state. Ganjam goats are distributed mostly in the districts of Ganjam, Gajapati, Kandhamal, Koraput and parts of Kalahandi, while Black Bengal is found in the coastal, western and northern districts. There are in addition a few minor breeds/strains of goat Malkangiri found in the Malkangiri district and Orissa Brown found in the Keonjhar and Mayurbhanj districts.

The characteristics of the major breeds of goat in Orissa are presented in the Table 9.5. For breeding of goats, the emphasis was always on improvement of body weight in case of both Ganjam and Black Bengal, for enhancing meat production. Initially the attempt was to cross the two Orissa breeds with each other, Ganjam x Black Bengal and Black Bengal x Ganjam; sometimes even reverse and back crosses, as well. This was an unsuccessful experiment as both the breeds lost out on their original qualities and the crosses were inferior to both parents, in all respects. The official breeding programme was to crossbreed, both the breeds, with heavier indigenous breeds like Beetal, Jamunapari, Barbari and recently with Sirohi by the ILDP Koraput. Crossbreds were reported to be heavier but comparative data on the improvements are not available. There are also reports that crossbreds are less prolific than the parental breed, at least in the case of Black Bengal. The programme for using the heavier breeds for crossbreeding still continues. Though this crossbreeding programme had been practised in goats for quite some time, its impact on the goat populations is not yet visible. This primarily is due to the sporadic and haphazard spread of the programme and its extremely disjointed application. These programmes were limited in their reach and coverage of the breeding populations. There had also been acute dearth of selected crossbred

TABLE 9.5: CHARACTERISTICS OF MAJOR BREEDS OF GOATS IN ORISSA

| | | | | | | |
|---|---|---|---|---|---|---|
| 1 | Ganjam | Meat | Medium | Male Ave.<br>Female Ave. | 44.05 kg<br>31.87 kg | Tall and leggy, coat colour black, white, brown or spotted |
| 2 | Black Bengal | Meat | Small | Male Ave.<br>Female Ave. | 32.37 kg<br>18.31 kg | Small body with short legs, coat colour vary from black to brown |

NOTE: The body weights reported by the task force is far higher than those reported by the LSR Team for the Meat Group. This at least is an indication of the possible selection differential that exist in the populations for improvement by selection.

SOURCE: Report of the Task Force on Sheep and Goat, GoI, 1996.

bucks for distribution to farmers, as the state goat breeding farms have totally failed in fulfilling the demand.

(D) SHEEP BREEDING PROGRAMME

Orissa has two identified and characterised breeds of sheep: Ganjam and Bolangir. The Ganjam sheep are found predominantly in the districts of Ganjam, Koraput, Kandhamal, Cuttack and parts of Puri district; while the Bolangir sheep are distributed mostly in Bolangir, Sambalpur and Sundargarh districts. Sheep are farmed in Orissa primarily for mutton, as the state has high rainfall and high humidity, which is not conducive for rearing sheep with high density of wool and do not favour wool variety of sheep. Characteristics of the sheep breeds in Orissa are presented in the Table 9.6.

The breeding programmes for sheep in the state place emphasis on improving the body weight, by use of improved crossbred rams, for meat production. The breeding programmes involve crossing local Ganjam and Bolangir sheep with Corriedale, Malpura or Bharat Merino rams. Presently crossbred rams are being supplied to farmers for breeding and stock improvement. Ram centres have been started at the premises of the progressive farmers, to make the rams available for mating the local sheep in the villages. The ILDP, Koraput has launched a programme for upgradation of the Ganjam sheep with Malpura rams. Though the crossbreeding programme

TABLE 9.6: CHARACTERISTICS OF SHEEP BREEDS IN ORISSA

| *Breed* | *Type* | *Size* | *Body Weight* | *Description* |
|---|---|---|---|---|
| Bolangir | Meat | Medium | Male Ave. 23.60 kg<br>Female Ave.17.85 kg | White, light brown or mixed, while black animals are not rare. Male are horned, female polled. Fleece quality is extremely coarse, hairy and open. |
| Ganjam | Meat | Medium | Male Ave. 30.00 kg<br>Female Ave. 24.18 kg | Brown to dark tan with white spots on face and body. Male are horned and female polled Fleece hairy and short. |

NOTE: The body weights reported by the task force is far higher than those reported by the LSR Team for the Meat Group. This at least is an indication of the possible selection differential that exist in the populations for improvement by selection.

SOURCE: Report of the Task Force on Sheep and Goat, GoI, 1996.

had been practised in sheep for quite some time, its impact on the sheep populations is not yet visible. This primarily is due to the sporadic and haphazard spread of the programme and its extremely disjointed application as in the case of goats. These programmes were limited in their reach and coverage of the breeding populations. There had also been acute dearth of selected crossbred rams for distribution to farmers as the state sheep breeding farms have totally failed in fulfilling the demand.

Goat and sheep breeding farms (see Table 5.6 in the Appendix) in the state are in very bad shape and are without proper staff and facilities. The farm areas are not adequately protected from grazing by the outside animals. Maintenance of records on the performance of animals is poor. The achievements of the farms are not commensurate with the expenses incurred on running them; nor are they consistent with the original objectives for which the farms were set up. Supervision of the farms, their technical programme for breed improvement and even the actual management of the farms leave much to be desired.

### (E) PIG BREEDING

Pig account for only some 2.19 per cent of the total livestock population and the population size is 0.53 mln. Pigs are reared predominantly in the districts of Sundargarh, Mayurbhanj, Koraput, Malkangiri, Kandhamal, Rayagada, Nabarangpur, Keonjhar, Sambalpur, Gajapati and Balasore. Some 0.23 mln households (5.00 per cent) keep pigs and the sole purpose of pig keeping is meat production. All pigs found in Orissa are primitive and nondescript. Average body weight under free-range conditions is some 50 kg and meat yield is 30 kg. Pig farming is largely confined to the SC and ST farmers and is entirely based on scavenging. Three pig breeding farms exist under the state government, located at Chipilima in Sambalpur district, Matkambeda in Keonjhar district and Bhanjanagar in Ganjam district, where the pure bred boars of exotic breeds are kept and mated with the indigenous variety of pigs to produce crossbred males. Presently the state follows a policy of crossbreeding the native breed with exotic breeds. Several donor breeds have been tried to improve the body weight of the animals. The breeds tried so far include Large White Yorkshire, Middle White Yorkshire, Hampshire, Landrace and Charmukha. Some of the breeds used for crossbreeding have been discontinued: Middle Yorkshire, Hampshire and Landrace, as they were not found suitable in the Orissa conditions. Pure bred boars of Large White Yorkshire and Charmukha, are bred in the state farms and crossbred boars are supplied to the farmers for breeding purpose.

### (F) BREEDING OF POULTRY

There is no notified breeding policy for poultry development in the state. Improvement of local stock by exchange of *desi* cocks with improved cocks and supply of WLH/RIR hatching eggs, was taken up in the early stages of planned development of poultry, but did not produce any tangible impact. During the fourth plan period improvement of T,V and M stocks of White Leg Horn (WLH) was taken up at Angul Poultry Breeding Farm, using family index that took into consideration individual production and its sire and dams family averages. No high producing strain, however, could be developed, as the foundation stock used was inferior. The improved birds of Rhode Island Red (RIR), WLH and other stocks that were available with the state farms were being multiplied and supplied to the public and the beneficiaries under various development programmes. Availability of high quality hybrid layers in the open market from private sources leaves no room for government farms, for supply of layer birds. Private commercial farms do not at all use the government farms as a source for layers or broilers. No breeding programme is in operation in the private sector poultry industry either, in the state. However, commercial hatcheries maintain parent stocks for production of commercial chicks and receive the grandparent stocks from the breeding companies in India or overseas. Private sector farms depend entirely on the commercial hatcheries for their supply of production stock, both layers as well as broilers.

The backyard poultry units need a brooding hen with good mothering instincts, as home hatching of eggs for production of table birds is the primary objective of the backyard farmer. *Crosses and grades of exotic breeds of poultry do not have these qualities and therefore are of no use in backyard units*. Development of the *desi* birds for faster weight gain under foraging conditions, is the direction that the state should follow in poultry breeding. There are many good *desi* breeds of poultry in India, selection among them and grading up of nondescript birds with them, has enormous scope.

In addition to the State Poultry Farm at Angul, there are seven other poultry farms in the state. At present, no systematic breeding programme is in operation in these farms and they do not have any long term objectives either. Currently they are all involved in supply of day-old commercial layer chicks to small and medium holders. These state farms do not have any support activities for the backyard poultry units, even though it is in the interest of the state to improve productivity and income generation capacity of the millions of backyard units. The state poultry farms should from now on be focussing on selection of *desi* birds for supply of genetic inputs to the backyard poultry system. These farms of the state government, however, have made some contribution to poultry development in the state in the form of multiplication and supply of day-old chicks to various state and centrally sponsored schemes. The state has two duck farms, at Chipilima and Cuttack. Though the state has some native strains of ducks like the Chilika, the policy for breeding and development of ducks is upgradation of local ducks with Khakhi Cambell.

Research for development of the broiler stock undertaken by the Orissa University of Agriculture and Technology, Bhubaneswar under the All India Coordinated Research Project on Poultry Breeding, is continuing. Emphasis of the scheme is on development of coloured broiler stocks, as they are considered more efficient to withstand sub-optimal conditions of management compared to white coloured industrial broilers. Research for development of high yielding commercial layer stock is going on at Central Poultry Breeding Farm, Bhubaneswar. Research carried out over the last 25 years at this farm has resulted in the development and release of a commercial hybrid marketed in the trade name *Kalinga Brown*. The Kalinga Brown is popular with the small scale organised poultry farmers in Orissa.

# 10 Institutional Set Up and Regulatory Framework in Orissa

## 10.1 Institutional Set Up

Institutional set up in the livestock sector in Orissa is predominantly with the state government, as in all other states in India. When the era of planned development started in India, with the launch of the first five year plan in 1951, a newly independent India was in a hurry to get on with the development process and to carry development to all corners of the country. The central government initiated along with it a massive national extension movement to smoothly usher in the technology changes accompanying development in agriculture and animal husbandry and to mobilise large scale involvement of the people in the development process. There were no participatory bodies or peoples' organisations in the country, even remotely connected with development tasks or equipped to handle development at the grass roots level. The government, therefore, had no alternative but to resort to direct action for development through government departments. Agriculture including animal husbandry, under the Indian Constitution, is a state subject and the responsibility for development of the sector vests with the state governments, barring the specific tasks assigned to the centre, vide the seventh schedule to the Constitution. The state governments were therefore charged with the responsibility of developing animal husbandry under the five year plans. The GoO naturally entrusted the task to its already existing State Department of Animal Husbandry and Veterinary Services. The State Department of Animal Husbandry and Veterinary Services was carved out of the Development Department of the then Orissa province in 1946, as an independent department under a director, with headquarters in Cuttack. The department in Orissa is the principal agency of the government for all matters connected with the health, production and development of the livestock in the state. Starting with the first five year plan the department grew steadily, adding to its institutional network and manpower enormously, most of the growth taking place in the services sector, for delivery of veterinary and AI services. Private sector involvement in livestock production in Orissa is confined to the commercial poultry industry, with its large farms and high-tech birds, involving just about 20 per cent of the poultry population in the state. There is a fairly successful cooperative movement in the dairy sector, the Orissa State Co-operative Milk Producers' Federation (OMFED), with a three tier co-operative network stretching across some fourteen districts in the state. This cooperative however covers only a very small percentage of the milk producers in the state. There is also an Orissa State Poultry Products Co-operative Marketing Federation (OPOLFED); the Utkal Gomangal Samity (UGS) a non-governmental organisation supporting and supplementing the department's activities in development; and a few other NGOs, active in the livestock sector in Orissa. These institutions are dealt with separately in this chapter.

## 10.2 Department of Animal Husbandry and Veterinary Services

Livestock sector development in Orissa is organised under the Department of Fisheries and Animal Resources Development, headed by the secretary (FARD). An additional secretary, two deputy secretaries and three under secretaries assist the secretary in this task. The secretary is the principal advisor to the government on all matters related to livestock development and is the chief executive of the government department in the secretariat. The Department of F & ARD formulates state policies in the livestock sector, oversees operations of all functional departments under it, controls the budget for the sector, orchestrates development plans and projects, provides the linkage with other development departments and is the nodal authority for all administrative approvals. The DAH & VS is the major functional arm of the GoO for livestock sector development. The department provides all the services in the sector, administers all development plans, schemes and projects, administers the regulatory framework and is equipped with infrastructure, institutional network and manpower for the task. The department's institutional structure state wide is organised in six tiers, starting with the director who is the chief executive and ending with the block level and *gram panchayat* level service institutions. The six structural tiers are: state level, range level, district level, sub-divisional level, block level and *gram panchayat* level.

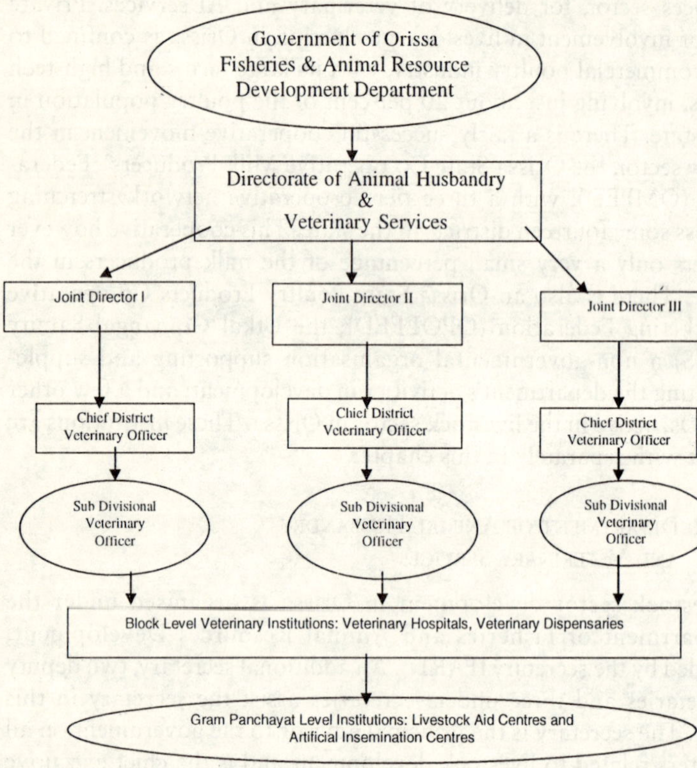


FIG. 10.1 STRUCTURAL ORGANISATION OF DAH & VS STATE WISE.

Functionally the directorate is organised into three working groups (see Fig. 10.1), each group headed by a joint director, under the overall supervision and guidance of the director, assisted by the additional director (post now vacant). The joint directors supervise and manage their respective group responsibilities in the entire state and in addition, each of them co-ordinates all activities of the department in a range of ten districts. Five deputy directors in turn assist the joint directors in the headquarters, heading five specific task groups in charge of range level institutions like the FSBS, OBPI, ADRI, SLBF and VOTI. The three working groups are:

Joint director I: Disease control, Planning, Artificial Insemination; Range Level Institutions OBPI, ADRI, CILs and FSBs; Co-ordination of all departmental activities in ten districts in the southern range. Joint director I is assisted by deputy director (Disease Control) and deputy director (Planning and AI), both located in the headquarters.

Joint director II: Dairy & Co-operative Cell, Livestock Breeding Farms, Fodder Development, Externally Aided Projects; Range Level Institutions SLBF, ISPO and ILDP; Co-ordination of all departmental activities in ten districts in the northern range. Joint director II is assisted by deputy director (Dairy & Co-operative Cell) and deputy director (Fodder), both located in the headquarters. The joint director II is also called JD-HID, as he is the head of the department's HID Cell.

Joint director-III: All small animal farms-sheep, goat, pig, rabbit, poultry and duck, Training, Extension, Public Relations and Publicity; Range Level Institution VOTI; Co-ordination of all departmental activities in ten districts in the central range. Joint director III is assisted by deputy director (Nutrition), located in the headquarters.

The '*Functional Organogram of the Directorate of AH & VS*' is presented as Chart 10.1 in the Appendix. In addition to the line functions allotted to the three working groups, there are the house keeping functions: administration and accounting, attended to by separate groups, located in the headquarters and reporting directly to the head of the department, the director. The DAH & VS has in its headquarters, a statistical cell headed by a statistician in the rank of deputy director and reporting to the director. The statistical cell is responsible for livestock statistics, data analysis, data update, reporting, sample surveys and state livestock census. The Information Bureau of the department is located in the headquarters office, as also the Marketing Cell, each manned by an officer in the rank of OVS Class II, one information officer and one marketing officer. There are also one post each of a cost accountant and a junior engineer, in the DAH & VS. Recently an HID Cell was created in the department, headed by the JD-HID. The functions of this cell are to co-ordinate all human and institutional development related activities, more specifically training, extension and veterinary information. The externally aided projects also fall under the JD-HID's domain.

A chief district veterinary officer (CDVO) heads the district level administration of the department of the 30 districts in the state 13 have a CDVO heading the district administration of the department, while in the remaining 17 newly created districts, posts of CDVOs are yet to be formally created by the government. Sub-divisional veterinary officers (SDVO) empowered to exercise the powers of the CDVO carry out district administration in these 17 districts. The structure of the district administration in the 13 old districts provides for senior level officers to assist the CDVO, to see through the various tasks of the department within his jurisdiction. Four assistant district veterinary officers (ADVO), one each for Disease Control, Artificial Insemination and Cattle Development, Poultry Development and a dairy specialist of the rank of an ADVO, designated the assistant dairy development officer, to assist the CDVO in dairy development activities. The district office in addition has the usual administration and account cells, an assistant fodder development officer, a co-operative inspector for promotion of village dairy co-operative societies and a statistical assistant for data handling. In the 17 new districts supporting staff described above are yet to be sanctioned by the state government. At the block level and the *gram panchayat* level, the departmental institutions are all service institutions, the main dispensing arm of the department delivering the professional services and inputs to the general public: veterinary hospitals and veterinary dispensaries manned by qualified veterinary professionals at the block level and livestock aid centres and artificial insemination centres at *gram panchayat* level, manned by para veterinary staff under the supervision of the block level professionals. The institutional network of the DAH & VS in Orissa, is exhibited in Table 10.2 in the Appendix. The budget of the DAH & VS made up of: state plan, state non-plan and central plan allocations annually (see Table 10.3 in the Appendix for details). Total expenditure on livestock development in Orissa over the nine five year plans, between 1951 and 1998, is Rs. 5648.54 mln. Exact proportion of its layout for capital and recurring expenses are not available. The indications are that substantial portions of this amount were spent on the establishment. The state non plan expenditure of Rs. 3746.37, some 66.32 per cent of the total expenditure, was exclusively for salaries, allowances, travel and transport. Of the remaining 33 per cent too, the bulk is for such expenses. The main financial drains on the state are the breeding farms for different species and the fodder seed farms, while their contribution to state's development efforts is highly debatable.

## 10.3 Development Linkages of the Department

The DAH & VS works closely with other development departments in the state and the centre; and a portion of the development budget of the department comes from the livestock components of such agencies. There are also two externally aided projects working with the DAH & VS, under bilateral collaboration arrangements of the government of India with the governments of Switzerland and Denmark (see Fig. 10.2)

## 10.4 Panchayati Raj Institutions

The 73rd Amendment to the Constitution of India is widely considered a watershed in the social and economic development of India, particularly development of the rural areas. The constitutional set

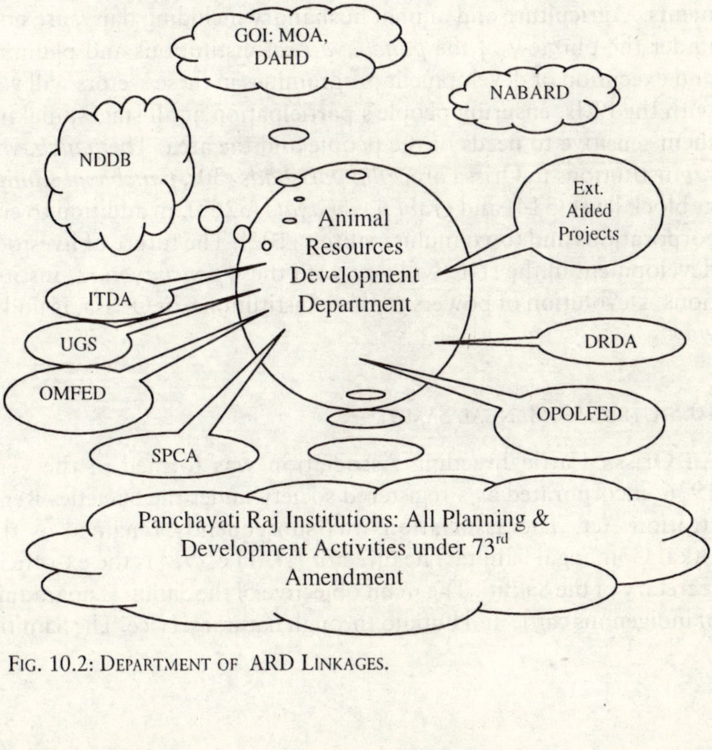


Fig. 10.2: Department of ARD Linkages.

up of India was originally designed as a three tier democratic structure with local self-governments at the grass roots, elected governments in the states and the centre. While the set up at the centre and state level were specified in the constitution and were unalterable without a constitutional amendment, local self-governments were creatures of the state statutes and were therefore at the mercy of the ruling political party in the state. For the first time, the *73rd amendment of the Indian Constitution notified in 1993*, has made the village *panchayats,* block level *panchayats*, district *panchayats* and municipalities, constitutional bodies and devolution of powers to these bodies formal and obligatory under the Constitution. However the law making powers continues to vest with the state legislatures. Subjects falling within the purview of the *panchayati raj* institutions and municipalities were added to the Constitution as the 11th and 12th schedules respectively. These subjects comprise virtually all development sectors and institutions along with the state departments dealing with them within their respective jurisdiction. A state finance commission set up under the amendment, facilitates sharing of the revenues between the state and the local self-governments. Agriculture and animal husbandry including dairy, are now under the purview of the *panchayati raj* institutions and planning and execution of development programmes in these sectors will vest with the PRIs, ensuring people's participation at all stages, making them sensitive to needs of the people and the area. The *panchayati raj* institutions in Orissa are: *zilla parishads* (30), *panchayat samitis* at block level (314) and *gram panchayats* (5263), in addition to city corporations and town municipalities (102). The future of livestock development in the state will vest with these *panchayati raj* institutions. Devolution of powers to these institutions, in Orissa, is under way.

### 10.5 Utkal Gomangal Samiti

An Orissa Cattle Breeding Association was formed in the year 1936, incorporated as a registered society under the Societies Registration Act. The association was subsequently renamed as the Utkal Gomangal Samiti. The director (DAH & VS) is the ex-officio secretary of the Samiti. The main objective of the Samiti is upgrading of indigenous cattle and buffalo through natural service. The Samiti's activities supplement the efforts of the department where artificial insemination facilities have not reached so far. To support the natural breeding programme, bull rearing and fodder cultivation are also taken up by the Samiti. The Utkal Gomangal Samiti receives grant in aid from the state, under the plan and non plan budgets every year, to meet expenditure on bull subsidy, rearing cost of bull calves, cultivation of fodder and the Samiti's establishment cost. In 1998-9 the grant provision for the UGS was Rs.1.00 mln under the state plan and Rs.2.20 mln under non-plan. The Samiti has set up four bull rearing units at Patha, Sagadi, Angul, and Bhogara, where selected Hariana, Red Sindhi, crossbred and Murrah buffalo bull calves procured from individuals, state farms or central government farms, are reared. The Samiti provides a grant of Rs.100 each per month to the custodians of the natural service bulls distributed by them, under the 'host system'. The UGS also has one large feed milling plant of 100 mt per day at Chipilima and a smaller one at Patha. Officers/staff of the Samiti are deputed from the department or are retired officials of the department.

## 10.6 The Orissa State Co-operative Milk Producers' Federation (OMFED)

The Orissa State Co-operative Milk Producers' Federation was incorporated under the State Co-operative Societies Act in 1980, as a part of the Operation Flood II project for Orissa. The milk co-operative set up under Operation Flood has a three tier set up with the federation as the state level apex society, the district unions and the village dairy co-operative societies as the primaries. The federation now has 8 milk unions affiliated to it and some 986 functional village dairy co-operative societies. The operational area of the federation is spread over 14 districts. The federation manages its affairs with its own business income and had been steadily making profits since 1993-4. The federation also receives state government grants for developmental activities. The provision for state grants to the federation during the ninth plan is Rs.26.00 mln. The federation now collects some 80000 lpd and has a total distributed processing capacity of some 200000 lpd and an animal feed plant with 100 mt per day capacity. The federation's organisational set up is presented in Table 10.1.

TABLE 10.1: ORGANIATION SET-UP OF THE MILK FEDERATION (OMFED)

| *Federation* | *Milk Unions* | *District covered* | *Total DCs/ members* |
|---|---|---|---|
| Orissa State Co-operative Milk Producers' Federation | Cuttack, Puri, Dhenkanal, Keonjhar, Sambalpur, | Cuttack, Puri, Balasore, Jagatsinghpur, Angul, Jajpur, Kendrapara, Khurda, Dhenkanal, Deogarh, | 986 of which 330 are women DCs |
| | [Sundargarh, Kalahandi] | Bargarh, Nayagarh, Jharsugada, Keonjhar, Sambalpur | |
| | [Ganjam, Gajapati] | | |

NOTE: [ ] shows Unions associated with the Federation but not affiliated.

## 10.7 THE ORISSA LIVESTOCK RESOURCES DEVELOPMENT SOCIETY (OLRDS)

The Orissa Livestock Resources Development Society was formed in the year 2000 and registered under the Society's Act as an independent body. The function of this society is to provide services to all actors in animal breeding in the state in the form of procurement, production and distribution of breeding inputs like semen and liquid nitrogen and training and promotional activities. The society was modelled after the livestock development boards in some of the other states in India as a condition of the central government for eligibility to grants under the National Programme for Cattle and Buffalo Breeding. All infrastructure related to the production and distribution of breeding inputs will ultimately be handed over to and managed by the society. The society is yet to become functional and the detailed modalities of it's functioning are still to be determined.

## 10.8 OTHER INSTITUTIONS IN LIVESTOCK SECTOR

There are a few voluntary organisations in the livestock sector in Orissa: (i) People for Animals, an all India body, mainly concerned with animal rights; (ii) Orissa Livestock Development Society (OLDS), a body of retired veterinary professionals, with headquarters at Cuttack, providing clinical services to animals, manning the SPCA dispensary and training; (iii) The SPCA, working closely with the department for prevention of cruelty to animals; and (iv) Animal Welfare Society, a registered society affiliated to the animal welfare board of India, for building up awareness in animal welfare. The society also offers an annual *Jibabandhu Award* for outstanding contribution to the cause of animal welfare in the state.

### 10.9 Indo-Swiss Project Orissa (ISPO)

The Indo-Swiss Project Orissa (ISPO) was established in 1991 under a bilateral agreement between the Government of India and the Government of Switzerland. The project partners are the Swiss Agency for Development and Cooperation (SDC) on the Swiss side and the Department of Animal Husbandry, Orissa and the Greater Ganjam Gajapati Milk Union on the Indian side. From 1999 the project became a component of the Indo-Swiss Natural Resources Management Programme Orissa (NRMPO), the other component being a livelihood and community organisation oriented programme in the tribal areas of Gajapati district, in partnership with a number of local NGOs. The project's objective is to contribute to the reduction of poverty in rural areas through increased productivity of the farm households with emphasis on viable small holder livestock and dairy production and sustainable land use. The major areas of intervention are:

- Human and Institutional Development (Institutional Development, Training and Extension),
- Fodder Technology Development and Extension, and
- Co-operative Dairy Development.

The project was initially located in Berhampur in Ganjam district of Orissa, but later moved its headquarters to Bhubaneswar. The project has so far completed four phases and entered it's fifth in July 2002. Focus during this phase will be on quality improvement of livestock services delivery through people's involvement and redefinition of the structure and functioning of the service departments and other organisations operating at state level.

### 10.10 Integrated Livestock Development Project (ILDP), Koraput

The ILDP is a bilateral collaboration project under an international agreement between the Government of India and the Government of Denmark. The project partners are the Danish International

Development Agency (DANIDA) on the Danish side and the Orissa State Department of Animal Husbandry on the Indian side. The project started operations in Koraput in 1993. The project primarily aims at tribal development. The major objective of the project is improved living standards for the tribal villagers, through increased awareness and better skills in animal husbandry and fodder production. The project's emphasis is on extension and human resource development in the livestock sector and it has established an effective, completely decentralised extension network of trained community link workers and target farmers, from among the beneficiaries, ensuring sustainability of the network. The project has established 157 self help groups (SHGs) in tribal villages, over 200 link workers and has virtually eradicated loss of birds in the backyard poultry system through timely vaccinations in the villages, by the link workers. The project has completed its fourth phase in March 2002. In a one-year's extension phase DANIDA will assist the GoO to replicate the link worker system in the neighbouring districts, after which the Danish government will withdraw from the project.

## 10.11 Analysis of the Organisation and Role of the Department of AH & VS

The most critically important administrative levels in the department's six tier organisational structure are: level one, the directorate itself; level three, the district administration; and levels five and six, the block and *gram panchayat* level service institutions. The director takes final decisions on all matters concerning the department's operations, setting priorities, thrusts; goals and crisis management are all the direct responsibilities of the directorate. Cohesive direction and network optimisation are the personal responsibilities of the director. The organisation of the directorate is therefore designed *prima facie* to help and enable the director to achieve this end. It appears that the present structure of the directorate is appropriate to satisfy these requirements. Only three functional groups, other than the in-house support groups like accounts and administration, report to the director. Powerful senior officers, with considerable professional experience behind them—the three joint directors, head these functional groups. This lightens the burden of the director, saving him from the routine and insulates him from the trivia. There seem to be no logic for an additional director in between; upgrading the three joint directors to additional directors, with wider powers would be a better option. Distribution of the portfolios to the joint directors can perhaps be rationalised, but beyond that, there is not much by way of improvements, needed. The only thing that can overwhelmingly improve matters would be a much wider delegation of financial powers to the director, heads of subordinate offices and CDVOs.

The objective of delegating financial powers should be that the director is empowered to exercise full powers within the sanctioned annual budget, subject to the ways and means position of the government, without having to seek approvals. Approval from the government should be necessary only for decisions exceeding the budget and for items not budgeted for. This can tone up the department's functioning, reduce *red tape* and consequent delays. This would particularly be extremely advantageous for implementation of 'project mode activities' and for maintaining 'project cash' flows. Rationalisation of the financial powers of the heads of the subordinate offices and CDVO would streamline the entire departmental administration, reducing bottlenecks and speeding up execution. The powers of these decision-making functionaries in the departmental hierarchy should be fixed in proportion to their respective tasks and responsibilities and not on the basis of their ranks. The current delegation of powers to these categories of officers is not commensurate with their tasks and responsibilities. The GoO would do well to have this matter examined by a high powered committee of the government.

*The overall role of the department of animal resources development in the livestock sector needs review, in the changing economic policy environment in the country. There are also historical errors in the priorities of the department, that need to be corrected.*

That India had enormous animal disease problems was well known even during the colonial days, in fact the imperial government appointed two commissions at the turn of the nineteenth century—the cattle Plague Commission and the Famine Commission, to look into the problem of animal diseases and recommend remedial measures. The Royal Commission on Agriculture followed these in 1926. The recommendations of all these commissions focussed on the need for disease control and containment measures as the basic requirement for rural poverty alleviation. All institutions established in the wake of these commissions were exclusively for disease investigation, control and containment of animal diseases. The veterinary departments that the imperial government set up, are the precursors of the present day state departments of animal husbandry (and of the DAH & VS in Orissa); but with one major difference: *The mandate of the veterinary departments under the British, were unambiguously animal disease control and prevention, while the departments of animal husbandry today concentrate on animal health care services, as a welfare measure.*

In 1951, when the first five-year plan was launched in Orissa, the state had only some 79 veterinary hospitals/dispensaries and 222 veterinary stockman centres. By the end of the year 2000 these increased to some 541 veterinary hospitals/dispensaries and 2939 livestock aid centres dispensing free veterinary service. The state's concern for animal health is apparent from the plan investments on these institutions, but unfortunately all of them are primarily involved in treatment and cure of animal diseases and not prevention and control. In the changing economic environment in India and the world as a whole, it is high time that the state government changed the mandate of the department of animal husbandry from animal health care services in the current sense, to exclusively prevention and control of animal diseases.

*Curative veterinary care generates only private good and does not alter the endemicity of animal diseases. Preventive veterinary care generates public good and logically public funds should be applied for generating public good.*

Orissa's losses on account of animal diseases annually is some Rs. 2500 million, some 15 per cent of the total annual output value of the state livestock sector. A fraction of this amount, spent annually on focussed, well orchestrated disease control programmes, would be more than adequate to effectively contain all the known epidemics among livestock in Orissa and perhaps even to eradicate some of them. This change in mandate is not really going to affect the common man adversely in any manner, as the so-called free service the department provides is more symbolic than physical. The state department's budget share for instruments, drugs, pharmaceuticals, vaccines and consumable is only 5 per cent of its total annual grants together from all sources, some Rs. 16.50 mln in 1997-8, or Rs.1.38 per case treated. The animal owner in any case receives only a prescription at the veterinary institution and he has to buy all medicines and consumables from the retail trade. This is to an extent corroborated by the pharmaceutical trade figures, see box below:

| | |
|---|---|
| Total National Trade Turn over on Veterinary Pharmaceuticals 1997 | Rs. 5000 mln. |
| Institutional Share (Govt. Departments of AH, all States together) | Rs. 250 mln (5%) |
| Approximate share of Orissa | Rs. 10 mln |
| Expenditure on medicines, etc., per case treated in Orissa, 1997 | Re. 0.88 |

See charts in Chapter 7 for market shares of veterinary pharmaceuticals by species and customer.

Another service that the state department is now providing free, is artificial insemination. The analysis in Chapters 3 and 9 of this report shows that the quality of the AI service is poor. The average conception rate in Orissa is less than 20 per cent. Less than 10 per cent of the breeding population of cows and not even 5 per cent of buffaloes in the state are bred by AI. The Government of India has already set in motion a national project for cattle and buffalo breeding which seeks to rationalise AI services country wide, by expanding coverage of AI to all breeding animals, delivery of a vastly improved AI service at the farmers' door-step, enabling all AI practitioners under the government to practice door-delivery of AI as a paid service, all co-ordinated viably by an autonomous state livestock board in each state (a registered society) as the principal implementing agency. Orissa should participate in the project and enable the state to make AI a self-generating service, moving progressively to the private sector. The government should also move towards a viable, decentralised, farmer to farmer, extension network following the model set up by the ILDP in Koraput. Veterinary services and AI delivery should move away from the government department and into self-generating mechanisms, home delivering the services as paid inputs. The department will then be in a position to devote its entire energies on disease prevention and control, sector development, professional ethics in veterinary and AI practice, and quality assurance in products and services; and the regulatory frame work in the livestock sector. These are truly the functions of the government and are now being grossly neglected.

The various breeding and fodder seed production farms run by the department are a millstone around the department's neck: they are money guzzlers, their annual receipts are less than a third of the expenditure on them and they contribute nothing to the department's development efforts. The livestock breeding farms alone have incurred losses of over Rs.78 mln between 1991-8. These farms are listed in Table 10.4 in the Appendix. With the proposed revision in the livestock breeding policy for the state, breeding farms become redundant, particularly in case of cattle. The state would then need only one or two farms primarily for raising young bulls and for ONBS. The remaining 11 livestock breeding farms can be wound up. Breeding farms for other species also do not provide any breeding inputs to the state livestock development programmes and are therefore fit candidates for closing down. The fodder seed farms too are totally non-performing units and the sooner they are wound up the better.

## 10.12 Regulatory Framework

Several Acts and Rules, both central and state, are involved in the regulation and promotion of the livestock sector. Some are sector specific like: laws on cow slaughter, Control of Animal Diseases Act, Livestock Improvement Act, Veterinary Council Act, Importation of Livestock Act; and Glanders and Farcy Act. Others are of an omnibus nature across several sectors, like the PFA Act, Essential Commodities Act, the Co-operative Societies Act, Weights and Measures Act, and BIS standards. State legislation relevant to the livestock sector are Orissa Cattle and Poultry Feed Regulation Act 1979, Orissa Livestock Improvement Act 1957, Orissa Prevention of Cow Slaughter Act 1966, Orissa Gosala Act 1961, Orissa Veterinary Practitioners Act 1969, Orissa Veterinary Council Act, Prevention of Cruelty to Animals Act, Orissa Animal Contagious Diseases Act 1957, and Orissa Animal Contagious Disease Act (Amendment) 1978. Milk and Milk Products Order and the Meat and Meat Products Order under the Central Essential Commodities Act are valid in the state. There are in addition state statutes on slaughter and slaughterhouses, regulation of meat and meat products.

Taxation and levies on animals and animal products in Orissa are generally restricted to packaged and value added products, which are subjected to both sales tax as well as excise duty. The state sales tax on these items is 8 per cent and central sales tax 4 per cent with

C or D forms. Excise duty rates vary from 10 to 15 per cent. Compounded animal feeds are liable for sales tax. Milk and milk products (except value added, packaged, products) and live animals do not attract any tax in the state. Animals and commodities like *ghee* and *desi* butter, marketed through regulated markets are liable for market cess.

## 10.13 Infrastructure: Livestock Sector Orissa

Infrastructure in the livestock sector in Orissa is all under the Department of Animal Husbandry, the local bodies and in the OMFED. These include a state wide network of veterinary hospitals, dispensaries, livestock aid centres, AI centres, running into thousands of institutions and an army of skilled manpower (see Table 10.2 in the Appendix); semen production stations, biological and vaccine production units, a host of production input generation institutions, breeding farms for different species of livestock and poultry. The Utkal Gomangal Samiti too has some production support infrastructure. There are no private sector investments on infrastructure except in the commercial poultry industry. A full list of the infrastructural facilities for the livestock sector in the state are listed in Tables 10.5, 10.6 and 10.8 in the Appendix. A list of the 93 slaughter houses is exhibited in Table 5.7 in the Appendix. The state has a large number of animal haats and markets for trading in live animals. A list of some 133 of these haats mostly under the control of local bodies and some privately operated, are presented in Table 11.1 in the Appendix. In addition to the cattle/poultry feed milling plants in the government and co-operative sector listed, there are 44 cattle and poultry feed milling plants in the private sector, mostly of small and medium capacity varying from 8 mtpd to 20 mtpd. The feed milling plants are also listed in Table 8.7 in the Appendix.

## 10.14 Human Resources

Almost all infrastructure in the livestock sector in Orissa is in the DAH & VS and the department provides all professional services. It is therefore natural that the largest single skill pool in the livestock sector too belongs to the department. The department also has all infrastructure and facilities for human resource development in the state. The department's skill pool in 1998 is presented in Table 10.2

TABLE 10.2: SKILL POOL OF THE DEPARTMENT OF AH & VS

| *Sl.No.* | *Category* | *Number* |
|---|---|---|
| 1 | Veterinary Graduates | |
| 1.1 | Director | 1 |
| 1.2 | Joint Directors | 3 |
| 1.3 | Deputy Directors | 14 |
| 1.4 | Chief District Veterinary Officers | 13 |
| 1.5 | Project Officer (CRP) | 1 |
| 1.6 | Project Officer ILDP | 1 |
| 1.7 | Progeny Testing Officer | 1 |
| 1.8 | Project Director ADRI | 1 |
| 1.9 | Sub-Divisional Veterinary Officers | 58 |
| 1.10 | Veterinary Assistant Surgeons | 515 |
| 1.11 | Additional Veterinary Assistant Surgeons | 209 |
| 1.12 | Assistant District Veterinary Officers | 45 |
| 1.13 | Specialists | 13 |
| 1.14 | Other Allied Posts | 180 |
| 1.15 | Junior Veterinary Officers | 105 |
| 2 | Para Veterinary Staff | |
| 2.1 | Veterinary Sub-Assistant Surgeons | 48 |
| 2.2 | Veterinary Technicians | 438 |
| 2.3 | Livestock Inspectors | 3477 |
| 3 | Other Professionals | |
| 3.1 | Dairy Officers, Inspectors, Supervisors (Dairy Specialists) | 23 |
| 3.2 | Fodder Development Specialists (Graduates in Agriculture) | |
| 3.2.1 | Deputy Director (Fodder) | 1 |
| 3.2.1 | Fodder Development Officers | 1 |
| 3.2.3 | Asst./Sub. /Asst. Fodder Development Officers | 53 |
| 3.2.4 | Field Man/Demonstrator (Diploma in Agriculture) | 30 |
| 3.3 | Statistical Officer (Senior) Statistician | 1 |
| 3.4 | Statisticians (Junior) Statisticians | 4 |
| 3.5 | Ayurvedic Medical Officers (Graduates in Ayurvedic Medicine) | 2 |
| 3.6 | Junior Engineer ( Graduate in Engineering) | 1 |

SOURCE: Table compiled based on the data provided by the DAH & VS and their publications.

and the HRD facilities of the department are briefly discussed in the following paragraphs (see Table 10.7 in the Appendix).

### ORISSA VETERINARY COLLEGE

Orissa Veterinary College was established in 1955. Initially the college was affiliated to the Utkal University and was later made a part of the Orissa University of Agriculture and Technology.

There are 14 departments in the college. The present annual intake capacity is 80 students for B.V.Sc. and AH degree, 56 for the M.V.Sc. degree and 6 for Ph.D. degree in different branches of veterinary and animal sciences. So far the college has produced 1943 veterinary graduates, 615 post graduates and 30 doctorates since its inception. The capacity of the college for the basic B.V.Sc. degree is adequate for satisfying the demand of the state for veterinary graduates for at least the coming two decades.

### VETERINARY OFFICERS TRAINING INSTITUTE (VOTI)

The Veterinary Officers' Training Institute is part of the department's human resource management efforts and provides refresher/orientation programmes to the in-service officers of the department. With the assistance of Indo-Swiss Project, Orissa, the institute has been equipped with modern teaching tools and audio visual aids. A senior officer of the department designated as the training officer is in charge of the institute and the training programmes. The programmes are tailor made for the department's requirements and vary in course content and duration.

### LIVESTOCK INSPECTORS' TRAINING CENTRE

Livestock inspectors are para veterinary technicians who undergo a one-year training programme in the department's Livestock Inspector Training Centres. There are three Livestock Inspector Training Centres in the state, one each at Bhanjanagar, Bolangir, and Chipilima. The intake capacity of each centre is 80 candidates per year. This is a residential programme with duration of one year and the institutes are well equipped with all facilities for board and lodge of the trainees. The classrooms are well equipped with modern teaching aids and audio visual aids.

### FROZEN SEMEN TECHNOLOGY AND AI TRAINING CENTRES

There are two Frozen Semen Technology and AI Training centres, one located at Khapuria, Cuttack, and the other at Bhawanipatna, both in the campus of the Frozen Semen Stations. The Cuttack centre imparts refresher training to veterinarians and livestock inspectors, whereas the centre at Bhawanipatna provides basic training in frozen semen technology and AI to livestock inspectors only. The deputy directors in charge of the Frozen Semen Stations, with the help of their staff, conduct the training courses.

### POULTRY TRAINING INSTITUTES

Poultry training in Orissa is offered by the DAH & VS, OPOLFED, the OUAT, some voluntary agencies and also private sector hatcheries (Table 10.9 in the Appendix). Most of these trainings are informal and need based; and are not carried on as regular structured courses. Only OUAT offers training on a regular off campus course of 6 months duration in 'Poultry Production', as a distance education programme. The Extension Department of the university together with the Poultry Science Department conducts this course. Any farmer who can read and write proficiently is eligible to register for the course and there are no number restrictions. The fee for the course is only Rs.20. Course materials, ten volumes in Oriya, is sent to the trainees and they are encouraged to interact through exchange of letters. The department conducts an examination at the end of the course and those who pass get a certificate. The course is essentially targeted at farmers, to encourage them to go in for poultry farming. The Central Avian Research Institute's regional centre in Bhubaneswar offers a 15 day poultry training course for farmers. They usually arrange the training four times in a year, but would be willing to offer courses more frequently if there is demand. The Department of Animal Husbandry and Veterinary Services had poultry training facilities in Bolangir, Bhanjanagar, Chipilima and Bhubaneswar but these facilities are not functional now.

### ORISSA STATE CO-OPERATIVE MILK PRODUCERS' FEDERATION (OMFED)

The OMFED has a multi-disciplinary skill pool comprising specialists in management, finance and accounts, marketing, veterinary and animal husbandry, fodder production, co-operative development, milk procurement, dairy technology, dairy, civil, electrical and mechanical engineering and a host of technicians and artisans in various technical areas. The OMFED skill pool is presented in the Table 10.3. The Federation's training needs for its cooperative network are taken care of by the OMFED Training and Demon-

TABLE 10.3: SKILL POOL OF OMFED

| *Category* | *Number* |
|---|---|
| Veterinary Professionals | 11 |
| Engineering Professionals | 5 |
| Dairy Professionals | 4 |
| Chartered Accountants | 1 |
| Dairy Technicians (all trades) | 50 |

stration Centre (OMTDC) and they have a package of custom made programmes varying in course content and duration (Table 10.8 in the Appendix). The centre's capacity was 40 candidates at a time to start with, but now has been raised to 100, in the wake of the massive training programmes they now have for women members. The programmes include Veterinary First Aid and AI for DCS staff for six weeks, DCS secretaries training programme for 4 weeks, managing committee members of the DCS 3 days, milk testers programme for 5 days, etc. The centre started operations in 1980 and has tiained so far some 11012 trainees in the various courses.

# 11 Livestock Sector Trade: Orissa

Almost all livestock produce in Orissa is consumed in the domestic market with the exception of some live animals, a sizable number of broilers, almost all skin and hide and all animal by-products. These are traded outside Orissa, as part of the export trade in animal products. In addition a large quantity of livestock products, eggs and animal feed are imported into the state. Global trading in livestock products or live animals from Orissa does not exist.

## 11.1 Milk and Milk Products

In 1999-2000, of the total 8.50 lmt of milk produced in the state, almost the entire quantity except some 20 per cent (1.70 lmt) consumed in producer households, was traded within the state, bulk of it for domestic consumption and some 6000 mt, as export to Calcutta in the form of *chhena* (1200 mt). Trading of milk for domestic consumption takes place in the traditional trade channels (except the quantities handled by OMFED) either from producers to consumers direct or through a chain of middlemen and urban milk vendors, primarily as liquid milk and about 20 per cent as milk based

TABLE 11.1: MILK PRODUCTS CONSUMED IN THE STATE

| *Product* | *Quantity (mt)* |
|---|---|
| *A. Imports* | |
| Dairy Whiteners Consumer Pack | 8000 |
| Skimmed Milk Powder: Bulk Pack | 6000 |
| SMP for Reconstitution by OMFED | 2000 |
| Ghee Bulk and Consumer Pack | 4000 |
| Table Butter Consumer Pack | 300 |
| Processed Cheese Consumer Pack | 15 |
| Liquid Milk (OMFED) | 1500 |
| *B. Exports* | |
| Liquid Milk (OMFED) | 850 |
| *Chhena* | 1200 |

SOURCE: Dairy Industry and Trade.

sweets. OMFED's milk procurement (25000 mt of rurally produced milk annually) too is traded entirely in the domestic markets, as branded, packaged liquid milk and very small quantities as products. The OMFED's share of milk produced in the state is only some 4 per cent. Micro studies conducted by the LSR teams indicate that total chenna manufacture in Orissa is equivalent to some 24500 mt of milk per year. Orissa in addition consumes large quantities of milk solids imported into the state, from other states in India, both as branded, value added products as well as unbranded bulk products. In 1998 the total imported milk products consumed in the state is exhibited in Table 11.1. Orissa also exports some quantities of liquid milk (8.50 lakh litres per year 2001-2) during the flush season and imports 10-15 lakh litres of liquid milk per year during the lean, for balancing the demand and supply of the organised dairy sector in the state. There is very little private, across the border trade in liquid milk and all large-scale import and export of liquid milk is done by the OMFED.

## 11.2 Meat, Co-products and By-products

All meat produced in Orissa, 43000 mt in 2000, is consumed in the state. There is no evidence of a substantial meat or meat product import into the state. But almost all the skin and hide from the slaughter as well as from fallen animals are traded outside the state. The total number of hide and skin produced in 1997 was some 2.66 mln and barring a small number processed in local tanneries, are exported to Calcutta or through Visakhapatnam to other consumption points like Kanpur, etc. The entire quantity of by-products salvaged is marketed outside the state. Trading in live birds for table purposes takes place all over the state, direct from producer to consumer, through haats and markets, or through middlemen. The total quantity of poultry meat from the backyard units in 2000 was 6200 mt and all of it is consumed in the state. Trading in culled birds from the commercial poultry stream is more organised and involves a two or three tier chain of middlemen. The total meat from culled birds and broiler consumed in the state was some 15600 mt in 2000 and all of it through the normal trade channels. Of the 16.50 mln broiler birds produced in Orissa, some 5 mln are exported to consumption centres outside Orissa, mainly to Calcutta, through established chain of middle men. Eggs produced in the state, 822 mln, are all consumed in the domestic market. Trade chains exist in egg marketing from the commercial poultry farms, but eggs from backyard units are traded locally and only small numbers reach the major urban demand centres in the state as a favoured item in small niche markets. Orissa in addition consumes some 350 mln eggs imported from out side the state annually. Small general and grocery shops sell eggs at the retail level.

## 11.3 Live Animals

Live animals are traded all over the state, all through the year. Many transactions take place directly between the buyer and the seller and many take place in the 134 well-known *haats* and fairs in the state (see Table 11.1 in the Appendix for the list of fairs and *haats*). These markets are under the control of regulated market committees, *gram panchayats*, notified area councils, municipalities and some under private management. Of the 134 markets some 57 are under regulated market committees, spread out in the 30 districts in the state, one each in the 45 sub-divisions, two each in 5 and none in 8 sub-divisions. Example of a private market is Hatabhadra in Bargarh district. Regional market committees are constituted under the Orissa Agricultural Produce Market Act 1956 and are regulated under the Orissa Agricultural Produce Market Rules 1958. The apex body of the RMCs is the State Agricultural Marketing Board. The state registrar of co-operatives is the ex-officio director of regulated markets. The Regulated Market Committees are made up of elected representatives of traders, producers, local bodies and officials nominated by the government. The Regulated Markets' marketing year is from 1 November to 31 October of the succeeding year. RMCs are allowed to charge a maximum of 3 per cent of the sale value of the produce/animal as their fees, but many RMCs charge much lower fees. Private markets invariably charge even lower fees than the official markets. Regulated markets deal in all agricultural produce as well as trading in livestock: milch cattle, draught animals, buffaloes, sheep, goat, pig and poultry. Market days for different animals vary, as all types of animals are not traded on the same day. For example, in RMC Bargarh, Saturdays are trading days for cattle and Fridays for small ruminants.

The markets provide shelter, trading space and water free. Veterinary care facilities are arranged on livestock market days. All markets charge an entrance fee of Re.0.50 per animal. In 1996 total trading in these markets was some 11.28 lakh animals. Trading in these markets does involve middlemen, although many transactions take place directly between the seller and the buyer. Livestock and poultry trading in these markets account only for a small percentage of the total trade of live animal/poultry in the state. Meat animal trade for the domestic markets is more organised and involves middlemen. In 1995 the total of animals traded for slaughter in Orissa was 22334 cattle, 1355182 goat, 1193190 sheep and 85649 pig. A large export trade exists for meat animals, especially goat and bovine. The estimates are that some 1.50 to 2.00 mln goat and 0.50 mln cattle and some buffalo were exported in 1995. Live animal export trade is controlled by well-established traders, who operate through a chain of middlemen in the state for regular procurement of animals from the villages.

## 11.4 Animal Feed Raw Materials

The total concentrate animal feed raw materials consumed in the state are some 2.12 mln mt. Of this some 0.74 mmt (0.15 mmt of oil cakes; 0.37 mmt brans and chunni; grains 0.14 mmt and balanced cattle/poultry feed 0.08 mmt) are produced in the state and the bulk of it is traded trough the retail grocery outlets, except for the small quantities home produced and consumed by the farmers. The remaining 1.38 mmt (1.23 mmt of brans and chunni; 0.07 mmt of oil cakes; and 0.08 mmt of grains) of feed raw materials are imported from other states. The entire quantity is handled by the traditional grocery whole sale and retails merchants and is available throughout the state in the retail grocery outlets in all villages and urban areas.

# 12 Livestock Sector in Orissa: Outlook for Future

## 12.1 Livestock Sector: Strengths

The large population of livestock, though low in productivity across all species, is the strength of the livestock economy in the state, in terms of its potential for rapid transformation into economically viable milch, meat and draught animals, generating livelihood opportunities for millions of rural households. *Desi* fowls, millions of them, in the backyards in rural households, are a strength in terms of their livelihood intensity: their ability to thrive under range conditions; forage for their feed and fend for themselves; and contribute additional household income and protective food, without any overheads, commitment of land or out of pocket expenditure, generating and protecting livelihoods for millions of the rural poor in Orissa.

A well-orchestrated institutional structure, vast infrastructure for livestock input generation, state wide infrastructure for processing of livestock produce and an extensive field network for delivery of livestock services, state wide, are all the foundation on which the state livestock sector can develop and expand in the next two decades. The large skill pool of well qualified professionals and technicians to mange the production enhancement efforts, human resources development, processing and marketing of livestock produces and products, that already exist in the state will facilitate the development process.

A large consuming public, some 75 per cent of them non-vegetarian, with steadily rising incomes and high elasticity of expenditure for livestock products, guarantee rapid growth of demand for all animal products: milk, meat, eggs and value added products. The organised milk procurement, processing and marketing system that exist in the form of the milk co-operative network, both under the OMFED and the state DAH & VS, will provide the market pull so essential to stimulate livestock production.

A responsive state government, sensitive to public demands and committed to rural development (and particularly improvement of the economic condition of the farming community), along with non-governmental organisations like the Utkal Gomangal Samiti and the OMFED to support and complement the government's efforts in livestock development, can orchestrate a perspective plan for the development of the sector over the next two decades.

## 12.2 Weaknesses in the System

Orissa can set in place astute policies to counter the following weaknesses:

Absence of a decentralised, farmer to farmer, extension support programme, leading to lack of awareness and skills among farmers; and the consequent tardy adoption of technology and development programmes in the livestock sector.

The vicious cycle of low productivity of livestock, acute feed and fodder scarcity, recurring ravages of animal epidemics, production organisation in millions of scattered tiny holdings; and fragmented, unorganised markets for many of the livestock produce and the consequent inability of the farmers to adopt change and newer technologies.

The present inefficient institutional set up: stationary AI centres delivering AI services at the centre, reduce access to AI, resulting in poor AI coverage of breeding animals and low conception rates, necessitating continued dependence on scrub bulls for breeding, perpetuating the scrub cattle population; and the institution based veterinary services delivery necessitating movement of animals over long distances to the veterinary institutions, severely restricting the farmers' access to services.

Absence of well orchestrated disease prevention and control programmes, leading to recurring epidemics, erodes viability of small holder farming enterprises (the core livestock production sector in the state), causes enormous production losses and precludes options for global marketing of livestock products.

Overwhelming dependence on draught animals for farm power, leading to very large work animal force; and consequently, unsustainably large bovine population. Slow progress in partial farm mechanisation and lack of access to alternate sources of farm power, compels the farmers to own draught animals for farm power, in spite of shrinking holding size and severe resource crunch in households, progressively impoverishing them.

### 12.3 Development Opportunities

The following opportunities exist to use livestock sector development as the instrument for ushering in rural prosperity:

Livestock sector, in Orissa, across all species, is highly livelihood intensive; over 80 per cent of the rural households own livestock and earn supplementary incomes out of them. Development of the sector is therefore the critical pathway to rural prosperity. Known technologies and very high potential exist to transform the low productive livestock population into comparatively high producing farm livestock, through grading up and crossbreeding in case of cattle, buffalo, and pig; selective breeding among sheep, goat and *desi* fowl.

Very high income and expenditure elasticity of demand for livestock products, relatively high private domestic consumption expenditure on livestock products; and steadily rising income state wide, assure burgeoning demand growth for all livestock products and therefore enormous scope for large investments in the development of the sector.

Possibility exists for maximising returns on investments already made on AI, breeding infrastructure and veterinary services, through new institutional models, restructuring of existing institutions, vastly enhanced quality and coverage: evaluated bulls for AI, doorstep delivery of AI services and veterinary services, both as paid inputs.

Changing economic policies of the governments at the centre and state; and reduction of controls on the economy, enabling capital flow into the livestock sector, particularly in processing, value addition and marketing areas.

### 12.4 Risks and Threats

There are of course risks:

Stagnation of the livestock sector will seriously affect livelihood generation and will result in major shifts in rural economy, increasing rural poverty.

Large ruminants account for over 90 per cent of the livestock load in the state in 'Cattle Equivalent' terms; failure to enhance productivity will further increase their population size, eroding ecological balance and greatly jeopardising sustainability of all animal agriculture. Failure to accelerate the pace of partial mechanisation of farming practices in the state will increase the dependence on draught animals for farm power and will in turn, defeat all attempts to rationalise bovine population size.

Continued delivery of AI and veterinary services by the government departments will in addition to compromises in quality and cost constraints, crowd out the emergence of free markets for these services.

Failure to control/eradicate animal diseases will neutralise all efforts for genetic improvement and production enhancement; entail huge production losses to the poorest of the poor among the rural households, greatly undermine farm economy and preclude Orissa livestock and livestock products from global markets under the sanitary and phyto-sanitary (SPS) regulations of GATT/WTO.

Failure to reduce production costs, improve efficiency and quality; and failure to generate competitive advantages in animal agriculture, will expose Orissa farmers to unequal and unfair global competition under the 'minimum access and other clauses' of the GATT/WTO regulations.

# 13 Livestock Products in Orissa: Processing and Value Addition

Livestock products are all highly perishable and would need immediate processing in order to enable the surpluses to be moved from the production areas to the demand centres, for increasing their shelf life, value and storage for marketing. Milk is the single most important livestock produce in Orissa and accounts for over 33 per cent of the value of all livestock output. The livestock output in 1998-9 (ISS: DAH & VS) are given in the Table 13.1. The marketable supply of milk in 1998 was some 2.00 mln lpd. Bulk of the marketable supply available is traded in the unorganised traditional sector. In 1998, the share of the unorganised traditional trade was some 1.80 mln lpd or 95 per cent of the supply. The share of the organised sector in milk marketing was only some 0.1 mln lpd, just 5 per cent of the supply. Meat supply available in 1998 was 38129 mt, made up of mutton, chevon, small quantities of pork and beef. In addition poultry meat and broiler added an additional supply of 16096 mt of meat. Egg supply from within the state was some 762.79 mln and an additional 300 mln was imported from neighbouring states.

TABLE 13.1: LIVESTOCK OUTPUT IN ORISSA

| *Sl. No.* | *Produce* | *Quantity* |
|---|---|---|
| 1. | Milk | 732740 mt. |
| 2. | Meat | 38129 mt. |
| 3. | Poultry Meat | 1591 mt. |
| 4. | Eggs | 762.79 mln. |
| 5. | Hide (C & B) | 16649 pcs. |
| 6. | Sheep & Goat | 3.63 mln. pcs. |
| 7. | Wool & Hair | 0.2 mln. mt. |
| 8. | Bones & Offals | 1000 mt. |

SOURCE: ISS, 1998-9, Department of AHD.

## 13.1 Marketable Supply of Milk: Current Scenario

The LSR field survey in March-April 1999 among other things studied the quantities of milk retained for home consumption in a representative sample of milk producing household, in the three zones' namely—coastal, midland and uplands. Quantities retained for home consumption varied widely among households depending on many factors: family size, quantity of milk produced, access to market, family income and prevailing milk price. The findings of survey are shown in the Table 13.2. Presently the marketable surplus is some 1.81 mln kg per day after accounting the retention of milk by the households.

Table 13.2: Consumption of Milk in Producer Households

| *Zone* | *No. of HH* | *Prod. kg.* | *Retention kg.* | *Per cent* |
|---|---|---|---|---|
| Coastal | 21 | 127.50 | 33.50 | 26.27 |
| Midland | 29 | 136.50 | 42.50 | 61.13 |
| Uplands | 15 | 70.00 | 19.50 | 27.85 |
| State | 65 | 334.00 | 95.50 | 28.59 |

Source: LSR Field Survey, 1999.

## 13.2 Disposal of the Marketable Supply

The available marketable supply of milk in Orissa villages, some 1.81 mln kg per day in 1998-9, by and large, is traded in the traditional channel (see Fig. 13.1). Traditional trading in milk by the middlemen form the major source of liquid milk supply for the urban areas in the state, except for Bhubaneswar, Cuttack, and Rourkela, where OMFED's pasteurised packaged milk is a major source for consumer supply, as also large quantities of milk produced within the city by the commercial city stables.

## 13.3 Milk Collection by the Organised Sector, 1998

Milk collection by the organised sector in Orissa is tiny, confined to the milk procurement by the dairy cooperative societies (DCS), promoted either by the OMFED or the DAH & VS. Their numbers are small, 1339 organised by the OMFED, 128 by the GGGMU and some 434 by the DAH & VS, a coverage of only 1901 villages and their satellites, out of the total 51057 villages in the state. The

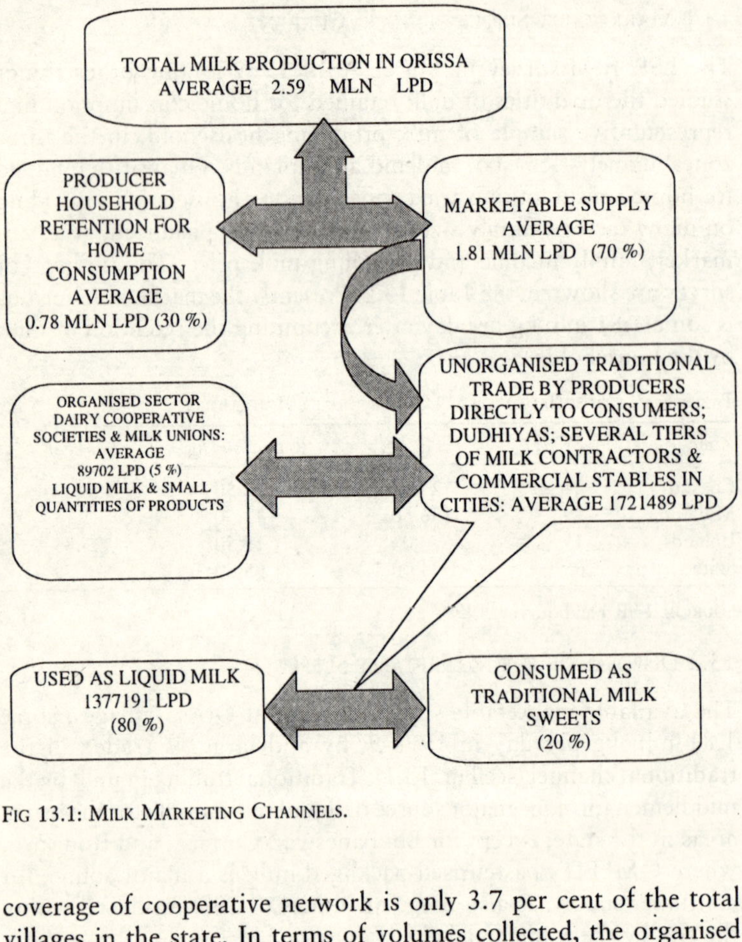


FIG 13.1: MILK MARKETING CHANNELS.

coverage of cooperative network is only 3.7 per cent of the total villages in the state. In terms of volumes collected, the organised sector accounts for only 5 per cent of the total marketable supply available in the state: some 71413 lpd by the OMFED, 5983 lpd by the GGGMU and 12306 lpd by the department (in all cases average of three years 1996-9).

Milk collection by the cooperative milk unions in the state through their DCS network in 1998-9 is presented in Table 13.1 in the Appendix. Collection volumes per DCS are so small, often well below their breakeven procurement, 100 lpd, making the entire operation unviable. See the chart below:

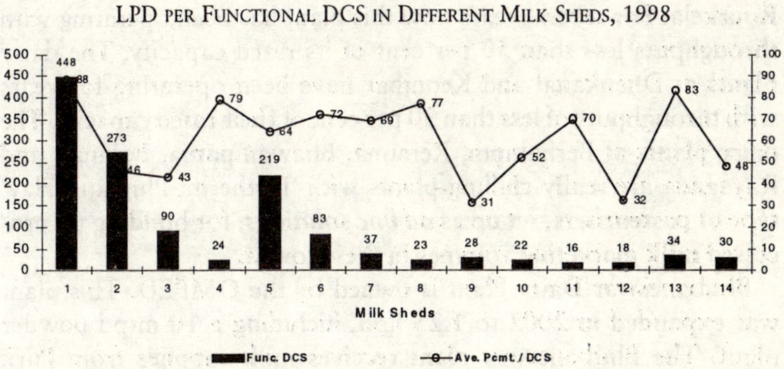


NOTE: The chart above is merely an illustration to highlight infirmities in procurement planning and not a graph establishing any trends.

FIG. 13.2: AVERAGE MILK PROCUREMENT VOLUMES.

TABLE 13.3: KEY TO MILK SHED NOS. 1–14 IN THE CHART

| *Milk Sheds* | *Milk Sheds* | *Milk Sheds* | *Milk Sheds* |
|---|---|---|---|
| 1. Cuttack | 5. Sambalpur | 9. Kalahandi | 13. Sundargarh |
| 2. Puri | 6. Ganjam | 10. Nuapada | 14. Mayurbhanj |
| 3. Dhenkanal | 7. Balasore | 11. Koraput | |
| 4. Keonjhar | 8. Bolangir | 12. Boudh | |

## 13.4 MILK PROCESSING FACILITIES IN ORISSA, 1998

The total milk processing capacity in the state in the form of milk plants and milk chilling centres in 1998 was 1.61 lakh lpd for milk processing and 1.45 lakh lpd of distributed chilling capacity. The major dairy plants existing in 1998 were the ones at Bhubaneswar, Rourkela, Dhenkanal, Keonjhar, Sambalpur and Behrampur. The existing milk processing capacity in the organised sector and their average daily throughput are presented in Table 13.2 in the Appendix.

Capacity utilisation by the dairy plants in Bhubaneswar and Sambalpur can be described as over 100 per cent, as all liquid milk plants have to carry spare capacities of at least 33 per cent over average procurement volumes, as the flush supplies are invariably much higher than the lean supply. Luckily the lean to flush supply ratio is only 2 : 3 in the case of Orissa, as these are predominantly cow milk areas. The other major dairy plant in Orissa is the one at

Rourkela. For several years now this plant has been operating with throughputs less than 50 per cent of its rated capacity. The dairy plants at Dhenkanal and Keonjhar have been operating for years with throughputs of less than 30 per cent of their rated capacity. The dairy plants at Berhampur, Remuna, Bhawanipatna, Bolangir and Rayagada are really chilling plants with 'Isotherm, Plug and Play' type of pasteurisers, set up as *ad hoc solutions,* for building up processed milk marketing volumes in these towns.

Bhubaneswar Dairy Plant is owned by the OMFED. This plant was expanded in 2002 to 1.25 llpd, including a 10 mtpd powder plant. The Bhubaneswar plant receives milk supplies from Puri, Cuttack, Dhenkanal and Keonjhar milk unions regularly. The OMFED annually imports milk from the national milk grid during the lean season in order to meet its marketing commitments. During 1997-8 this accounted for some 1.50 mln litres, adding an average of 4200 lpd to the plant's daily throughput. The Bhubaneswar plant also reconstitutes small quantities of SMP for balancing the SNF in the market milk. The average throughput of the plant for the past three years, pooling supplies from all sources, was some 68528 lpd (this has gone up to some 100000 lpd by August 2002). The Rourkela plant's throughput shown accounts for only what is supplied from the Sundargarh milk shed. This plant receives additional supplies from dairy plants in Bhubaneswar and Sambalpur, and its three year average throughput was 14634 lpd.

### 13.5 Meat and Meat Products: Current Scenario

Meat animals in Orissa are mainly small ruminants: goat and sheep; followed by poultry, in the order of output volumes. Cattle and pig are also used for meat purposes, but only in limited numbers and the use of their meat is restricted to very specific communities. The DAH & VS department's Integrated Sample Survey reported (see Table 13.4) that in 1998-9 the number of animals slaughtered were: goats 2.75 mln, sheep 0.88 mln, pig 0.11 mln and 0.016 mln cattle. The total output of meat was 3812000 mt. Meat output in Orissa grew by over a hundred percent between 1980 and 1998 from 16843 mt to 38129 mt. The growth and production of different kinds of meat vary from year to year. Organised commercial broiler production in the state commenced in the late 1980s and grew to some 12 mln broilers a year in 1996-7, contributing to some eight million

TABLE 13.4: MEAT PRODUCTION SPECIES WISE

| *Species* | *Nos. in mln* | *Qty. in mt* |
|---|---|---|
| Sheep | 0.88 | 8582 |
| Goat | 2.75 | 24654 |
| Cattle | 0.016 | 1691 |
| Pig | 0.11 | 3201 |
| Total | 3.76 | 38129 |
| Poultry | 5.42 | 6496 |
| Broiler | 8.00 | 9600 |
| Total | 13.42 | 16096 |
| Eggs | 762.8 | |

SOURCE: Integrated Sample Survey, 1998-9.

birds or 9600 mt of poultry meat for consumption in the state. In addition poultry meat from the back yard poultry units contributes some 5696 mt and culled birds from the commercial farms add some 800 mt of poultry meat.

## 13.6 SLAUGHTERHOUSES IN ORISSA, 1998

Slaughterhouses in the state are all owned by the local self-governments, 93 of them (see Table 5.7 in the Appendix) scattered in cities, towns and notified areas, all of them primitive, unkempt and without any hygiene or sanitation. Meat inspection is cursory and is carried out, if at all, by under qualified sanitary inspectors. More often than not meat sold in the market was seldom subjected to any sort of inspection. Processing and value addition facilities for pork and poultry do not exist in Orissa. Slaughter of animals, meat production, meat handling and vending are all carried out exclusively in the unorganized sector all over the state.

Slaughter of meat animals in almost all villages and even in most of the towns and cities, never the less takes place in open spaces, wherever convenient. Meat inspection, strangely enough, is the responsibility of the municipalities and other local self government bodies and not of the Department of Animal Husbandry, the main repository of all skills and knowledge in this area. Sanitary inspectors in the local bodies do not have adequate training in meat inspection. The largest slaughterhouses in the state are the ones in Cuttack and Bhubaneswar. Cuttack has two slaughterhouses one at Kesarpur and the other at Patopala Baxibazar; Bhubaneswar has only one located at Jharpada, some 5 km from the town. All three of them are primitive, lack basic facilities like running water, drainage or any kind of effluent collection or treatment. These three slaughterhouses hardly handle even 50 per cent of quantity of meat consumed in the cities of Cuttack and Bhubaneswar annually. The slaughterhouses in the smaller towns and notified area councils, over ninety are all open spaces without any basic facility required for the slaughter of animals. Beef and pork are slaughtered and vended in open spaces in villages and towns as well. There is no modern bacon factory in Orissa even though all the neighbouring states have one each. Many states in India initiated organised pig breeding programmes and established bacon factories (pig slaughter and pork processing facilities) sometime during the second to fourth five year plan period. Orissa has not benefited under this national programme. Bacon factories in the neighbouring states: at Gannavaram in Andhra Pradesh, Ranchi in Bihar and Haringhatta in West Bengal, are close enough to Orissa for drawing supplies, but their presence has not influenced the course of organised pig breeding in Orissa, even though these plants have always faced short supply of raw material-ready to slaughter pigs. Meat vending outlets are open spaces with the backyard for slaughter of animals. This sort of arrangement exists everywhere, even in the villages.

## 13.7 Egg Production and Consumption in Orissa, 1998

Of the 600 million eggs produced in Orissa, almost 55 per cent (320 mln) are *desi* eggs from the millions of back yard poultry holdings. *Desi* eggs are by and large used for hatching and table bird production; only some 40 per cent are consumed as table eggs, mostly in the producing households and villages, traded in the village *haats* and markets by the producer families themselves along with *desi* table birds, or through petty middle men who operate in rural *haats*. Eggs in Orissa are marketed by the private trade, as supplies to the major towns and cities come from the large, organised layer farms in the state. The entire trade in this sector is managed by well-established contractors who pick up eggs from the farms and distribute to retail points in all urban markets and even to a large number of semi urban and large rural markets. In addition to the roughly 280 mln eggs produced in the commercial poultry farms in Orissa, these markets consume an additional 350 mln eggs imported from other states annually, all through established private traders. Only a small number of *desi* eggs reach the *urban niche markets*, through a chain of middlemen. This affinity for local markets is because *desi* eggs from backyard holdings are all fertilised eggs and have very limited shelf life.

## 13.8 Poultry Meat and Pork Processing, 1998

There is no processing or value addition infrastructure for eggs in Orissa, justifiably because Orissa has no surplus eggs and at least for the time being, the state is a net importer of eggs. It is unlikely that Orissa becomes a surplus state for eggs during the next ten years. Reported consumption of poultry meat in Orissa is some 5 million *desi* birds and over 8 million broilers, some 16096 mt of poultry meat in a year. It is also reported that Orissa exports some 4 mln broilers to neighbouring states annually. Orissa's back yard poultry system has a total of over 16 mln *desi* birds, of which 3.49 mln are layers. They produce an average of 90 eggs per layer per year and the major end use of *desi* eggs (over half the production) is hatching for table bird production. Therefore, the table bird production would actually be somewhere near 20 mln. While the estimate of broiler consumption is nearer to the actual consumption, *desi bird consumption should at least be four times higher (20 mln) than the reported consumption of 5.42 mln.* Be that as it may, the important point is that Orissa is a *surplus state for poultry meat*, *desi* as well as broiler and therefore there is considerable scope for processing and value addition for poultry meat, in the private sector. Orissa now has no infrastructure for processing and value addition for poultry meat.

Growth in pork production in Orissa is stymied as the present scavenging scrub pigs repulses even the most ardent pork lovers. Changes in swine husbandry practices and modern meat processing and handling will enormously encourage pork production and will enhance livelihood generation in the most backward districts of the state, as good quality pork has a flourishing market in the neighbouring megalopolis of Calcutta. Other metro cities in India, as well as many states like Goa, West Bengal and Kerala have large demand for clean pork and pork products. Orissa in 1998, however, had no processing and value addition facilities for pork. Private trade markets eggs in Orissa, as supplies to the major towns and cities come from large commercial farms in the state.

## 13.9 Future Scenario: Dairy and Meat Sector, 2008

Supply projections for the different livestock produces for 2008 indicate that there will be considerable growth in all produces, under the impact of the ten year perspective plan now under the consideration of the state government, provided the plan is implemented as recommended by the Steering Committee (LSR), on the suggested time frame and with the institutional restructuring proposed. These development plans will alter favourably: (i) the quality of the inputs for production enhancement; (ii) their delivery system; and (iii) thereby the quality of the cattle and buffaloes: increasing productivity per head of animal and per livestock/poultry owning household.

### (A) Dairy Sector

Milk production will grow from 0.73 mln mt in 1998-9 to some 1.30 mln mt by 2008, the marketable supply of milk will increase to some 2.50 mln lpd and per capita availability of milk will improve to 84 g per day for an increased population of some 42.66 mln in Orissa, 2008. The increase in milk output would essentially be on account of the increase in crossbred cows, which will by then account for some 12.53 per cent of milch animal population as shown in the Fig. 13.3 below:

Milk collection by the organised dairy sector in the state, the milk cooperative movement, will go up to some 324000 lpd, 13 per cent of the vastly increased supply and the matching growth in processing will necessitate a capacity of some 450000 lpd for processing and over 500000 lpd of distributed chilling. To ensure the projected 2008 throughputs for the proposed dairy plants in Orissa, the organized sector in the state dairy industry therefore needs a well conceived

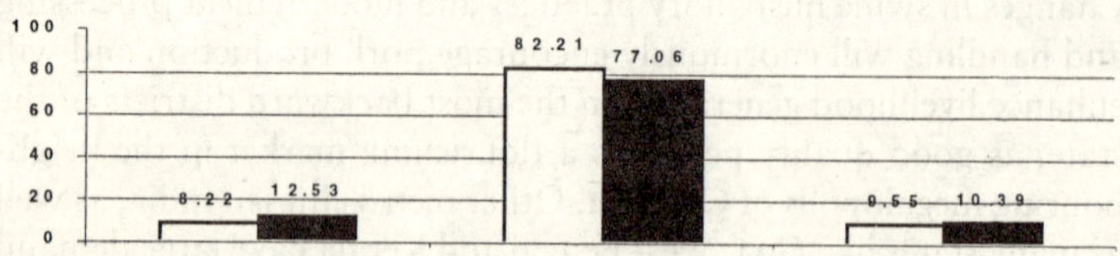


Fig. 13.3: Adult Female Population Composition (%).

supply management strategy, comprising: (a) reorganization of the milk sheds in the state, (b) expansion of DCS net work in the rural areas, (c) procurement price of milk and its payment schedule, (d) distributed milk chilling facilities in the milk shed, (e) rationalisation of procurement transport, (f) quality as the basis for price, and (g) provision of essential production input supply. The projected milk procurement in the year 2008 is presented in Table 13.3 in the Appendix. Expanding the existing major dairy plants and building new capacities will accomplish this. The most important addition will be a new dairy plant of some 100000 lpd capacity in Cuttack, expansion of the Bhubaneswar plant from 75000 lpd to 100000 lpd and of the Rourkela plant from 30000 lpd to 60000 lpd. The Bhubaneswar dairy will be Orissa's link with the national milk grid and will be receiving and pouring liquid milk from/to the national milk grid, both road and rail tankers, to balance the state milk grid and to sustain its own supply commitments to the different state markets. There will be a complete reorientation of the milk chilling approach and chilling plants will be the basis for organising rural milk collection. Under this approach bulk coolers of the appropriate sizes will be installed in DCSs, one for a cluster of 3 to 5 DCSs and chilled milk transported to the dairies by insulated road milk tankers, once on alternate days.

There would be by 2008, five key milk sheds, namely, Cuttack, Puri, Balassore, Ganjam and Sambalpur as core components of the state milk grid and these would justifiably deserve special attention for the production enhancement inputs under the ten year perspective plan. The projected market share of the major dairy plants by 2008 are: Bhubaneswar 70000 lpd liquid milk, 60 per cent of the local milk market; Cuttack 60000 lpd, 64 per cent; Rourkela 50000 lpd, 48 per cent and Puri 25000 in Puri and Khurda together, 50 per cent. The proposed infrastructure for 2008 in Orissa is presented in Table 13.4 in the Appendix.

### (B) PROCESSING INFRASTRUCTURE MEAT SECTOR: BY PRODUCTS AND CO-PRODUCTS

Meat supply too will go up considerably by 2008, quantities of meat available will be some 60279 mt comprising mutton, chevon, pork and beef. In addition there will also be an enhanced supply of poultry meat and broiler totalling to 22000 mt. Matching processing facilities in the meat sector are expected to come up for handling and processing poultry and pork meat and limited facilities for mutton and chevon. Poultry meat and pork processing in Orissa has considerable commercial and livelihood implications. Broiler surpluses of over 10 mln birds per year are projected and therefore one large and three medium capacity poultry processing plants, all in the private or co-operative sector, are likely to come up in the state. One pork processing plant is already coming up in Balasore district, promoted by PRIYA, a voluntary organisation. Fully automatic plants for processing poultry and pork are available in India and there are several fabricators ready to supply on turnkey basis.

Modern slaughter houses, with all required hygiene and sanitation facilities, one each for Bhubaneswar, Cuttack and Rourkela are required, to be established in the joint sector and with management entrusted to the private sector partner, the capacity for each should be up to 1000 sheep/goat per day. Simpler slaughter facilities should be developed for the remaining 27 district headquarter towns for slaughter of up to 50 sheep/goat per day; and experimental slaughter sheds for six major *gram panchayats*. For the meat sector the recommended measures aim at stable supply relationship between plants and producers; and identification and nurturing of supply sheds/producers by plants, through a variety of measures like provision for genetic inputs, production support and feed, all on the commercial plane.

Supply of meat animals for slaughter is in private hands or with butchers themselves who are unorganized and follow the traditional channels. With the large investments proposed for the meat industry (processing plants and slaughter houses) it is imperative to bring some order and reforms in this area. Large scale production of beef is out of question in Orissa as slaughter of cows is banned by the state: and more important, beef is not a popular or preferred meat. The people generally favour sheep and goat meat.

### (C) POULTRY MEAT: SUPPLY, PROCESSING AND VALUE ADDITION, 2008

Broiler production is estimated to grow at an annual rate of 15 per cent and the total broiler production in the state will cross 25 mln by 2008. Consumption of broiler in the state will go up from 8 mln in 1996 to some 14 mln by 2008, leaving nearly 10 mln broiler birds for export; a volume large enough to promote processing and value addition. With increasing output of broiler in the state, helping to establish processing plants for broiler is one area where the state government's promotional role should actively come into play. Agro-tech entrepreneurs (not broiler farmers) in the state should be encouraged to set up fully automated but medium scale broiler processing business, leading to products like: dressed broiler meat, special cuts, processed meat products, ready to eat meat products; for the state as well as the national markets. Very large, fully automated plants for poultry meat processing are available in the international markets and will need to be imported. But as these are equipment for processing and value addition to farm/food produces, they will attract considerable assistance and support from the central government. Medium scale fully automated plants for broiler processing are now fabricated in India and there are several suppliers in the country. Their capacity ranges from 500 birds to 1000 birds per hour. The processing includes: electrical stunning of birds, sticking, bleeding, scalding, de-feathering, evisceration, washing and chilling. Plants for further processing and manufacture of ready to eat meat products are also available in India.

The most important districts in Orissa for large, medium and small commercial broiler farms are: Cuttack, Balasore, Puri, Ganjam, Sundargarh, Sambalpur, Dhenkanal and Bolangir; together these districts account for 80 per cent of the total broiler production in the state. Therefore a large, state-of-the-art, multi product poultry processing plant can be set up in Cuttack, processing and producing poultry meat products for the international markets, particularly targeting East Asian and South-East Asian countries. The state government may use the services of reputed international consultants for technical and commercial assessment of the possibilities; and also to promote foreign direct investments in this sector. Under the WTO Regulations, the '*most favoured nation status*' that India enjoys with the United States and the European Community, as well as, *the 'minimum access clause of the Uruguay Round Agreement*' will enable Orissa to market these products in any of the world markets including the USA, provided they satisfy the '*Sanitary and Phyto Sanitary Standards (SPS)*' of the WTO. Medium scale plants for poultry processing in the private sector should be encouraged in the districts of Ganjam, Balasore, and Sundargarh. These plants will have a capacity of 500 birds per hour. In addition to the plants already mentioned, the cold chain for marketing, comprising distributed cold storages (-20° C storages), special transport for frozen cargo and retail outlets with -20° C horizontal deep freezes 4° C cold storage and handling cabinets would also be needed. All these of course will evolve as part of the emerging meat processing industry, not only for poultry but for the meat processing industry in general.

### (D) PORK AND PORK PRODUCTS: PROCESSING AND VALUE ADDITION, 2008

Pork and pork product processing too has good prospects in Orissa, provided raw material of good quality becomes available in the pig breeding districts of Orissa, under the livestock development plan. Pig meat production in Orissa will grow, in response to the growing market pull, at the rate of 20 per cent per year and the total pork supply will reach some 7000 mt, by 2008. In addition to planned breeding and husbandry schemes, processing and value addition will enormously encourage growth of pig production in the state. Districts important for pig breeding and for pig meat processing as well are: Balasore, Mayurbhanj, Sundargarh, Koraput, Malkangiri and Subarnapur. In Balasore a non-governmental organisation, People, Rural Research and Youth Action (PRIYA), has already entered into a contract with Swadeshi Agrotech, Bhopal, for the turnkey execution of a pig processing plant, with a capacity to process 50 pigs per day (1500 kg of meat per day); and to be located at Sankumari. This will be the turning point in the history of swine husbandry and piggery development in the state. One more plant in Mayurbhanj district could be set up to handle 50 pigs per day. Additional facility can be added to these plants to produce ready to eat pork products like bacon and ham.

### (E) SMALL RUMINANTS: SLAUGHTER HOUSES AND MEAT HANDLING, 2008

Cuttack and Bhubaneswar are the largest demand centres for mutton and chevon in Orissa and the combined consumption of the two cities, was estimated as some 4500 mt annually, nearly 13 per cent of the total meat output (small ruminant) in the state in 1997. By 2008 the estimated consumption in Cuttack and Bhubaneswar would be 7900 mt (16 per cent of total sheep and goat meat output in 2008) involving slaughter of over 2000 sheep and goat per day.

To ensure that a good part of the meat supply to the two cities, say 70 per cent of what is consumed, comes from safe and hazard free sources: modern slaughter houses with high standards of hygiene and meat inspection, the government has to take immediate action to:

(i) Revamp the meat inspection rules and procedures in the state and put qualified veterinarians, specialised in meat inspection and veterinary public health, in charge of meat inspection.

(ii) As the existing three slaughter houses are beyond redemption, the state government should encourage and support the municipal corporations in Cuttack and Bhubaneswar, to build two new, modern slaughter houses, one each in Cuttack and Bhubaneswar, preferably in the joint sector, with management entrusted to the private sector partner and inspection and hygiene under the control of the specialist veterinarians, employed by the corporations.

(iii) Rourkela needs a modern slaughter house of almost the same sophistication and size, as the ones recommended for the cities of Cuttack and Bhubaneswar.

(iv) As consumers in Orissa are used to and prefer fresh meat, the slaughter houses need be equipped only for production of fresh chilled meat, with the cold handling facilities limited to overnight hanging of carcasses to get over the rigor mortis and in the meat handling and packaging/dispatch rooms.

(v) Private management of such a slaughter house is of paramount importance, as the installations need constant and regular upkeep and maintenance. As commercial slaughter facilities, they will then be able to offer the butchers excellent services and conveniences, all on payment of market-determined charges.

(vi) This will also mark the emergence of commercial meat complexes in the major demand centres, in the private sector, leaving the municipalities and the city corporations free to enforce the slaughter and meat inspection laws and procedures.

(vii) The system will then evolve as an independent enterprise and will equip itself with the down stream services required, such as transport for chilled meat, cold chain and air-conditioned meat retail outlets with cold handling cabinets for retail sale of cut meat.

The demand centres for meat, next in the order of priority are the remaining 27 district headquarters towns in the state. The district headquarters towns of all districts need new but smaller slaughter-houses capable of handling up to 50-100 small ruminants for slaughter per day, with all the hygiene and sanitation standards prescribed under revised statutes. These slaughter houses at least in the initial years of the ten year programme recommended, will have to be built and managed by the municipalities, with the help of the state government. The municipalities in these towns and the state government should actively try to involve the private sector in the venture as joint sector partners, at least in the district towns like Berhampur, Balasore, Baripada (Mayurbhanj) and also Sundargarh, where there will be a private sector/nongovernmental organisation owned meat processing units for poultry/pig; and the combined larger volumes of meat handled will enable viable commercial operations.

The slaughter sheds in the villages in Orissa, approximately 60 in all, are best left alone for the time being, as the vast majority of the slaughter, in any case, take place in open air, minimising the public health hazard; and as it will be impractical for the government/*gram panchayats* to enforce hygiene and sanitation standards in all of them.

#### (F) MEAT SECTOR: BY-PRODUCTS AND CO-PRODUCTS: PROCESSING AND VALUE ADDITION

Skin and hide as well other by products like offal, bone, hair, and even very small quantities of wool are all exported from the state to West Bengal, Uttar Pradesh and Andhra Pradesh, as raw materials for the tanneries, bone crushing plants and by-product processing units. There are one or two small scale tanneries in the state, but these are in the private sector and have no scope for expansion. Also from the environmental point of view, it is advantageous to the state, to encourage export of these products as raw materials to processing units outside the state.

### 13.10 Animal Feed Milling Plants

Animal feed milling capacity in the state existing today is adequate (see Table 8.7 in the Appendix). Compounded feeds for livestock production is not a very popular ingredient in the daily rations of any species of animals in the state, except for the high yielding crossbred cows and the commercial birds in the layer and broiler farms in the state. Against a total installed capacity of some 600 mt per day, the capacity utilisation is only some 20 per cent for the three large plants (100 mtp) in the public sector; and less then 50 per cent for 44 small plants in the private sector. Total compounded feed production in the state was only some 80000 mt in 1997. Therefore, there is no scope for additional capacity creation. The increased demand for compounded feeds likely for supporting the enhanced production under the impact of the ten year perspective plan, will all be met by the spare capacity that now exists and if necessary by incremental capacities in the private sector.

## 13.11 Supply Management, 2008

### (A) Dairy Sector

To ensure the projected 2008 throughputs for the proposed dairy plants in Orissa, the organised sector in the state dairy industry therefore, will need a well conceived supply management strategy, comprising: (a) reorganisation of the milk sheds in the state; (b) expansion of the DCS network; (c) distributed milk chilling facilities within the milk shed; (d) rationalisation of procurement transport; (e) procurement price of milk and its payment schedule; (f) quality as basis of price; and (g) provision of essential production input supply. If the strategies recommended are aggressively pursued by the cooperative set up in the state, the organised dairy sector will

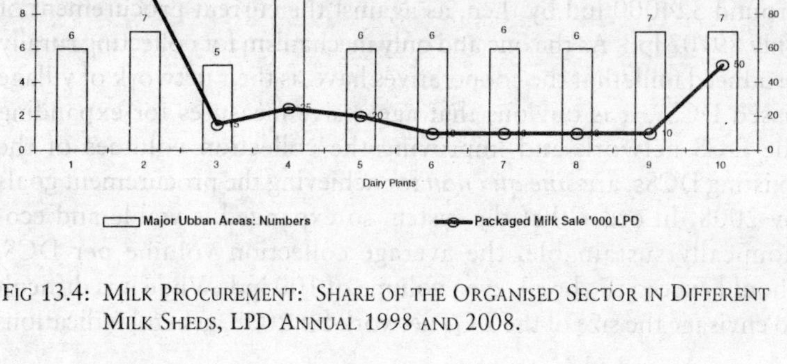


Fig 13.4: Milk Procurement: Share of the Organised Sector in Different Milk Sheds, LPD Annual 1998 and 2008.

TABLE 13.5: LIST OF REORGANISED MILK SHEDS 1-10 IN THE CHART

| *Milk Shed* | *Districts falling within each proposed Milk Shed* | | |
|---|---|---|---|
| 1. Cuttack | Cuttack | Jagatsinghpur | Kendrapara |
| 2. Puri | Puri | Khurda | Nayagarh |
| 3. Balasore | Balasore | Bhadrak | Mayurbhanj |
| 4. Ganjam | Ganjam | Gajapati | |
| 5. Sambalpur | Sambalpur | Bargarh | Subranapur |
| 6. Kalahandi | Kalahandi | Kandhamal | Bolangir, Boudh, Nauapara |
| 7. Dhenkanal | Dhenkanal | Angul | |
| 8. Keonjhar | Keonjhar | Jajpur | |
| 9. Koraput | Koraput | Nawarangpur | Rayagada, Malkangiri |
| 10. Sundargarh | Sundargarh | Devgarh | Jharsugada |

be able to enhance its share to 13 per cent of the vastly increased marketable supply, compared to the 5 per cent share it had in 1998 see Fig. 13.4.

*Expansion of DCS Network in Orissa Milk Sheds*

The promoting agencies, the OMFED, ISPO and the DAH & VS, together organised some 1901 dairy co-operative societies (DCS) in the state up to March 1999. However the functional DCSs in March 1999 were only 1345: 1054 under OMFED, 83 in the GGGMU and 291 under the AHD (see Appendix for details). The Ten Year Perspective Plan for Cattle and Buffalo Development, recommended by the Steering Committee constituted by the Orissa government, assuming time bound implementation of the perspective plan, indicates that annual milk production in the state will go up to 1.30 mln mt by 2008 and will generate a marketable supply of some 2.50 mln lpd. Projections of possible milk procurement by the organised sector (dairy cooperatives) indicate a collection volume of around 324000 lpd by then, as against the current procurement of only 89702 lpd. As the one and only mechanism for collecting rurally produced milk that the cooperatives have, is their network of village based DCSs, it is obvious that aggressive measures for expanding the DCS network and improving the collection volumes of the existing DCSs, are *sine qua non* for achieving the procurement goals by 2008. In order that the system so expanded is viable and economically sustainable, the average collection volume per DCS, should exceed the break even volume of 100 lpd. While it is difficult to envisage the size of the DCS network for 2008, general indications are that the number of viable, functional DCSs would be some where between 1800 and 2500. The effort should also be to double the collection volumes of the existing DCS network.

*Distributed Milk Chilling Facilities in Milk Sheds*

The distributed milk chilling capacity as recommended is a total of 502000 litres per day, for the collection and transportation, initially of some 324000 lpd together from all the 10 milk sheds and supplying to the 10 milk processing plants of widely varying sizes. The proposal is to locate small bulk coolers (a mix of 500 lpd, 1000 lpd and 2000 lpd depending on collection potential) in selected DCSs, jointly for the use of a cluster of DCSs surrounding the DCS with the bulk cooler. Normally at levels of milk collection in Orissa, one bulk cooler can be shared by 3 to 5 DCSs depending on the size of the cooler. The advantages of the system are: (a) better quality of milk reaches the milk plants from the DCS, (b) two time collection, i.e. morning and evening collection will be possible at the DCS, this will raise the average milk collection per DCS, (c) small volumes, transported over long distances daily, are costing the plant heavily and milk transport cost is the main reason for high overheads for the unions and the dairy plants. Bulk coolers in DCSs will allow the dairy to rationalise procurement transport, and (d) reception of chilled milk by road tankers, offers many advantages (lower investments and running costs for refrigeration) to dairy plants as well.

*Rationalisation of Milk Procurement Transport*

The reorientation of the milk chilling system discussed above will entail, as a sequel, complete change over from cans and trucks, to road milk tankers (RMT) for milk collection, as all milk coming to the dairy will exclusively be chilled milk, from the bulk coolers. All milk procurement transport will then be by insulated road milk tankers. Dairy plants state wide will receive raw chilled milk in tankers and dairies no longer will need can reception docks, but will have tanker reception bays. In order to streamline and standardise milk transport, both for procurement as well as for inter-dairy movement of milk in the state milk grid, the recommendation is that all dairies in the state be equipped with standard size road milk tankers which can be used for both purposes. Experience under Indian conditions in many milksheds in the country has proved that 9000 litre capacity, fixed chassis, road milk tankers are ideal as standard equipment for all dairy plants, where the volumes moved inter-dairy are not very large.

*Procurement Price of Milk and Payment Schedule*

All milk unions in Orissa have a sustained good record for regularity in payment for the milk procured and the price paid by and large, has been fair and reasonable. However, payment to the producers is made only once in ten days. Milk supplied by producers to the DCSs in Orissa, however, is invariably diluted with water and the DCSs have so far not been able to train them to supply clean, undiluted milk. The average SNF per cent of milk reaching the dairy dock in most milksheds in Orissa had never exceeded 8.1 per cent. Milk producers in Orissa are invariably very poor, a vast majority of them live below the poverty line and many of them are illiterate. Denying them access to daily cash for commodities sold by them every day, is therefore unfair. Be that as it may, daily payment of the milk prices in the DCSs will have many advantages, in addition to the question of fairness. The most important of them is that the DCS will be able to attract all the milk the producer has, into its collection bucket. The daily cash income from milk means for him, deliverance from the clutches of the village trader for daily necessities. *One litre of milk in Orissa sold to the DCS, gives the milk producer an income equivalent to 50 per cent of the average per capita daily income in the state. This is a powerful incentive for him to pour progressively larger volumes in the DCS and to supply milk twice a day. For the DCS it will mean 4 times increase in its daily collection volumes, instantly.*

Another dimension of immense importance to the producer as well as to the DCS, is the correlation of price to quality that daily cash payment can inculcate in the mind of the milk producer. Yet another social and economic dimension is the changes daily payment of milk brings about in the producers' ability for capital formation. *Daily cash incomes enable producer families to meet the daily cash needs for obtaining daily household necessities, without having to run up a growing debt to the village trader. Cash payments further enables the family to choose what they want and how much; and consequently gets them much better value for money and better terms of trade for what they buy. In the long run it helps the family to avoid creating charges on their bulk income from crops or sale of commodities, services or livestock, leading to much better capital formation and financial viability. All Milk Unions and DCSs in Orissa should, therefore initiate daily payment for milk, forthwith.*

*Quality as the Basis for Producer Price*

Producer price for milk in the Orissa DCSs is set on the basis of quality with reference to composition of milk: determined on the basis fat and SNF content. While this has indeed had considerable influence on the composition of the milk collected, difficulties in accurate measurement of SNF at DCS level have lead to some amount of dilution of milk supplied to DCS, with water. As there is very little buffalo milk in Orissa, DCSs can really buy milk on fat test alone and can discourage dilution. Quality in terms of the bacteriological standards of milk however is not considered for price setting in the Indian dairy industry. Raw milk procured from the milksheds in Orissa therefore already has high bacterial count even as it is received in the DCS. While chilling of milk in the DCS and movement of chilled milk by insulated road milk tankers will undoubtedly help, the ideal solution to good quality milk procurement will be paying for milk on bacteriological quality as well. For this individual samples of milk delivered in the DCS can be subjected to Somatic Cell Count/MBR test and payment based on Fat/SNF adjusted for bacteriological quality through bonuses and penalties, depending on their bacteriological quality. It is therefore desirable that *all DCSs and Milk Unions in Orissa should start milk procurement on the basis of quality, both composition as well as bacteriological, forthwith.*

*Provision for Essential Production Input Supply*

Finally enabling the milk producer access to essential inputs for enhancing milk production is the surest way for enlarging supply, as well as for building up rapport with the producers and ensuring their loyalty. While the milk union and federation take care of major input supply programme for the entire milk shed and all milk sheds in the state, the DCS should market the most essential among them directly to the milk producers. The most important input for milk production, which can help the milk producer as well as the DCS with immediate supply response is compounded balanced cattle feed. *Every DCS should therefore stock and sell balanced cattle feed, made by the OMFED, in small quantities, enabling producers to buy their daily need, with the daily price paid to them.* The input next in the order of priority is AI for crossbreeding of cattle/grading up of buffalo. While AI may not yield production responses in the immediate term, it does over the short term bring many benefits to the DCS village: it improves the regularity of calving of the milch animals in the village, increases the number of cows in milk and generates improved milch animals with much higher yields generation after generation. *AI is an input that the DCS can arrange on its own, either through an AI centre in the DCS or in* association with nearby DCSs, through a mobile AI practitioner.

### (B) MEAT SECTOR

Supply of meat animals for slaughter, in the case of all species is managed by private contractors, or the butchers themselves. This is also entirely in the unorganised traditional channel. With large investments going into meat processing plants and modern slaughterhouses, it will become necessary in the immediate future to bring some order and continuity in this area. Large scale beef production is out of question in Orissa as the slaughter of cows is banned by the state. Sheep and goat supply channel would, on the other hand, need reorganisation, as mutton and chevon are the most favoured meats. The modern slaughter houses in Bhubaneswar, Cuttack and Rourkela, are the major bulk consumers of meat animals and therefore it is in their interest to streamline supply for their plants. The slaughter house managements should enter into long term supply arrangements with the sheep and goat breeders' associations, non-governmental organisations helping the sheep and goat farmers, as well as, with private contractors, for regular supply of slaughter animals on the basis of agreed standards and specifications, essential for good meat production. Pig meat processing plants are all recommended in the co-operative or the private sector. For some time to come in the immediate future, the plants will have to work with the OLRDS to keep track of the organised pig farmers they promote and to arrive at long term supply arrangements with the farmers. The evolving supply link would depend on the organisation and continued support the plant offers the pig farmers for modernising their farming practices, as well as, the genetic and production input supply the plants establish for promoting pig production. Each plant should ideally select a supply area and build up a mutually beneficial long term business relationship with the pig farmers in the area, constantly promoting their farming efforts and assuring them a stable, lucrative market.

Poultry processing plants too are all recommended in the cooperative and private sector. The raw material in the case of these plants are invariably broilers and it should be comparatively easy for the plants to register and nurture their long term suppliers, for year round supply. Broiler farms are all in the semi intensive or intensive farming systems and are part of the commercial stream. They have visibility and are specialists in production. To organise them into a producers' co-operative or to engage them in business relationships should pose no problems. Here too the plants should take initiative to ensure quality genetic inputs, feed supply and production support, all on a mutually beneficial commercial relationship.

### 13.12 Milk and Milk Products Marketing in Orissa

Milk and milk products marketing in Orissa takes place predominantly in the unorganised traditional sector. Of the total daily milk production of some 2.59 mln litres in 1998-9, nearly 30 per cent, 0.78 mln litres per day, are retained in the milk producer households, for home consumption. Over 95 per cent of the marketable supply available, some 1.81 mln litres are traded daily in the traditional channels: from the producers directly to the consumers, through petty traders (Dudhias), or through several tiers of milk contractors to urban and semi urban consumers, both households and institutions. Some 20 per cent of the milk traded in the traditional channels, always through middlemen with long term supply relationships, is consumed by traditional sweetmeat manufacturers for making milk based sweets. The current share of the organised sector of the dairy industry in the state, in milk marketing, is only some 5 per cent, 0.09 mln litres per day. The milk cooperative movement in the state, promoted by the Orissa State Co-operative Milk Producers' Federation (OMFED), the state Department of Animal Husbandry and the Indo-Swiss Programme, is the exclusive organised channel for milk marketing in Orissa and they constitute the organised sector of the state dairy industry.

In 1998 these cooperative institutions: milk unions and the federation together, marketed some 123031 litres of milk mostly as pasteurised, packaged milk in 500 ml polypacks, in over 60 cities, towns and other urban and semi urban demand centres. In addition,

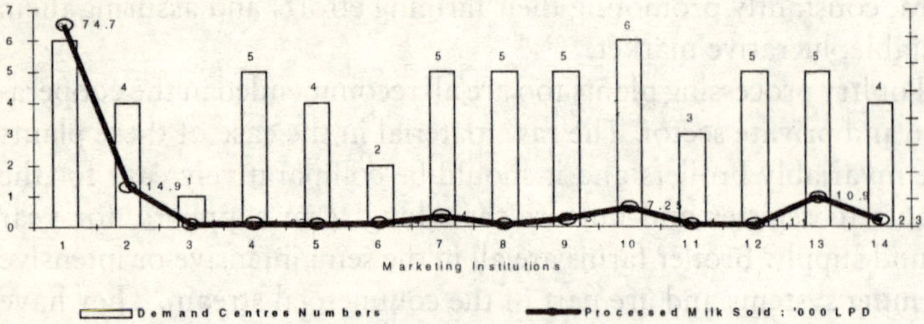


FIG. 13.4: PROCESSED, PACKAGED, MILK MARKETING IN ORISSA BY THE ORGANISED DAIRY SECTOR, 1998.

TABLE 13.6: LIST OF MILK MARKETING INSTITUTIONS 1-14 IN THE CHART

| *Marketing Institutions* | *Marketing Institutions* |
|---|---|
| 1. Bhubaneswar Dairy, OMFED | 8. Puri Milk Union |
| 2. Ruorkela Dairy, OMFED | 9. Balasore Milk Union |
| 3. Kalahandi Milk Union | 10. Greater Ganjam Gajapati Milk Union |
| 4. Koraput Milk Union | 11. Bolangir Milk Union |
| 5. Boudh Milk Union | 12. Nuapara Milk Union |
| 6. Mayurbhanj Milk Union | 13. Sambalpur Milk Union |
| 7. Dhenkanal Milk Union | 14. Keonjhar Milk Union |

the Cooperative Institutions, primarily the OMFED, markets small quantities of milk products as well. The liquid milk marketing in 1998-9, by the Cooperative Institutions is presented in the Fig. 13.4. With the processing infrastructure build up recommended, total liquid milk marketing by the organised sector (the milk cooperatives) will go up to some 350000 litres per day by 2008. Almost all of it will be marketed as pasteurised, packaged milk in 500 ml poly packs. The milk shed/plant wise marketing profile, indicating the number of major demand centres that will be covered and the quantity sold in each of them (including sale in their satellites as well) is presented in the Fig. 13.5. All milk sheds by then will have dairy plants capable of pasteurising and packaging milk. Place names within brackets in Table 13.7, are the locations of the dairy plant in each milk shed.

Processed milk supply will be available in 66 major urban areas and the surrounding demand centres near them, by 2008. However, astute marketing strategies by the milk marketing institutions, supported by strong legal interventions by the government, will be

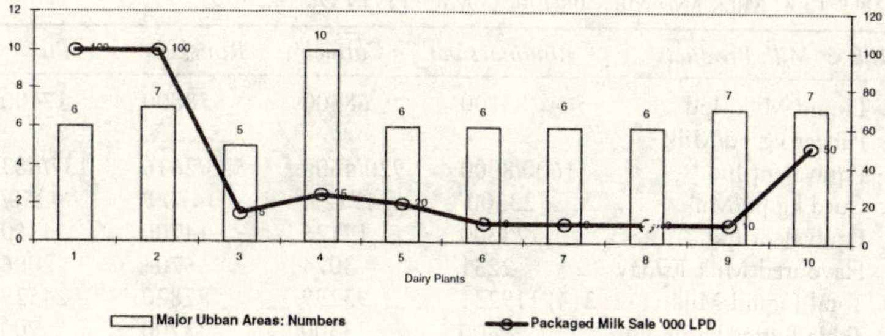


FIG. 13.5 PROCESSED LIQUID MILK MARKETING BY DAIRY PLANTS, 2008.

TABLE 13.7: LIST OF DAIRY PLANTS 1-10 IN THE CHART

| *Milk Shed and Dairy Plant* | *Milk Shed and Dairy Plant* |
|---|---|
| 1. Cuttack (Cuttack) | 6. Kalahandi (Bhawanipatna) |
| 2. Puri (Bhubaneswar) | 7. Dhenkanal (Dhenkanal) |
| 3. Balasore (Balasore) | 8. Keonjhar (Keonjhar) |
| 4. Ganjam (Berhampore) | 9. Koraput (Koraput) |
| 5. Sambalpur (Sambalpur) | 10. Sundargarh (Rourkela) |

required to dislodge the supply coming from well entrenched urban commercial milk producers and to capture a commanding share of the market in the cities and towns like Bhubaneswar, Cuttack, Rourkela and Berhampur. *Commercial milk production in the major urban centres in the state poses serious environmental and public health hazards and should be sternly discouraged by the government, for the good of man and animal alike.* The most important markets for milk and milk products in Orissa are Bhubaneswar, Cuttack, Rourkela and Puri, in that order. The Indian Market Research Bureau (IMRB), Calcutta, studied the markets for milk and milk products in these centres in 1997. The market estimates for the four centres made by the IMRB are presented in the Table 13.8. Market share of the OMFED for milk was estimated by the IMRB as: Bhubaneswar: 15400 lpd, 18 per cent; Cuttack: 16200 lpd, 23 per cent; Rourkela: 9200 lpd, 14 per cent and Puri: 2800 lpd, 12 per cent. The share of the *khatals* (city stables of the commercial city milk producers) however had the lions share of the market in all the four cities: Bhubaneswar: 70000 lpd, 66 per cent; Cuttack: 52300 lpd, 62 per cent; Rourkela: 49000 lpd, 57 per cent and Puri: 14500 lpd, 60 per cent. The IMRB study does not indicate the OMFED's share of the product market.

TABLE 13.8: MILK AND MILK PRODUCTS MARKETS IN ORISSA, 1997

| *Milk & Milk Products* | *Bhubnaeswar* | *Cuttack* | *Rourkela* | *Puri* |
|---|---|---|---|---|
| 1. Liquid Milk, lpd | 85700 | 68500 | 58800 | 17400 |
| 2. Paneer kg pd/Milk Equivalent lpd | 1600/8000 | 920/4600 | 523/2616 | 137/683 |
| 3. Curd kg pd/Milk Equivalent lpd | 23300/ 23300 | 17125/ 17125 | 14700/ 14700 | 4350/ 4350 |
| 4. Flavoured Milk lts/day | 2231 | 3074 | 6704 | 2096 |
| Total Liquid Milk (1+2+3+4) | 119231 | 93299 | 82820 | 24529 |
| 5. Table Butter kgs/month | 5600 | 3300 | 3700 | 700 |
| 6. Ghee kgs/month | 23900 | 20000 | 18700 | 7600 |

SOURCE: IMRB Study 1997. IMRB estimates for curd appears to be an underestimate and therefore figures for curd in table 21 are estimates by this study.

Population growth in Orissa between 1981-91 was 20.06 per cent. Population projection for 2008 at this rate of growth is presented in the Table 13.9. Milk consumption per capita in 1997, was estimated by the IMRB survey as 185 gm, for Bhubaneswar, Cuttack 138 gm, Puri 123 gm and Rourkela 131 gm. The estimated growth in per

TABLE 13.9: DEMAND FOR LIQUID MILK IN IMPORTANT URBAN CENTRES BY 2008

| *Sl.* | *Town* | *Human Population* | | | *Demand lpd* | |
|---|---|---|---|---|---|---|
| *No.* | | *1991* | *1997** | *2008** | *1997* | *2008** |
| 1. | Cuttack | 440295 | 494715 | 590356 | 68500 | 93276 |
| 2. | Bhubaneswar | 411542 | 462408 | 551803 | 85700 | 116982 |
| 3. | Rourkela | 398864 | 448163 | 534804 | 58800 | 106960 |
| 4. | Puri | 125199 | 140673 | 167869 | 17400 | 24508 |

NOTE: *Study Estimates 1999.

TABLE 13.10: ESTIMATED MILK AND MILK PRODUCTS MARKETS IN ORISSA 2008

| *Sl. No.* | *Milk & Milk Products* | *Bhubaneswar* | *Cuttack* | *Rourkela* | *Puri* |
|---|---|---|---|---|---|
| 1. | Liquid Milk lts/day | 116982 | 93276 | 106760 | 24508 |
| 2. | Paneer kg pd/Milk Equivalent lpd | 1909/9546 | 1098/5489 | 624/3121 | 163/815 |
| 3. | Curd kg pd/Milk Equivalent lpd | 34898 | 20435 | 17541 | 5190 |
| 4. | Flavoured Milk lts/day | 3096 | 3668 | 8000 | 2501 |
| | Total Liquid Milk (1+2+3+4) | 164522 | 122868 | 135422 | 33014 |
| 5. | Table Butter kg/month | 6682 | 3937 | 4415 | 835 |
| 6. | Ghee kg/month | 32798 | 27446 | 22315 | 9069 |

capita consumption in 10 years by 2008, would be: Bhubaneswar 212 gm; Cuttack 158 gm; Puri 146 gm; and Rourkela 200 gm.

The share of the Bhubaneswar Dairy in the liquid milk market by 2008 (see Table 13.10) would be some: Bhubaneswar: 70000 lpd, 60 per cent; Cuttack dairy: Cuttack city: 60000 lpd, 64 per cent; Rourkela dairy: Rourkela city: 50000 lpd, 48 per cent; and Puri 25000 lpd, together in Puri, Khurda and other small urban areas nearby, 50 per cent (marketed by the Bhubaneswar Dairy Plant as there is no proposal for a processing plant in Puri).

Larger procurement volumes, consequent lower transport cost and lower processing costs per litre will all enable the federation to hit the *khatals* where it hurts most. The *khatals* have much higher milk production costs in the urban areas where they are, compared to the cost of production in villages and they would not be able to cut prices or in other words enter into a price war with the federation. Another area where the federation has to bring in reforms is the retailing network for OMFED milk. Today the federation has some 199 booths and 80 shop agencies for retailing milk in the city of Bhubaneswar. The booths are invariably in commercial areas and the booth owners consume the milk supplied to the booths for vending tea. Very little milk from these booths reaches the housewives in Bhubaneswar. Shops near or in residential colonies are ideal, as retailing agents for liquid milk and the federation should entrust milk retailing to such shops. Price, quality, regularity of supply and convenience are what wins customers for OMFED and the federation should strive to win as many as possible. Finally, the federation in their enthusiasm to reach out to as many markets as possible has spread themselves too thin. This does not auger well for the federation's own interests nor does it help the unions to increase their procurement because the quantities sold are far too small to make an impact.

# 14 Livestock Sector Policy: Orissa

Neither the Government of India nor the Government of Orissa had managed to articulate a unified agricultural or livestock policy framework until the mid nineties and had operated all along pretty much without a comprehensive policy framework. Policies had often been ad hoc responses to development needs. By and large these policies had been more restrictive than liberating; it has made extensive use of direct action by the government: a host of departmental and public sector initiatives have dominated the livestock sector. Many of these have worked in an unco-ordinated manner at best and at cross-purposes at worst. Following on the recommendations contained in the Report of the Steering Committee for Livestock Sector Review (1999), the GoO has now finalised a draft Livestock Sector Policy Frame for the state. The draft policy paper formulated by the GoO and pending formal approval processes is presented in the following paragraphs.

## 14.1 Current Policy Environment

The Orissa government's policy on agriculture development, including livestock seeks to ensure the welfare of the vast majority of its people living in the rural areas and stresses social justice and equality of opportunity as important considerations in the development strategy. Within the confines of this basic objective, the state's policy intends in general to build a progressively modern and dynamic agricultural livestock economy in the state leading to improved employment potential, increased income, self-sufficiency in food and food security for the state. During the past five decades of the planned development era post independence, the state however, has operated pretty much without a comprehensive policy framework in the agriculture and livestock sectors. The state formulated its first comprehensive agricultural policy framework, including a component of animal husbandry, only in 1996.

Livestock sector in Orissa is highly livelihood intensive and over 80 per cent of its rural households own livestock of one species or the other and earn supplementary incomes from them. Livestock holding is less iniquitous than land holding and income from livestock is more equitably distributed. The sector contributes 7.25 per cent of the state's net domestic product and, therefore, development of the livestock sector is the critical pathway to rural prosperity. However, livestock sector policy so far, had only a marginal presence in the sectoral economy and the policies, in general, have failed to galvanise purposeful action.

The Government of Orissa, therefore, appointed a high-powered Steering Committee in 1998 to make a comprehensive review of the state livestock sector and to recommend new policy directions in order to enable the state government to formulate a new Livestock Sector Policy Framework. The Steering Committee felt that, in the wake of the changing economic policies nationally and globally, the state livestock sector policy has to take a more holistic view of the sector and find ways of catalyzing rapid economic growth and development in the decades to come. The Steering Committee recommended that the state should formulate a comprehensive new policy framework for its livestock sector in order to help the sector to play its appointed role in the development of the state in the decades to come. These proposals for a new policy framework are based on the recommendations of the Steering Committee.

## 14.2 Goals of New Livestock Sector Policy

On the basis of the livestock sector review 1999, it is apparent that the over-arching goals that Orissa's new livestock sector policy should pursue, shall be:

14.2.1 Use the livestock sector as an engine for the social and economic development of the rural population enabling steady growth of rural household income, increasing rural employment opportunities and improved quality of life, cutting across caste, class and gender.

14.2.2 Enable the small producers to actively participate in the process of development and equip them with information, skills and technologies to transform the growing challenges of the market place, into comparative and competitive advantages through improved livestock quality and higher productivity.

14.2.3 Ensure the ecological and environmental sustainability of the livestock sector growth and modernization; constantly monitoring the environmental impact of the growth process and designing policies and programmes to effectively mitigate their adverse impact.

14.2.4 To capacitate the marginalized sections, especially women, SCs and STs with supplementary inputs and services, so that they are enabled to have equal access to the opportunities offered under this new livestock development and management policy.

For achieving the proposed policy goals, the Department of Fisheries and Animal Resources Development (F & ARD), the administrative and nodal Department in the State Government for Livestock Development, will interact and liaise with other state departments like agriculture, cooperation, finance, planning & coordination, revenue, forest & environment, rural development and *panchayat raj*, labour & employment and with the Government of India.

The Department of F & ARD will co-ordinate interaction between government and industry, between cooperatives, NGOs and private enterprises, between research establishment and industry and among a host of other actors whose actions will shape Orissa's competitive advantage. The most decisive role for the government is to design a policy framework for the livestock sector for the coming decades and of orchestrating the actions of the multitude of actors involved in the sector.

## 14.3 Proposed Policy Framework and Strategies

Orissa's new Livestock Sector Policy Framework is proposed along the following seven Key Thrust Areas:

14.3.1 Capacitate and equip the rural poor to use livestock production as the instrument to enhance household income, supplement family nutrition and to protect rural livelihood systems, giving special emphasis to women.

Livestock production in Orissa is predominantly the endeavour of the small holders. Marginal and small farmers account for some 80 per cent of the total operational holdings. Together with the landless they own 60 per cent of the milch animals, 55 per cent of the draught animals, 75 per cent of the poultry, over 80 per cent of the goat and almost the entire sheep and pig populations and over half of them live below the poverty line. Women play a crucial role in the day to day management of livestock.

Income from livestock is therefore a substantial supplement to the overwhelmingly subsistence farming systems in rural Orissa. Enabling them to maximize livestock income can make all the difference between subsistence and progressively viable farming systems. A critical role the government proposes to play, therefore, is to help them maximize returns on hitherto free resources of crop residues, grazing and family labour. For this several specific policies are proposed.

14.3.1(a) Redesign and reconfigure the input delivery service under the government to serve as protective armour around the small producers and their subsistence farming systems.

Animal health care and breeding services are the two most important services that the state now provides free to the livestock producers. Improving the quality of these services and their usefulness to the producers is the prime consideration under the new policy. There is increasing evidence that farmers prefer good quality paid services to poor quality free service.

In order to make these services improve their quality, reach out to the farmers whom it seeks to serve and becomes accountable, the government will progressively make veterinary and artificial insemination services, mobile practices operating within their existing jurisdictions and delivering the services at the farmers door-step, as paid inputs. Under the new policy the government will permit the government employed veterinarians, livestock inspectors and inseminators to practice their profession/trade and to charge for the services delivered at the farmers' door-step at market rates. These reforms will be implemented in a phased manner; first in well developed areas, which can absorb the change and work it to their advantage. Extension of the policy and introduction of the new delivery systems in other areas will follow an economic change scale.

14.3.1(b) Equip and empower the small producers with information and skills to maximize returns, through appropriate technologies and self help approach to problem solving.

There are many services and inputs needed by livestock owners in the day to day management of their livestock enterprise and most of these do not need the services of a qualified veterinarian or livestock inspector. The magnitude of the task is so large that the only solution is to create such skills among the users—the small holders themselves—in their villages. The tasks are veterinary first aid, vaccination of birds and animals, ecto and endo parasite control, innovative feed supplementing techniques, shelter innovations and candling of *desi* eggs for hatching. These are all simple skills needed in villages constantly. Young men and women from the small holder households can be trained to practise these skills, provide service to the small holders and even earn a small income for their services, addressing men and women equally.

14.3.1(c ) Promote and nurture grass root level participatory bodies all over the state, as the organic link between the Animal Husbandry Department and the small holders.

Just as in the case of inputs and services to the scattered small holders, training them for various skills required for the day-to-day management of their livestock enterprise, is also a task outside the size and scope of the State Department of Fisheries and Animal Resources Development. The department's task is to assess and quantify the training needs, to structure and package the training programmes and to farm them out to grass root level bodies all over the state for implementation.

Several forms of such grass root level bodies are possible: producers co-operatives, breeders' associations, self help groups and voluntary organizations. These organizations can form the organic link between the department and the small holders as well as the conduit for transfer of technologies, skill training, extension support and even inputs.

The government and the department will kick start the movement of promoting grass roots bodies in a few chosen districts and nurture them as live models for other districts and areas to follow on their own. The government would encourage and support local initiative in building up such organizations/groups, in any area in the state. A budget for structuring and promoting the organic link would be a part of the policy implications.

14.3.2 Promote adoption of appropriate technologies, enhance productivity, increase effectiveness and ensure returns proportionate to the investment of time, energy and resources that small holders, particularly women, make for livestock development and management.

Government policy would focus on aggressive strategies to integrate the small producer in the larger process of sectoral growth. A critical area for experimentation and promotion towards this, is the intermediate production system, which enables the small holder to gradually integrate the highly productive modern technology and management into his traditional system. Introducing half bred milch animals into the traditional small holder households is an excellent example for the intermediate production system, which not only gives some high production features, but also preserves some of the ruggedness of the local animals he is used to. There are many others like this involving other species of livestock and poultry.

These intermediate production systems depend on high technologies like artificial insemination (AI), the most critical tool that the science has given to animal production. Orissa is yet to exploit the tool to the full advantage of its many milk producers, in spite of establishing very large infrastructure and skill pool. Restructuring the management of the AI system is the critical reform for establishing intermediate production systems. The new livestock sector policy seeks to transfer the task of generating high quality AI inputs like genetically evaluated AI bulls, frozen semen and liquid nitrogen and their supply to all AI practitioners, to a new organization, incorporated as a registered society, The Orissa Livestock Resources Development Society. AI delivery itself will be reorganized as mobile service delivering a vastly improved AI service at the farmers' door-step.

Graded pigs with exotic donors for higher body weights, moving in genetically selected bucks and rams for goat and sheep breeding into small holder units for selective breeding and custom bred *desi* breeding cocks for the backyard poultry are other examples for engineering intermediate production systems in small holdings.

To promote intermediate production system, government will mobilize credit through commercial banks for mini dairy schemes, small animals and poultry schemes. There will also be a subsidy package similar to the Government of India scheme 'Special Livestock Breeding Programme'

(SLBP), along with concessional credit scheme for the bottom end of the small holder spectrum.

14.3.3 Encourage growth and modernization of the livestock sector in a well balanced format where all species of livestock are allowed to grow and develop in proportion to their livelihood intensity and potential to enhance livelihoods; not merely in proportion to their population size.

Development of the livestock sector in Orissa so far, had largely been monopolized by the bovine. Sheep, goat, pig and poultry are far more livelihood intensive and are owned by the bottom end of the small holder households. The new livestock sector policy will incorporate adequate safeguards to balance the specieswise outlay of the state and central plan, largely in proportion to the livelihood implication of these species of livestock.

These interventions actually will comprise measures for: (i) skill training, subsidies for acquiring breeding stock like genetically selected cocks for the backyard system, bucks, rams and boars for goat, sheep and pig breeding respectively; and concessional credit for household level enterprises, on one plane; (ii) breeding and selection programmes for all species, on the second; and (iii) aggressive promotional activities for building up an organic link of peoples' bodies outside the government, so essential for the sub sector, on the third plane.

14.3.4 Resolute direct action by the Government in such areas as disease control and eradication and quality control mechanisms.

Curative veterinary care generates only private good while prevention and control of animals disease generates enormous public good to the advantage of the state and the nation as a whole. Control of diseases will reduce the yield gap and cut down the annuals losses due to diseases Rs.2.5 billion in the case of Orissa. Under the new livestock policy, public funds will increasingly be directed towards public good disease prevention and control and less for curative veterinary care.

The new livestock policy will enable the launch of a state wide FMD control programme as part of a national control programme, an active and responsive disease reporting system and disease containment zone in the most productive areas in the state.

14.3.5 Devise ways to ensure that the sector grows with the active and gainful participation of the resource poor throughout the state.

For quite some time to come, the state government needs to devise and implement specific policies and programmes to enable the small holders to progressively approach viable levels of efficiency and output, through better access to credit, better quality credit and some subsidy support.

The government is not in favour of subsidy as an instrument of development but under the prevailing poverty scenario it will develop a creative policy to generate positive response which will not be antithetical to the interest of the resource poor, progress and efficiency and by which the small holders will progressively reach viable levels of efficiency and output with access to better quality credit and subsidy support.

The State will have two kinds of credit inflow for the livestock sector:

1. Commercial Credit for the upper end of the smallholder producers engaged in livestock enterprises to enable them to move into intermediate production system.
2. A concessional and liberalised credit scheme for the bottom half of the small holder spectrum, in the IRDP format, to enable them to move above the poverty line and to achieve the efficiency levels for entering into intermediate systems.

14.3.6 Ensure the ecological and environmental sustainability of livestock sector growth and modernization; mitigating their adverse impact through appropriate policies and programmes.

The very large and growing population of bovine is a major threat to sustainability of all animals and agriculture in Orissa. Reduction in cattle numbers is possible only if the dependence on draught animals for farm power declines. The new livestock policy will encourage a set of measures to reduce the dependence on draught animals for farm power and to reduce their numbers: (i) optimal sharing of work animals by farmers; (ii) improved quality of work animals through grading up of local animals with Haryana breed; (iii) vigorously encouraging lease markets for work animals, promoting team labour; and (iv) Encouraging establishment of agro-service centres in major villages, enabling custom hiring of farm machinery and tractors.

Another major ecological concern is the deterioration of common property resources. The problem of designing the interface between livestock owners and common property resources is complex and intractable. For the new livestock policy it makes best sense to encourage and support a variety of experiments and approaches to: (i) generate alternatives that reduce pressure on rural people to pursue livelihood strategies detrimental to their habitat, and (ii) promote symbiotic and synergetic relationships between local communities and their environment, through participatory natural resource management.

14.3.7 Restructure and revitalize existing institutional set up in the livestock sector, enhance institution level efficiency and promote new institutional models to handle the emerging challenges in sector development.

Under the regime of the new policy, two major initiatives are proposed: (i) existing institutional structure will be reoriented and geared up to play a far bigger and demanding role, partly through restructuring and partly by redefining its mission; and (ii) there are many tasks that need to be performed, for which the best strategy would be to promote institutions outside the government.

The mandate of the Department of Fisheries and Animal Resources Development under the new policy would be: (i) control, containment and eradication of animal diseases; and (ii) livestock sector development. Department will progressively move away from delivery of veterinary care and AI services, first converting them into mobile practices; gradually retreating towards the privatization of the services. The department will have a bipolar structure, reflecting the mandate—one group engaged in disease control and the other in livestock development. Disease control will be the direct action by the department; but for livestock development the department will work in a participatory format. The department's training capacity will be geared up to cater to the needs of intensified participatory extension service and empowerment of non-governmental organisations active in livestock development.

The development tasks under the new policy will necessitate the promotion of a new autonomous body 'the Orissa Livestock Resource Development Society' (OLRDS), a registered society under the Societies Act, which will take over the entire AI infrastructure, except the field AI centres. It will generate all the genetic inputs for breeding of cattle and buffalo and will establish a state-wide infrastructure for the distributed bulk movement and bulk storage of liquid nitrogen. Frozen semen and liquid nitrogen will be delivered to all AI practitioners at their doorstep by the OLRDS, against payment.

The Orissa State Co-operative Milk Producers' Federation (OMFED) and the milk unions affiliated to it will be re-promoted with greater autonomy, greater member control and reduced government interventions in order to enable it to pursue its charter and business interest as a commercial enterprise of producer members.

The Utkal Gomangal Samiti (UGS) will take up larger responsibilities in promoting natural breeding service and use of cross bred bullocks.

The Orissa State Poultry Products Co-operative Marketing Federation (OPOLFED) will be re-promoted as a development co-operative to take up the responsibility of supplying the genetic inputs and appropriate technologies for the backyard poultry system in addition to assisting small producers to market their products.

The Orissa University of Agriculture and Technology (OUAT) through its constituent colleges will provide necessary technical input and guidance in matters relating to overall livestock sectoral growth.

Agricultural Promotion and Investment Corporation of Orissa Ltd, (APICOL) will promote dairy and poultry industries on commercial scale through entrepreneurship development programme. A food processing unit will be within the ambit of its objective.

District Rural Development Agency (DRDA)/Zilla Parisad will disseminate developmental work under Animal Husbandry sector at grass root level under panchayati raj system.

Breeders associations, voluntary agencies and non-governmental organisations will be promoted to activate the grass root level bodies and for imparting training and transfer of skills as may be defined by the state government.

## 14.4 Perspective Plan for Livestock Development

The proposed policy framework will be translated into specific actions through a 'ten year perspective plan for the development of livestock in the State', which forms a part of the Steering Committee Report and has been submitted for sanctioning by the GoO, as a supplement to the above policy. The plan covers all species of livestock including poultry and spans a ten year period from 2002 to 2012 for implementation in two phases, each of five years: Phase I: 2002-7 and Phase II: 2007-12. The Government of India has finalised a National Project for Cattle and Buffalo Breeding, spanning ten years, more or less overlapping the state development plan discussed in the Steering Committee Report and it has many commonalities with the cattle and buffalo breeding part of this plan. The strategies and action plan for cattle and buffalo breeding in both are identical and the state plan is designed to merge with the national project and to receive full funding for it. The OLRDS has been earmarked as an important implementer of this plan.

The action plan under the state livestock development plan (SLDP) is designed area and species specific, staggering the implementation process in accordance with the development status of the area and ability of the farming community there to absorb the changes to their advantage. All the 30 districts in the state are grouped into three economic categories (see Table 14.1): Category A: most potential; B: potential and C: least potential, based on several criteria specifically relevant to dairy production. Choice of areas for develop-

TABLE 14.1: GROUPING OF DISTRICTS

| *Most Potential Districts (A)* | *Potential Districts (B)* | *Low Potential Districts (C)* |
|---|---|---|
| Cuttack | Bolangir | Koraput |
| Puri | Dhenkanal | Gajpati |
| Ganjam | Keonjhar | Jharsuguda |
| Khurda | Angul | Boudh |
| Jagatsinghpur | Sambalpur | Kandhamal |
| Bargarh | Sundargarh | Nawapara |
| Balasore | Mayurbhanj | Deogarh |
| Kendrapara | Rayagada | Nawarangpur |
| Jajpur | Kalahandi | Malkangri |
| Bhadrak | Nayagarh | Subranpur |

ment of other species is on the basis of specific animal population size, households owning the different species of livestock and production aggregates of livestock produce.

The plan will be implemented in the state by a consortium of implementing agencies: the State Department of Animal Husbandry; the proposed Orissa Livestock Resource Development Society; the Orissa State Co-operative Milk Producers' Federation; the Utkal Gomangal Samity; the Orissa State Poultry Products Co-operative Marketing Federation and any other agencies like NGOs; VOs; Bilateral Assistance Projects that the GoO designates as 'Implementing Agencies'. Project funding will come from three major sources: (i) state plan and non-plan budgets, (ii) central plan assistance, and (iii) institutional finance. The major investment for cattle and buffalo breeding component will be sourced from the proposed central project for cattle and buffalo breeding.

# APPENDICES

TABLE 1.1: AGRO-CLIMATIC ZONES IN ORISSA

| *Sl. No.* | *Agro-Climatic Zone* | *Climate* | *Mean annual rainfall (mm)* | *Soil Group* |
|---|---|---|---|---|
| 1. | North-Weatern Plateau | Hot & Moist | 1648 | Red & Yellow |
| 2. | North-Central Plateau | Hot & Moist | 1535 | Red & Loamy |
| 3. | North-Eastern Coastal Plateau | Hot & Moist and Humid | 1569 | Alluvial |
| 4. | East & South-Eastern Plateau | Hot & Humid | 1449 | Coastal Alluvial Saline |
| 5. | North-Eastern Ghat | Hot & Moist Sub-Humid | 1597 | Laterite & Brown Forest |
| 6. | Eastern Ghat Highland | Warm & Humid | 1522 | Red |
| 7. | South-Eastern Ghat | Warm & Humid | 1522 | Red, Red & Yellow Mixed |
| 8. | Western Undulating | Warm & Moist | 1527 | Black, Mixed Red & Black |
| 9. | West-Central Table Land | Hot & Moist | 1527 | Red Heavy Textured Colourous |
| 10. | Mid Central Table Land | Hot & Dry Sub-Humid | 1421 | Red Loam, Laterite Mixed Red & Black |

SOURCE: Economy Survey, Govt. of Orissa, 2000-1.

TABLE 1.2: GROUPING OF DISTRICTS IN DIFFERENT ZONES BASED ON AGRO-CLIMATIC CLASSIFICATION

| *Sl. No.* | *Caostal Districts* | *Midland District* | *Highland District* |
|---|---|---|---|
| 1. | Balasore | Angul | Gajapati |
| 2. | Bhadrak | Bargarh | Ganjam (part) |
| 3. | Jagatsinghpur | Bolangir | Kalahandi |
| 4. | Jajpur | Boudh | Koraput |
| 5. | Kendrapara | Cuttack | Malkangiri |
| 6. | Khurda | Deogarh | Nawapara |
| 7. | Nayagarh | Dhenkanal | Nabarangpur |
| 8. | Puri | Jharsguda | Kandhamal |
| 9. | Ganjam (part) | Keonjhar | Rayagarh |
| 10. | | Mayurbhanj | |
| 11. | | Sambalpur | |
| 12. | | Subranpur | |
| 13. | | Sundargarh | |

TABLE 2.1: ASSET VALUE OF LIVESTOCK IN ORISSA (PRICES 1998)

| *Sl. No.* | *Species* | *Numbers* | *Unit Value Rs.* | *Value Rs. mln.* | *Per cent Contribution* |
|---|---|---|---|---|---|
| 1. | Cattle (Male) | | | | |
| | a. Indigenous Adult | 5327622 | 3780 | | |
| | b. Young Stock (Adult Equivalent) | 971494 | – | | |
| | Total Male (a+b) | 6299116 | – | 23810.65 | 56.28 |
| 2. | Cattle (Female) | | | | |
| | a. Indigenous Cows | 3667753 | 1500 | | |
| | b. Young Stock (Adult Equivalent) | 1106701 | – | | |
| | Total Indigenous Female (a+b) | 4774454 | – | 7162 | 16.92 |
| | c. Crossbred Cows | 380424 | 5000 | | |
| | d. Young Stock (Adult Equivalent) | 137508 | – | | |
| | Total Crossbred Cows (c+d) | 517932 | – | 25890 | 6.12 |
| 3. | Buffalo | | | | |
| | a. Adult Male | 575619 | 3750 | | |
| | b. Young Stock (Adult Equivalent) | 86279 | – | | |
| | Total Male (a+b) | 661898 | – | 2482 | 5.87 |
| | c. Adult Female | 369329 | 3000 | | |
| | d. Young Stock (Adult Equivalent) | 127241 | – | | |
| | Total Female (c+d) | 496570 | – | 1490 | 3.52 |
| 4. | Sheep | 1765288 | 500 | 882 | 2.08 |
| 5. | Goat | 5772114 | 500 | 2886 | 6.82 |
| 6. | Pig | 601917 | 800 | 481 | 1.14 |
| 7. | Poultry | 18434613 | 30 | 533 | 1.26 |
| | Grand Total | 42306 | 100 | | |

NOTES: (1) Young stock of all together, among cattle and buffalo, reckoned as 0.50 adult unit per head for valuation purpose.

(2) Crossbred male accounted for along indigenous male, as numbers are very small.

(3) Percentage fraction rounded off to the nearest whole number.

SOURCE: Orissa LSR Report 1999: Updated.

TABLE 2.2: BROAD SECTOR WISE NET STATE DOMESTIC PRODUCTS AT FACTOR COST AT CURRENT PRICES AND AT 1993-4 PRICES (RS. IN CRORE)

| *Sector* | *1994-5* | *1995-6* | *1999-7* | *1997-8* | *1998-9* | *1999-2000* | *2000-1* |
|---|---|---|---|---|---|---|---|
| 1. Primary Sector (agriculture, animal husbandry forestry, fishing, mining, quarrying ) | 9175.88 | 11817.05 | 10678.12 | 13885.59 | 14584.46 | 15344.65 | 13114.23 |
| | (48.39) | (50.77) | (48.12) | (50.54) | (48.86) | (48.88) | (42.59) |
| | *7857.20* | *8106.11* | *7310.81* | *8777.57* | *8703.91* | *8693.20* | *7870.14* |
| | *(47.55)* | *(46.91)* | *(45.34)* | *(47.52)* | *(46.72)* | *(44.97)* | *(42.11)* |
| 2. Secondary Sector (manufacturing, construction, electricity, gas and water supply) | 3443.63 | 3941.03 | 3301.97 | 3771.13 | 3664.45 | 4310.23 | 4094.26 |
| | (18.17) | (16.93) | (14.88) | (13.74) | (12.27) | (13.17) | (13.30) |
| | *2966.96* | *3024.12* | *2380.67* | *2496* | *2171.84* | *23.9.52* | *1998.63* |
| | *(17.96)* | *(17.50)* | *(14.76)* | *(13.52)* | *(11.66)* | *(11.95)* | *(10.63)* |
| 3. Tertiary Sector (transport, communication, trade, storage etc.) | 3002.67 | 3652.90 | 3686.89 | 4607.24 | 5058.27 | 5540.23 | 5257.43 |
| | (15.84) | (15.69) | (16.61) | (16.79) | (16.95) | (16.93) | (17.07) |
| | *2649.77* | *2942.02* | *2901.41* | *3371.12* | *3456.23* | *3694.70* | *3645.38* |
| | *(16.04)* | *(17.02)* | *(17.99)* | *(18.25)* | *(18.55)* | *(19.11)* | *(19.50)* |
| 4. Service Sector (banking and insurance, real estate, public administration, other services) | 3338.07 | 3865.56 | 4522.32 | 5193.53 | 6543.12 | 7533.89 | 8329.28 |
| | (17.60) | (16.61) | (20.35) | (18.93) | (21.92) | (23.02) | (27.05) |
| | *3048.85* | *3209.02* | *3532.73* | *3825.50* | *4297.73* | *4632.36* | *5176.10* |
| | *(18.45)* | *(18.57)* | *(21.91)* | *(20.71)* | *(23.07)* | *(23.97)* | *(27.69)* |
| Net State Domestic Product at factor cost | 18960.25 | 23276.55 | 22189.30 | 27437.49 | 29850.30 | 32728.80 | 30795.20 |
| | (100.00) | (100.00) | (100.00) | (100.00) | (100.00) | (100.00) | (100.00) |
| | *16522.76* | *17281.27* | *16125.62* | *18470.57* | *18629.71* | *19329.31* | *18690.25* |
| | *(100.00)* | *(100.00)* | *(100.00)* | *(100.00)* | *(100.00)* | *(100.00)* | *(100.00)* |
| Per Capita Income (Rs.) | | | | | | | |
| At current prices | 5638 | 6806 | 64401 | 7831 | 8435 | 9152 | 8547 |
| At 1993-4 prices (Rs.) | *4913* | *5053* | *4652* | *5272* | *5264* | *6411* | *5187* |

NOTE: A. Figures in italics represent the cost at 1993-4 prices. B. Figures in parenthesis indicate the percentages.
SOURCE: Economy Survey of Govt. of Orissa, 2000-1.

TABLE 2.3: LIVESTOCK SECTOR OUTPUT VALUE 1999–2000 AT CURRENT PRICES

| *Sl. No.* | *Output* | *Quantity* | *Unit Price in Rs.* | *Value mllion Rs.* | *Per cent* |
|---|---|---|---|---|---|
| 1. | Milk | 847.78 (000 mt) | 13.00 | 11021.14 | 47.13 |
| 2. | Meat | 43000.00 (000 mt) | 80.00 | 2925.60 | 12.51 |
| 3. | Work out put | 194.40 kwh | 3.00 | 582.00 | 2.49 |
| 4. | Eggs | 822.21 (mln) | 1.45 | 1192.20 | 5.10 |
| 5. | Poultry Meat | 24478.90 mt | 50.00 | 1468.80 | 6.28 |
| 6. | Hide & Skin | 3.00 mln nos. | 500.00 large animal | 8.25 | 0.80 |
| | | | 60.00 for small animal | 179.01 | |
| 7. | Dung / Manure | 20.00 mln mt | 200.00 per mt | 4000.00 | 17.10 |
| 8. | Wool / Hair | 0.50 mln mt | 2500.00 mt | 5.00 | 0.00 |
| 9. | Bone Offal | 1000.00 mt | 2000.00 per mt | 2000. 00 | 8.55 |
| | Total | 23381.99 | 100.00 | | |

SOURCES: Steering Committee (LSR) Report 1999; Integrated Sample Survey, AHD, 1998-9; Economic Survey 2001-2.

TABLE 2.4: RETAIL PRICES OF LIVESTOCK PRODUCTS IN ORISSA (PRICES 2002)

| *Sl. No.* | *Products* | *Price* |
|---|---|---|
| | *OMFED* | |
| 1. | Liquid Milk | |
| 1.1 | Full Cream Milk | 500 ml. polypack Rs. 7.50 1 ltr policy pack Rs. 14.60 |
| 1.2 | Toned Milk (3 per cent fat & 8.5 snf) | 500 ml. polypack Rs. 6.75 & 1 ltr pack Rs. 13.50 |
| 1.3 | Double Toned Milk (1.5 per cent fat & 8.5 per cent snf) | 500 ml. polypack Rs. 6.00 & 1 lt pack Rs. 12.00 |
| 2. | Ghee | 1kg MRP Rs. 160.00 |
| 3. | Table Butter | 100 gms Rs. 13.00 & 500 gm Rs. 63.00 |
| 4. | Misthi Dhai | 100 gms MRP Rs. 6.50 |
| 4.1. | Plain Curd | 200 gms. MRP Rs. 8.00 & 500 gm MRP Rs. 15.00 |
| 5. | Flavoured Milk | 200 ml. Bottle MRP Rs. 8.00 & Rs. 9.00 (in disposable bottle) |
| | *Unorganised Market* | |
| 6. | *Liquid Milk* | |
| 6.1 | Cow Milk | Rs. 10-12 per litre |
| 6.2 | Buffalo Milk | Rs. 12-14 per litre |
| 7. | Meat | |
| 7.1 | Mutton | Rs. 120-130 per kg |
| 7.2 | Pork | Rs. 40-60 per kg |
| 7.3 | Beef | Rs. 35-60 per kg |
| 7.4 | Broiler / Poultry Meat / *Desi* Chicken | Rs. 50-70 for br. & poultry, *desi* chicken Rs. 90-100 per kg |
| 8. | Egg | |
| 8.1 | Egg Commercial Farms | Rs. 155-180 per 100 eggs |
| 8.2 | Egg from *Desi* bird (Back yard) | Rs. 200-220 per 100 eggs |
| 8.3 | Egg from Ducks | Rs. 200-275 per 100 eggs |

SOURCE: Market Scan by NRMPO / OMFED 2002.

TABLE 2.5: SECTORAL GROWTH OF EMPLOYMENT IN RURAL AREA (1972-88) ALL INDIA

| Sl. No. | Sector | Employment (million) | | | | Average annual growth rate | | | |
|---|---|---|---|---|---|---|---|---|---|
| | | 72-3 | 77-8 | 82-3 | 87-8 | 72-8 | 77-83 | 82-8 | 72-88 |
| 1. | Agriculture* | 167.3<br>(85.62) | 183.4<br>(83.35) | 196.6<br>(81.50) | 196.8<br>(78.01) | 1.96 | 1.27 | 0.39 | 1.1 |
| | Livestock | 9.03<br>(4.62) | 10.6<br>(4.82) | 29.43<br>(.47) | 16.65<br>(6.6) | 7.41 | 10.1 | 18.3 | 4.2 |
| 2. | Mining & Quarrying | 0.68<br>(0.35) | 0.89<br>(0.40) | 1.16<br>(0.48) | 1.48<br>(0.59) | 5.83 | 4.94 | 5.56 | 5.4 |
| 3. | Manufg. | 10.46<br>(5.35) | 13.73<br>(6.24) | 16..32<br>(6.77) | 18.51<br>(7.34) | 5.89 | 3.19 | 2.84 | 4 |
| 4. | Electricity Gas & Water | 0.14<br>(0.07) | 0.28<br>(0.13) | 0.34<br>(0.14) | 0.43<br>(0.17) | 15.7 | 3.59 | 5.36 | 7.9 |
| 5. | Construction | 2.7<br>(1.38) | 2.9<br>(1.39) | 4.05<br>(1.68) | 8.5<br>(3.37) | 1.52 | 6.26 | 17.9 | 8.1 |
| 6. | Trade | 4.8<br>(2.49) | 7.24<br>(3.29) | 8.37<br>(3.47) | 10.31<br>(4.09 | 8.75 | 2.67 | 4.74 | 5.3 |
| 7. | Transport | 1.29<br>(0.66) | 1.79<br>(0.81) | 2.61<br>(1.08) | 3.33<br>(1.32) | 7.14 | 7.1 | 5.56 | 6.6 |
| 8. | Services | 7.97<br>(4.08) | 9.8<br>(4.45) | 11.77<br>(4.88 | 12.9<br>(5.11) | 4.45 | 3.39 | 2.06 | 3.8 |
| | Total | 195.4<br>(100) | 220<br>(100) | 241.2<br>(100) | 252.2<br>(100) | 2.53 | 1.68 | 1 | 1.8 |

NOTE: * Agriculture includes employment in livestock sector.

SOURCE: National Sample Survey Organisation, New Delhi.

TABLE 2.6: LIVESTOCK INSURANCE PREMIUM RATES

| Sl. No. | Type of Cover | Premium Rates |
|---|---|---|
| 1. | Scheme Animals (Cattle & Buffalo) | 2.25 per cent |
| 2. | Non Scheme Animals (Cattle & Buffalo) | Cooperative Societies 4.00; farmers (General) 5.00 per cent |
| 3. | PTD (All Categories, Cattle & Buffaloes) | 0.85 per cent, extra premium scheme; 1.0 per cent, non scheme |
| 4. | Exotic Cattle | 2.25 per cent scheme; 5 per cent non scheme |
| 5. | Master Policy Animals Bovines, without PTD | 3 yrs 5.06; 4 yrs 6.75; 5 yrs 8.44 per cent |
| 6. | Master Policy Animals Bovines with PTD | 3 yrs 6.98; 4 yrs 6.75; 5 yrs 11.63 per cent |
| 7. | Bullocks Working Males Buffalo | 2.25 per cent scheme; 4 per cent non scheme |
| 8. | Calves | 2.25 per cent scheme; 4 per cent non scheme |
| 9. | Sheep & Goat, *Desi* Breed | 2.75 per cent scheme; 4 per cent non scheme |
| 10. | Sheep & Goat, Crossbred | 2.75 per cent scheme; 5 per cent non scheme |
| 11. | Sheep and Goat, Exotic | 2.75 per cent scheme; 6 per cent non scheme |
| 12. | Pig, *Desi* Breed | 2.75 per cent scheme; 5 per cent non scheme |
| 13. | Pig, Crossbred / Exotic | 2.75 percent Scheme; 6 percent non scheme |
| 14. | Broiler (under IRDP) | 0.25 per cent per bird in groups; Re. 1.00 per bird per single |
| 15. | Broiler non IRDP | 1.5 per cent of peak value for batches; other options available |
| 16. | Layers | 5.5 per cent peak value for cover 1-72 weeks other options exists |

NOTES: Insurance for different types of animals (i) milch cow from 2 yrs or first calving to 10 yrs (ii) milch buffalo 3 yrs or first calving to 12 yrs (iii) Studs bulls: 3 yrs to 8 yrs; (iv) calf: under calf rearing schemes for female: from 4 months to 1st calving; (v) sheep and goat: 4 months to seven yrs; (vi) pig: 4 months to six yrs; (vii) poultry: no cover for local birds, cover of improved birds layers, broiler, and crossbred birds; unit insurance cover 100 broilers/ 500 layers, minimum.

SOURCE: User's Guide United India Insurance Company Ltd. 1996

*From April 2002, the Insurance Companies (all 4 of them) have withdrawn all schemes mentioned above. Because of heavy claim ratio Premium rate now is 8 per cent of the sum assured for all animals Plus 5 per cent of it surcharge. Government Scheme Animals, however continue to be insured at the concessional premium rate of 2.25 per cent.*

TABLE 3.1: DISTRICT WISE PRODUCTIVITY OF MILCH ANIMALS, PRODUCTION OF MILK AND PER CAPITA AVAILABILITY OF MILK PER DAY

| *Sl. No.* | *District* | *Milk Production per day per animal in milk in kg.* | | | *Total Production* | *Per Capita Availability / Day* |
|---|---|---|---|---|---|---|
| | | *Indigenous* | *Crossbred* | *Buffalo* | *Milk ('000) mt* | *Gms. per day* |
| 1. | Angul | 0.486 | 3.006 | 1.977 | 23.74 | 57 |
| 2. | Balasore | 0.484 | 2.211 | 2.411 | 27.14 | 40 |
| 3. | Bargarh | 0.706 | 4.668 | 1.686 | 39.58 | 80 |
| 4. | Bhadrak | 0.478 | 2.917 | 1.410 | 17.62 | 36 |
| 5. | Bolangir | 0.454 | 2.395 | 1.529 | 24.22 | 49 |
| 6. | Boudh | 0.421 | 2.079 | 2.218 | 8.93 | 65 |
| 7. | Cuttack | 0.833 | 5.179 | 2.752 | 75.56 | 88 |
| 8. | Deogarh | 0.345 | 2.346 | 1.535 | 4.73 | 47 |
| 9. | Dhenkanal | 0.538 | 3.177 | 1.972 | 27.16 | 70 |
| 10. | Gajapati | 0.393 | 2.265 | 1.547 | 8.14 | 32 |
| 11. | Ganjam | 0.506 | 4.005 | 2.380 | 60.07 | 52 |
| 12. | Jagatsinghpur | 0.646 | 4.541 | 1.948 | 49.04 | 127 |
| 13. | Jajpur | 0.418 | 3.627 | 2.826 | 19.60 | 33 |
| 14. | Jharsuguda | 0.369 | 3.025 | 1.333 | 6.25 | 33 |
| 15. | Kalahandi | 0.408 | 2.316 | 1.446 | 22.27 | 94 |
| 16. | Kendrapada | 0.512 | 3.177 | 1.972 | 20.20 | 42 |
| 17. | Keonjhar | 0.465 | 3.058 | 1.553 | 22.77 | 40 |
| 18. | Khurda | 0.691 | 4.900 | 2.032 | 51.82 | 75 |
| 19. | Koraput | 0.408 | 2.138 | 1.501 | 16.66 | 39 |
| 20. | Malkangiri | 0.447 | 1.859 | 1.761 | 8.97 | 51 |
| 21. | Mayurbhanj | 0.466 | 2.240 | 1.933 | 20.56 | 25 |
| 22. | Nawapara | 0.363 | 1.804 | 1.757 | 9.38 | 48 |
| 23. | Nawarangpur | 0.365 | 2.138 | 1.372 | 9.85 | 26 |
| 24. | Nayagarh | 0.387 | 2.723 | 1.768 | 12.06 | 38 |
| 25. | Kandhamal | 0.410 | 1.749 | 1.669 | 10.05 | 42 |
| 26. | Puri | 0.634 | 4.892 | 2.277 | 64.45 | 117 |
| 27. | Rayagada | 0.456 | 2.051 | 1.385 | 18.04 | 60 |
| 28. | Sambalpur | 0.669 | 4.356 | 1.869 | 19.16 | 56 |
| 29. | Subarnapur | 0.417 | 2.037 | 1.583 | 7.74 | 39 |
| 30. | Sundargarh | 0.454 | 3.329 | 3.063 | 26.98 | 40 |
| | State | 0.505 | 3.925 | 1.345 | 732.74 | 57 |

SOURCE: Compiled from the Integrated Sample Survey 1998–99, Directorate of Animal Husbandry & Veterinary Services.

TABLE 3.2: PERFORMANCE RECORDS OF FIRST BATCH OF TEST DAUGHTERS

| *Sl. No.* | *Recorded traits* | *Performance record data* | *Deviation* |
|---|---|---|---|
| 1. | Number of test bulls in the batch | 10 | – |
| 2. | Number of daughters recorded | 706 | – |
| 3. | Average 300 days lactation yield | 1956.41 kg. | + / - 32.21 |
| 4. | Average fat per cent | 4.8 per cent | – |
| 5. | Average SNF per cent | 8.73 per cent | – |
| 6. | Age at puberty | 901 days | + / - 16.74 days |
| 7. | Age at conception | 960.55 days | + / - 18.59 days |
| 8. | Age at first calving | 1243.33 days | 18.21 days |
| 9. | Body weight at first calving | 285.03 kg. | – |

SOURCE: OUAT Study by B.K. Prusty quoted in the Report of the Milk Group: Livestock Sector Review.

TABLE 3.3: DISTRICT WISE COMPARISON OF CATTLE & BUFFALO POPULATION (IN '000)

| *Sl. No.* | *District* | *Cattle* | | | *Buffalo* | | |
|---|---|---|---|---|---|---|---|
| | | *1996* | *2001* | *% change* | *1996* | *2001* | *% change* |
| 1. | Angul | 521.5 | 562.9 | + 7.93 | 51.3 | 44.8 | - 12.67 |
| 2. | Balasore | 912.9 | 949.0 | + 3.95 | 7.2 | 4.7 | - 34.72 |
| 3. | Bargarh | 513.1 | 507.0 | - 1.18 | 63.5 | 38.4 | - 42.67 |
| 4. | Bhadrak | 550.2 | 560.2 | + 1.81 | 14.2 | 12.1 | - 14.78 |
| 5. | Bolangir | 599.1 | 508.4 | - 15.13 | 117.1 | 99.9 | - 14.68 |
| 6. | Boudh | 231.9 | 237.1 | + 2.24 | 55.2 | 38.9 | - 29.52 |
| 7. | Cuttack | 640.9 | 623.0 | - 2.79 | 62.6 | 37.2 | - 40.57 |
| 8. | Deogarh | 181.3 | 178.9 | - 1.32 | 32.7 | 13.0 | - 60.24 |
| 9. | Dhenkanal | 487.4 | 496.2 | + 1.80 | 75.1 | 63.1 | - 15.97 |
| 10. | Gajapati | 272.7 | 239.9 | - 12.02 | 18.1 | 27.7 | + 53.03 |
| 11. | Ganjam | 1029.4 | 841.6 | - 10.24 | 151.9 | 131.3 | - 13.56 |
| 12. | Jagatsinghpur | 437.9 | 287.1 | - 34.43 | 15.7 | 13.5 | - 14.01 |
| 13. | Jaipur | 634.4 | 632.8 | - 0.25 | 11.9 | 11.9 | 00 |
| 14. | Jharsuguda | 193.4 | 173.3 | - 11.07 | 38.2 | 11.5 | - 69.89 |
| 15. | Kalahandi | 540.3 | 481.0 | - 10.97 | 125.9 | 95.5 | - 24.14 |
| 16. | Kendrapada | 471.1 | 247.5 | -47.56 | 22.2 | 31.7 | + 42.79 |
| 17. | Keonjhar | 696.0 | 713.3 | 2.48 | 52.2 | 36.4 | - 30.25 |
| 18. | Khurda | 566.9 | 406.5 | - 28.29 | 25.4 | 19.6 | -22.83 |
| 19. | Koraput | 424.7 | 467.7 | +10.12 | 143.3 | 135.5 | -5.44 |
| 20. | Malkangiri | 366.8 | 403.3 | + 9.95 | 39.1 | 35.4 | - 9.46 |
| 21. | Mayurbhanj | 874.3 | 979.2 | + 11.99 | 42.3 | 26.3 | - 92.90 |
| 22. | Nawapara | 289.6 | 208.9 | -27.86 | 70.2 | 32.2 | - 54.13 |
| 23. | Nawarangpur | 380.4 | 384.0 | + 0.94 | 106.9 | 78.4 | - 26.66 |
| 24. | Nayagarh | 390.6 | 324.5 | - 16.92 | 62.3 | 47.0 | - 24.55 |
| 25. | Kandhamal | 308.7 | 305.1 | - 1.16 | 76.2 | 62.2 | - 18.37 |
| 26. | Puri | 461.4 | 462.0 | + 0.13 | 26.2 | 16.6 | - 36.64 |
| 27. | Rayagada | 405.5 | 361.6 | - 10.82 | 115.6 | 112.2 | -2.94 |
| 28. | Sambalpur | 429.5 | 405.5 | - 5.58 | 36.6 | 28.5 | -22.11 |
| 29. | Subarnapur | 258.3 | 240.9 | - 6.73 | 30.1 | 28.2 | -6.31 |
| 30. | Sundargarh | 675.1 | 720.5 | + 6.72 | 102.1 | 54.9 | - 46.22 |
| | Total | 14766.0 | 13510.4 | (-) 8.50 | 1652 | 1358.0 | (-)17.79 |

SOURCES: 1. District Profile 1995-6, DAH & VS Department;
2. Livestock Census Orissa, 2001 (Provisional data).

TABLE 3.4: LIVESTOCK AND POULTRY POPULATION IN DIFFERENT CENSUS YEARS (NO. '000) IN ORISSA

| *Sl. No.* | *Species* | *1956* | *1966* | *1977* | *1995* | *2001 Nos. / per cent change* |
|---|---|---|---|---|---|---|
| 1. | Cattle | 8220 | 11496 | 12121 | 14766 | 13810 / 65.00 |
| 2. | Buffalo | 888 | 1399 | 1350 | 1652 | 1388 / 56.00 |
| 3. | Sheep | 1117 | 1369 | 1432 | 1865 | 1719 / 54.00 |
| 4. | Goat | 1695 | 3082 | 3416 | 5412 | 5772 / 241.00 |
| 5. | Pig | 129 | 180 | 295 | 572 | 601 / 366.00 |
| 6. | Total no. | 12128 | 16122 | 18626 | 24267 | 23290 / 92.00 |
| 7. | Poultry | 4991 | 7696 | 9490 | 16008 | 18434 / 269.34 |

SOURCES: 1. Integrated Sample Survey, 1994-95, DAH & VS.
2. Livestock Census Orissa, 2001 (Provisional data).

TABLE 3.5: NUMBER OF HOUSEHOLDS KEEPING LIVESTOCK (NOS. '000S)

| *Sl. No.* | *District* | *Bovine* | *Sheep* | *Goat* | *Pig* | *Poultry* |
|---|---|---|---|---|---|---|
| 1. | Angul | 92 | 16 | 39 | 6 | 63 |
| 2. | Balasore | 198 | 35 | 84 | 13 | 135 |
| 3. | Bargarh | 120 | 21 | 51 | 8 | 82 |
| 4. | Bhadrak | 109 | 19 | 46 | 7 | 74 |
| 5. | Bolangir | 134 | 23 | 57 | 9 | 91 |
| 6. | Boudh | 38 | 7 | 16 | 3 | 26 |
| 7. | Cuttack | 144 | 25 | 61 | 10 | 98 |
| 8. | Deogarh | 31 | 5 | 13 | 2 | 21 |
| 9. | Dhenkanal | 100 | 18 | 43 | 7 | 68 |
| 10. | Gajapati | 50 | 9 | 21 | 3 | 34 |
| 11. | Ganjam | 327 | 57 | 139 | 22 | 222 |
| 12. | Jagatsinghpur | 81 | 14 | 34 | 5 | 55 |
| 13. | Jajpur | 150 | 26 | 64 | 10 | 102 |
| 14. | Jharsuguda | 34 | 6 | 14 | 2 | 23 |
| 15. | Kalahandi | 108 | 19 | 46 | 7 | 74 |
| 16. | Kendrapada | 108 | 19 | 46 | 7 | 74 |
| 17. | Keonjhar | 140 | 25 | 60 | 9 | 96 |
| 18. | Khurda | 115 | 20 | 49 | 8 | 78 |
| 19. | Koraput | 151 | 26 | 64 | 10 | 102 |
| 20. | Malkangiri | 44 | 8 | 19 | 3 | 30 |
| 21. | Mayurbhanj | 215 | 38 | 91 | 14 | 147 |
| 22. | Nawapara | 96 | 9 | 22 | 7 | 34 |
| 23. | Nawarangpur | 110 | 19 | 47 | 7 | 75 |
| 24. | Nayagarh | 100 | 17 | 42 | 7 | 68 |
| 25. | Kandhamal | 55 | 10 | 23 | 4 | 37 |
| 26. | Puri | 116 | 29 | 69 | 11 | 111 |
| 27. | Rayagada | 98 | 17 | 42 | 7 | 67 |
| 28. | Sambalpur | 70 | 12 | 29 | 5 | 47 |
| 29. | Subarnapur | 49 | 9 | 21 | 3 | 34 |
| 30. | Sundargarh | 110 | 19 | 47 | 7 | 75 |
| | State | 3293 | 577 | 1399 | 223 | 2241 |

SOURCE: District Profile 1995–6, Directorate of Animal Husbandry & Veterinary Services, Orissa.

TABLE 3.6: LOCAL STRAINS OF CATTLE IN ORISSA

| *Sl. No.* | *Name of local strain* | *Habitat* | *General Characteristics* |
|---|---|---|---|
| 1. | Binjharpuri | Sujanpur, Bari, Binjharpur, and Neighbouring areas of Jajpur and Cuttack | Graded Hariana Stock, colour white, sturdy bullocks and good cows with daily average yields of 4 kg of milk |
| 2. | Ghumusari | Bhanjanagar, Aska and up to Chhatrapur in Ganjam district | Small white coloured animals, with short horns, mild mannered. Cows yield 2-3 kg milk per day, bullocks small but swift and sturdy |
| 3. | Khariar | Khariar area in Nawapara district | District, small, colour red or brown, low milk yield, hardy bullocks |
| 4. | Mottu | Malkangiri-Mottu tract of undivided Koraput district | Compact dwarf animals, brown or gray colour, short legs, bred by Koya tribals for beef and milk |

SOURCE: LSR Milk Group Report, 1999

TABLE 3.7: LOCALS STRAINS OF BUFFALO IN ORISSA

| *Sl. No.* | *Name of local strain* | *Habitat* | *General Characteristics* |
|---|---|---|---|
| 1. | Parlakhemundi | Parlakhemundi and Gunpur areas in Orissa; Mandasa; Bobli and Shrikakulam in Andhra Pradesh | Small to medium sized animals, blackish gray in colour, with a white ring around the chest in some cases, low milk yields, good work animals. Grading up with Murrah improves body weight, body size, and all aspects of productivity. Grading with Murrah highly popular among farmers in the area |
| 2. | Manda | Kakriguma, Laxmipur, hills of Damanjodi and Patraput, Petta hills near Jeypore, Gupteswar Balimela, Pedabahal and Arku Valley hills of Koraput, natural habitat hill of 1000-3500 ft altitude, graze in forests. | Medium sized animal, black and shades of black in colour, large and broad horns, draught animal |
| 3. | Jirangi | Jirang, Ramgiri, Udayagiri, Labanyagada, agency areas of Mohana Block in Gajapati district | Small draught animals and numbers fast dwindling |
| 4. | Sambalpuri | Jungles of Redhakho and nearby areas | Brownish black colour, medium to large body size, good for milk and work, too few in numbers, almost extinct |
| 5. | Dhenkanal | Dhenkanal district | Animals resemble Sambalpuri buffaloes, but smaller in size, good for both milk and work |
| 6. | Paradip / Kujang | Swampy areas of Mahanadi Basin | Medium size, black colour, exclusively milch breed Murrah grades of the breed good milch animals |
| 7. | Bheda | Bheda area of coastal Bhadrak and Chandbali area of Balasore districts | Medium to large animals, exclusive milch breed, Black colour |
| 8. | Parikuda / Chilika | Marshy areas of Parikud, Balugaon, Bhusandpur; Brahmagiri to Satpada in Chilika | Medium size, black colour, good draught animals |
| 9. | Kalahandi | Kalahandi plains | Medium size, black colour, draught animals |

SOURCE: LSR Milk Group Report, 1999.

EXHIBIT 3.8: A NOTE ON THE CHROMOSOME NUMBER OF BUFFALO IN ORISSA

Studies on the chromosome number of buffalo in Orissa was started in Department of Animal Breeding and Genetics, Orissa Veterinary College. Dr. P.K. Rao (1981) worked on nondescript and Murrah buffaloes found in and around Bhubaneswar for his M.V.Sc. degree. He found that the nondescript animals had 48 chromosomes and Murrah had 50 chromosomes. He could get one crossbred buffalo (nondescript x Murrah), the Chromosome number was 49.

*Bidhar (1985) collected blood sample from Paralakhemundi bulls stationed at the semen collection centre, at Paralakhemundi and females owned by a progressive farmer Shri Murty Mohan Rao for his M.V.Sc. research. He subjected the blood sample to a peripheral blood lymphocyte culture in the department of A.B.G. as in case of Dr. P.K. Rao and found that the chromosome number was 48. Dr. B.R.Yadab from N.D.R.I. analysed some blood samples of Paralakhemundi buffaloes and observed that number of buffaloes with 2n = 48 chromosomes were very less in number. Most of the animals had 50 chromosomes. Reports of analysis done at the Andrology Laboratory, Vishakapatnam also show that Paralakhemundi buffalo had 2n = 50 chromosomes.

The cause of this difference in chromosome number of buffalo in Paralakhemundi area may be due to 1. Existence of two population with different chromosome number in that area; 2. Animals with Murrah inheritance either brought from Andhra Pradesh or generated in Orissa are studied as Paralakhemundi buffalo. This possibility seems less likely. The actual position will be known after studying a large number of animals from different parts of the bordering districts. It will be tried in ICAR Scheme.

Three more M.V.Sc. students have collected blood from different areas like Balugoan, Aska, Paradeep and Bhubaneswar and found that the chromosome number of the nondescript buffaloes is 48 and in Murrah 50.

At present the chromosome number of buffaloes in different parts of the state are studied in a I.C.A.R. adhoc scheme operating in the department of A.B.G. Results so far obtained in Paradip / Kujang buffalo, Chilika buffalo and buffalo in Bhubaneswar and Dasapala area indicate that the chromosome number is 2n = 48 employing peripheral whole blood lymphocyte culture.

Published in Buffalo bulletin 1986, vol. 5, no. 3.

Title: Chromosome Number And Morphology Of Paralakemundi Buffaloes in Orissa
By G.C. Bidhar, G.R. Patnaik, P.K. Rao, B.N. Patro

EXHIBIT 3.9: SPECIAL SCHEMES UNDERTAKEN FOR THE DEVELOPMENT OF CATTLE AND BUFFALO BETWEEN 1951-98

- Key Village Schemes, which started under the first five year plan (1951-6), were expanded and continued under the different five year plans; and are still continuing
- Hill Cattle Development Scheme, Koraput
- Intensive Cattle Development Projects
- Natural Service Breeding Programme under the Utkal Gomangal Samiti
- ICAR Scheme for Ghumusari Cattle Development for Draught Animal Production
- Chilika Buffalo Development / Conservation Scheme
- Special Calf Rearing Programmes under SLBP
- Heifer Rearing Programme under Integrated Rural Development Programme (IRDP)
- Danish International Development Agency (DANIDA) assisted Jersey Bull Mother Farm, Chiplima
- DANIDA assisted Project for Frozen Semen Technology, Cuttack
- IRDP Scheme for Poverty Alleviation through Cattle and Buffalo Loans to families living below poverty line
- Livestock Insurance Scheme by the General Insurance Corporation
- District Rural Development Agency (DRDA) Assistance, Drought Prone Area Programme, Integrated Tribal Development Agency, Dispersed Tribal Development Programme, Modified Area Development Agency (MADA) and other micro projects for strengthening cattle and buffalo development
- National Watershed Development Programme for Rural Areas (NWDPRA) and Swedish International Development Agency (SIDA) assisted Watershed Development Projects with livestock components
- Centrally Sponsored Scheme for Extension of Frozen Semen Technology
- National Bull Production Programme
- Field Progeny Testing Programme for Cattle and Buffalo
- Operation Flood Project for Dairy Development
- Integrated Dairy Development Programmes for Non-Operation Flood Districts
- Technology Mission on Dairy Development
- Training and Development of Inseminators and Gosevaks on large scale, state plan scheme
- Scheme for Door-step Delivery of AI through Trained Lay Inseminators
- Development of Cattle and Buffalo through Embryo Transfer Technology using Multiple Ovulation Embryo Transfer Technology (MOET)
- Dairy Programme through Prime Minister's Rozgar Yojana
- Action programme for Livestock Development in Orissa, 1992
- Women's Dairy Programme
- Indo-Swiss Project Orissa (ISPO); for Live Stock, Dairy, Human and Institutional Development

TABLE 3.10: DEPARTMENT OF AH & VS: INFRASTRUCTURE FOR BREEDING SUPPORT

| *Sl. No.* | *Infrastructure* | *Numbers* | *Location / District* |
|---|---|---|---|
| 1. | Sperm Stations | 2 | Cuttack; Bhawanipatna |
| 2. | Frozen Semen Banks | 5 | Sambalpur, Bolangir, Koraput, Kandhamal, Cuttack |
| 3. | Liquid Nitrogen Plants | 12 | Cuttack, Khurda, Phulbani, Koraput, Chiplima, Bolangir, Bhawanipatna, Balasore, Keonjhar |
| 4. | Cattle Breeding Farms | 12 | Cuttack, Sundargarh, Bhanjanagar, Balasore, Chiplima, Baripada, Bhawanipatna, Phulbani Boudh, Bolangir, Keonjhar Khurda and Koraput |
| 5. | Training Institutions | 2 | FSB Cuttack, FSB Bhawanipatna |
| 6. | Progeny Testing Scheme | 1 | Cuttack |
| 7. | Embryo Transfer Technology | 1 | Cuttack FSB |
| 8. | AI Centres (AHD) | 1510 * | All the thirty districts in the state |

NOTE: Institutions under the state department of ARD are discussed in detail in Chapter 9 on Institutional Set Up and Infrastructure.

SOURCES: District Profile 1995–6, DAH & VS, Orissa; *from the Economy Survey of Orissa, 2001-2.

TABLE 3.11: PROGRESS OF ARTIFICIAL INSEMINATION ACTIVITY IN ORISSA: CENTRES, TOTAL NUMBER OF AI, YEARLY AVERAGE AI PER CENTRE AND CALF BORN PER CENT

| *Sl. No.* | *Year* | *Number of AI Centres* | *Number of Inseminations* | *Yearly Average AI / Centre* | *Calf born rate %* |
|---|---|---|---|---|---|
| 1. | 1985-6 | 1370 | 200313 | 146 | 37.04 |
| 2. | 1986-7 | 1456 | 194231 | 133 | 46.14 |
| 3. | 1987-8 | 1574 | 232537 | 147 | 41.70 |
| 4. | 1988-9 | 1569 | 253039 (1276) | 161 | 37.86 |
| 5. | 1989-90 | 1572 | 261561 (1509) | 166 | 43.16 |
| 6. | 1990-1 | 1626 | 271256 (2681) | 167 | 34.28 |
| 7. | 1991-92 | 1618 | 278198 (3363) | 172 | 39.21 |
| 8. | 1992-3 | 1623 | 321624 (3453) | 198 | 35.14 |
| 9. | 1993-4 | 1594 | 320463 (3460) | 201 | 40.04 |
| 10. | 1994-5 | 1721 | 409158 (4370) | 238 | 36.39 |
| 11. | 1995-6 | 1818 | 589406 (7959) | 324 | 30.40 |
| 12. | 1996-7 | 1971 | 633554 (8744) | 321 | 36.73 |
| 13. | 1997-8 | 2091 | 666246 (8829) | 319 | 32.22 |
| 14. | 1998-9 | – | 604000 | | |
| 15. | 1999-2000 | – | 478000 | | |
| 16. | 2000-1 | – | 233000 | | |

NOTES: 1. Includes the centres and AI done by the co-operative organisations.
2. Figures in parenthesis are number of inseminations performed in Buffaloes.

SOURCE: LSR Report 1999, updated with DAH & VS data.

TABLE 3.12: SPERM STATIONS IN ORISSA, CAPACITY AND PRODUCTION

| *Sl. No.* | *Location* | *Capacity* | *Production 1996 / 2001* | *Bulls** | |
|---|---|---|---|---|---|
| | | | | *Cattle* | *Buffalo* |
| 1. | Cuttack | 1.00 mln doses | 0.70 mln doses / 0.11 mln doses | Jr. 20; Cb. 15 RS. 9; Hariana 3 | Murrah 5 |
| 2. | Bhawanipatna | 0.40 mln doses | 0.17 mln doses / 0.03 mln doses | Jr. 30; Cb. 5 RS. 4; | — |
| 3. | Total | 1.40 mln doses | 0.87 mln doses / 0.14 mln doses | Jr. 50; Cb. 20 RS. 13; Hariana 3 | Murrah 5 |

NOTE: * Information pertains to 1996.

SOURCE: DAH & VS.

TABLE 3.13: PROGRESS OF AI SERVICES IN THE CO-OPERATIVE SECTOR IN THE STATE

| *Sl. No.* | *Year* | *Number of AI Centres* | *AI performed* | *Average AI / Centre* |
|---|---|---|---|---|
| 1. | 1985-6 | 110 | 7318 | 66 |
| 2. | 1986-7 | 71 | 1425 | 20 |
| 3. | 1987-8 | 118 | 7581 | 64 |
| 4. | 1988-9 | 113 | 10231 | 90 |
| 5. | 1989-90 | 116 | 10186 | 88 |
| 6. | 1990-1 | 106 | 10721 | 101 |
| 7. | 1991-2 | 98 | 14813 | 151 |
| 8. | 1992-3 | 93 | 16424 | 177 |
| 9. | 1993-4 | 97 | 22136 | 228 |
| 10. | 1994-5 | 157 | 31907 | 203 |
| 11. | 1995-6 | 200 | 54721 | 274 |
| 12. | 1996-7 | 219 | 56695 | 259 |
| 13. | 1998-9 | 303 | 70313 | 232 |
| 14. | 2001-2 | 309 (48) | 100558 | 325 |

NOTE: Figures in bracket are the mobile cluster centres.
SOURCES: Orissa LSR Report 1999 and OMFRD 2002.

TABLE 3.14: BULLS SUPPLIED FOR NATURAL SERVICES IN THE STATE

| *Sl.No.* | *Year* | *Utkal Gomangal Samiti* | | *OMFED* | | *Others* |
|---|---|---|---|---|---|---|
| | | *Cattle* | *Buffalo* | *Cattle* | *Buffalo* | |
| 1. | 1987-8 | 129 | 35 | – | – | – |
| 2. | 1988-9 | 221 | 51 | 18 | – | – |
| 3. | 1989-90 | 224 | 48 | 31 | – | – |
| 4. | 1990-1 | 185 | 41 | 45 | – | – |
| 5. | 1991-2 | 162 | 54 | 55 | – | – |
| 6. | 1992-3 | 188 | 55 | 93 | – | – |
| 7. | 1994-4 | 190 | 56 | 75 | – | – |
| 8. | 1994-5 | 147 | 68 | 81 | – | – |
| 9. | 1995-6 | 130 | 81 | 56 | | *146 N.S. Bulls |
| 10. | 1996-7 | 106 | 78 | 41 | | during the last |
| 11. | 1997-8 | 99 | 79 | 29 | | three years |

NOTE: * Bulls distributed by National Watershed Development Programme for Natural Service.
SOURCE: Orissa LSR Report 1999.

EXHIBIT 3.15: GUIDELINES ISSUED BY THE GOVERNMENT OF ORISSA IN OCTOBER 1998, VIDE ITS ORDER NO. 17808 DATED 15.10.98, FOR THE BREEDING POLICY AND THE AI PROGRAMME IN THE STATE

Quote"

*Breeding Policy*

(a) Cross breeding of 50 % indigenous cows with pure HF semen should be adopted to limit exotic inheritance at 50 %.

(b) Effort should be made to up grade the local indigenous stock through AI or natural breeding with Hariana and concentrating such draught power regeneration oriented breeding programmes in specific areas of Cuttack, Jajpur, Nayagarh and Kandhamal districts.

(c) Jersey, the milch breed of choice, should be made available throughout the state for crossbreeding programme, with maximum 50 % exotic inheritance.

(d) Since the Red Sindhi breed is not markedly beneficial either for Milch or for draught purpose and does not have specific mention in the breeding policy, the dept. should retreat using this breed for up-grading purpose.

(e) Wherever advanced farmers are serious about raising the exotic level to 62 %, they may be encouraged to do so.

*Conversion of FSAI centres from German Land Shut system to French Mini*

As per the present recommended standards French Mini straws (0.25 ml) are being produced at frozen semen banks. For use of these straws at FSAI centres, substituting the German Landshut, 600 FSAI centres should be converted every year and total conversion completed within a period of 3 years. However, initially such conversion shall be done in FSAI centres in operation flood districts.

*Re-orientation of livestock Breeding Farms*

(i) The state livestock breeding farms at Chipilima and district livestock breeding farm at Remuna are to be reoriented exclusively to function as bull-mother farm for production of CB bulls for breeding purpose

(ii) The district livestock farm at Kathapal (Mayurbhanj district) and Bhanjanagar, Ganjam district shall function as bull mother farms for production of Hariana bulls for breeding purposes.

(iii) The district livestock breeding farm Kaunamunda, Sundargarh district and Khapuria, Cuttack district, shall function as heifer rearing farms to rear cross breed heifers and cows in early lactation to supply to be beneficiaries under anti-poverty programs and other income-generating schemes.

*Training Institutes*

As usual training in FSAI and infertility management are to be imparted to veterinary assistant surgeons, Junior Veterinary officers and livestock inspectors at FSAI Training Institute in Cuttack. At Bhawanipatna training to LIs in FSAI is also to continue. Considering the under utilisation of the infrastructure at Cuttack, now training schedules for Senior veterinary officers, farmers, refreshers training for all technical staff in FSAI are to be formulated and implemented after due approval

*Progeny Testing Scheme*

The Progeny testing scheme implemented in the state out of central plan assistance should be suitably stepped-up to identify more no. of proven sires for utilisation of their semen.

*Storage and transportation of Liquid Nitrogen (LN2) and semen straws*

(i) Semen straws produced at FSB Khapuria and Bhawanipatna will henceforth be stored at all the eleven place where liquid nitrogen plants are located so that while taking delivery of LN2 semen straws required for the districts will be taken.

(ii) Steps should be taken to locate funds from state plan or central plan budgets for purchase of 100 small storage cryocans (3 ltr. capacity) required for doorstep AI I.C.D./ K.B./ urban areas.

"Unquote

TABLE 3.16: INFORMATION ON BREEDING POLICY OF SELECTED STATES IN INDIA

| *Sl. No.* | *Name of the State* | *Exotic Breeds used according to policy* |
|---|---|---|
| 1. | Andhra Pradesh | Jersey: in Chittor, Ananthpur, Cuddaph, Kurnool, Vizianagram, Vishakapatanam<br>Holstein: East & West Godavari, Guntur, Krishna Praksham, Nellore and Medak |
| 2. | Haryana | Jersey: Part of Ambala dist., Hilly areas<br>Holstein & Jersey Kurukshetra, Karnal, Sonepat, Faridabad, Hissar, Sirsa, Jind and part of Ambala Plains area |
| 3. | Himachal Pradesh | X-breeding in low areas & pure breeding in high altitude with Jersey & Holstein |
| 4. | Karnataka | Replacement of Red Dane with Jersey & Holstein<br>Exotic blood level 50 & 62.5% |
| 5. | Tamil Nadu | Holstein: Nilgiris, Kodaikanal, and Kanyakumari<br>Jersey: Rest of the state |
| 6. | Pondicherry | Jersey: for non descript cattle |
| 7. | Gujarat | Holstein & Jersey for crossbreeding<br>Exotic blood level 50-62.5% |
| 8. | Punjab | Holstein & Jersey for crossbreeding<br>Exotic blood level 50-62.5% |
| 9. | Uttar Pradesh | In plains excluding Bundelkhand div., parts of Allahabad, Mirzapur and Varanasi dist.<br>Jersey & Holstein |
| 10. | Madhya Pradesh | Jersey & Holstein in districts where grading is not practiced with selected indigenous breeds |
| 11. | Orissa | Jersey for cross breeding in areas which are not covered under grading with Hariana<br>in cities of Cuttack, Rourkela, Puri, Berhampur, Sambalpur, Paradeep and Talcher triple crossing of Jersey & Holstein having 25% blood of each breed and 50% blood of local breed. |
| 12. | West Bengal | Jersey, Holstein, Red Dane and Brown Swiss in and around industrial towns of Calcutta, Howrah, Asansol, Durgapur, Kharagpur, Siliguri and Darjeeling<br>Rest of the state Jersey / Holstein |

SOURCE: Orissa LSR Report, 1999.

TABLE 4.1: THE MALE-FEMALE (CATTLE & BUFFALO) RATIO IN CENSUS YEARS ALL INDIA AND ORISSA

| *Sl. No.* | *Year* | *Male in '000* | *Female in '000* | *Total in '000* | *Percentage M:F* | *Ratio M:F* |
|---|---|---|---|---|---|---|
| | | | All India | | | |
| *Cattle* | | | | | | |
| 1. | 1966 | 71431 | 51771 | 123202 | 57.96:42.04 | 1.379 |
| 2. | 1972 | 72567 | 52275 | 124842 | 58.13:41.87 | 1.388 |
| 3. | 1972 | 73227 | 54616 | 127843 | 57.28:42.72 | 1.340 |
| 4. | 1982 | 61137 | 58693 | 119830 | 51.01:48.99 | 1.041 |
| 5. | 1987 | 63596 | 60939 | 124535 | 51.07:49.93 | 1.043 |
| 6. | 1992 | 63193 | 62657 | 125850 | 50.21:49.76 | 1.006 |
| *Buffalo* | | | | | | |
| 1. | 1966 | 7592 | 25515 | 33197 | 22.93:77.07 | 0.279 |
| 2. | 1972 | 7612 | 28617 | 36229 | 21.01:78.99 | 0.265 |
| 3. | 1972 | 7934 | 31265 | 39199 | 20.24:79.76 | 0.253 |
| 4. | 1982 | 5975 | 32384 | 38359 | 15.57:84.43 | 0.184 |
| 5. | 1987 | 6561 | 38634 | 45195 | 14.51:85.49 | 0.169 |
| 6. | 1992 | 7359 | 42460 | 49819 | 14.77:85.23 | 0.173 |
| *Cattle* | | | Orissa | | | |
| 1. | 1966 | 4396 | 3418 | 7815 | 52.26:43.74 | 1.286 |
| 2. | 1972 | 4553 | 4041 | 8704 | 53.57:46.43 | 1.153 |
| 3. | 1972 | 4868 | 4185 | 9053 | 53.78:46.22 | 1.163 |
| 4. | 1982 | 4827 | 4162 | 8989 | 53.69:46.31 | 1.159 |
| 5. | 1987 | 6909 | 6727 | 13636 | 50.66:49.34 | 1.026 |
| 6. | 1992 | 7048 | 6796 | 13844 | 50.91:49.09 | 1.037 |
| 7. | 2001 | 7273 | 6536 | 13809 | 52.66:47.33 | 1.100 |
| *Buffalo* | | | | | | |
| 1. | 1966 | 598 | 391 | 989 | 60.43:39.57 | 1.527 |
| 2. | 1972 | 630 | 440 | 1071 | 58.86:41.14 | 1.430 |
| 3. | 1972 | 593 | 435 | 1029 | 57.71:41.58 | 1.364 |
| 4. | 1982 | 560 | 398 | 969 | 58.42:41.58 | 1.405 |
| 5. | 1987 | 878 | 876 | 1654 | 53.08:46.92 | 1.131 |
| 6. | 1992 | 844 | 695 | 1539 | 54.84:45.16 | 1.214 |
| 7. | 2001 | 748 | 640 | 1388 | 53.89:46.11 | 1.167 |

SOURCES: Integrated Sample Survey 1994-5, DAH & VS; and Livestock Census 2001.

TABLE 4.2 CHANGES IN THE ADULT MALE CATTLE AND MALE BUFFALO POPULATION 1966-2001

| *Sl. No.* | *Year* | *Indigenous Male Cattle Numbers* | *Changes in per cent* | *Buffalo Male Numbers* | *Changes in per cent* |
|---|---|---|---|---|---|
| 1. | 1966 | 43,96,954 | N.A. | 5,96,170 | N.A. |
| 2. | 1972 | 46,63,330 | (+) 6.06 | 6,30,348 | (+) 5.38 |
| 3. | 1977 | 48,68,676 | (+) 4.40 | 5,93,870 | (-) 5.79 |
| 4. | 1982 | 48,27,403 | (-) 0.85 | 5,60,564 | (-) 5.61 |
| 5. | 1991 | 48,39,446 | (+) 0.25 | 6,30,440 | (=) 12.47 |
| 6. | 1996 | 55,24,517 | (=) 14.16 | 6,37,118 | (=) 1.06 |
| 7. | 2001 | 52,28,519 | (-) 5.36 | 5,72,338 | (-) 10.17 |

SOURCE: Livestock Census 2001, DAH & VS (Provisional data).

TABLE 4.3: CHANGES IN NUMBERS OF WORKING BOVINES, TRACTORS & POWER TILLERS AND NUMBER OF PUMPS IN ORISSA & INDIA.

| *State* | *Year* | *Per 100 hectares operated area* | | *Per 10,000 hectares operated area* | |
|---|---|---|---|---|---|
| | | *Working bovines* | *Pumps electrical & diesel* | *Power tiller* | *Tractor* |
| Orissa | 1991-2 | 122 | 2 | 2 | 5 |
| | 1981-2 | 102 | 0 | 0 | 6 |
| | 1971-2 | 113 | 0 | 0 | 0 |
| India | 1991-2 | 59 | 12 | 41 | 109 |
| | 1981-2 | 62 | 7 | 21 | 41 |
| | 1971-2 | 68 | 3 | 0 | 7 |

SOURCE: Land & Livestock Holding Survey, NSS 48th Round, 1992, pp. 37.

TABLE 5.1: MEAT PRODUCTION IN ORISSA (MT)

| *Year* | *Sheep* | *Goat* | *Pig* | *Cattle & Buffalo* | *Total* |
|---|---|---|---|---|---|
| 1980-1 | 4750 | 6382 | 80 | 5630 | 16843 |
| 1981-2 | 5047 | 7395 | 79 | 6123 | 18645 |
| 1982-3 | 5327 | 7549 | 87 | 6681 | 19645 |
| 1983-4 | 6088 | 8409 | 94 | 7147 | 21882 |
| 1984-5 | 5700 | 6940 | 167 | 7932 | 20740 |
| 1985-6 | 4766 | 7674 | 250 | 8597 | 21286 |
| 1986-7 | 5561 | 7727 | 409 | 9627 | 23323 |
| 1987-8 | 5595 | 8097 | 465 | 7877 | 22033 |
| 1988-9 | 6018 | 8426 | 825 | 5955 | 21224 |
| 1989-90 | 6398 | 8622 | 1034 | 8664 | 24718 |
| | | | | **Cattle* | |
| 1990-1 | 6960 | 8848 | 1253 | 8991 | 26053 |
| 1991-2 | 9148 | 10611 | 2445 | 4792 | 27197 |
| 1992-3 | 10026 | 11479 | 2523 | 5400 | 29428 |
| 1993-4 | 11443 | 11763 | 2525 | 2305 | 28036 |
| 1994-5 | 12027 | 12361 | 2536 | 2294 | 29218 |
| 1995-6 | 12427 | 12840 | 2434 | 3867 | 31568 |
| 1998-9 | 8582 | 24654 | 3201 | 1691 | 38129 |

NOTE: *Slaughter of buffaloes was discontinued from 1998-9.
SOURCES: 1. Statistical Outline of Orissa 1997;
2. Statistical Hand Book 1994, DAH Orissa.

TABLE 5.2: CHARACTERISTICS OF MAJOR GOAT BREEDS OF ORISSA

| *Sl. No.* | *Breed* | *Type* | *Size* | *Body Weight* | *Description* |
|---|---|---|---|---|---|
| 1. | Ganjam | Meat | Medium | Male Ave. 44.05 kg<br>Female Ave. 31.87 kg | Tall and leggy, coat clour black, white Brown or white |
| 2. | Black Bengal | Meat | Small | Male Ave. 32.37 kg<br>Female Ave. 18.31 kg | Small body with small legs, coat colour, black to brown |

SOURCE: Orissa LSR Report, 1999.

TABLE 5.3: CHARACTERISTICS OF MAJOR BREEDS OF SHEEP IN ORISSA

| *Sl. No.* | *Breed* | *Type* | *Size* | *Body weight* | *Description* |
|---|---|---|---|---|---|
| 1. | Bolangir | Meat | Medium | Male Ave. 23.60 kg<br>Female Ave. 17.86 kg | White, light brown or mixed, white black animals are not rare. Male horned, Female polled. Fleece quality is extremely coarse, hairy and open. |
| 2. | Ganjam | Meat | Medium | Male Ave. 30.00 kg<br>Female Ave. 24.18 kg | Brown to dark tan with white spots on face and body. Male horned, female polled. Fleece hairy and short. |

SOURCE: Orissa LSR Report, 1999.

TABLE 5.5: DISTRICT WISE ANIMAL RESOURCES IN ORISSA: LIVESTOCK CENSUS 2001

| Sl. No. | District | Cattle | | Buffalo | | Sheep | Goat | Pig | Poultry |
|---|---|---|---|---|---|---|---|---|---|
| | | Male | Female | Male | Female | | | | |
| 1. | Angul | 297139 | 266007 | 23772 | 21066 | 64440 | 231001 | 3432 | 334445 |
| 2. | Balasore | 498175 | 450878 | 2239 | 2501 | 9121 | 369540 | 18736 | 1078850 |
| 3. | Bargarh | 294630 | 222394 | 24655 | 13778 | 57915 | 177082 | 8261 | 408660 |
| 4. | Bhadrak | 292144 | 268099 | 2573 | 9565 | 7319 | 177370 | 4792 | 416229 |
| 5. | Bolangir | 302324 | 206109 | 54063 | 45925 | 119403 | 268112 | 3391 | 848338 |
| 6. | Boudh | 123653 | 113537 | 20139 | 18846 | 77294 | 98168 | 1147 | 149242 |
| 7. | Cuttack | 247502 | 375594 | 17870 | 19408 | 88681 | 274446 | 3851 | 499901 |
| 8. | Deogarh | 96613 | 82394 | 7539 | 5482 | 4929 | 78280 | 4206 | 175931 |
| 9. | Dhenkanal | 242961 | 253330 | 26321 | 36801 | 39217 | 103078 | 1158 | 382193 |
| 10. | Gajpati | 138860 | 101130 | 13365 | 11335 | 10492 | 122391 | 17039 | 369781 |
| 11. | Ganjam | 398814 | 442847 | 56907 | 74398 | 145914 | 218370 | 13571 | 1437489 |
| 12. | Jagatsinghpur | 118638 | 168517 | 1854 | 11703 | 29658 | 118077 | 4048 | 289949 |
| 13. | Jajpur | 294506 | 339302 | 4328 | 7668 | 38301 | 273291 | 5285 | 543866 |
| 14. | Jharsuguda | 101565. | 71843 | 8356 | 3180 | 9491 | 44501 | 5154 | 159762 |
| 15. | Kalahandi | 287363 | 195242 | 58.871 | 36661 | 100928 | 221848 | 7689 | 826130 |
| 16. | Kendarapara | 15457 | 232051 | 4992 | 26743 | 43367 | 104474 | 9231 | 351681 |
| 17. | Keonjhar | 429816 | 283563 | 18589 | 17860 | 144133 | 403218 | 22710 | 1121636 |
| 18. | Khurda | 157519 | 248993 | 9445 | 10199 | 54990 | 88837 | 5416 | 1280999 |
| 19. | Koraput | 249848 | 217541 | 80309 | 55264 | 125154 | 182521 | 50351 | 748039 |
| 20. | Malkangiri | 2222982 | 180351 | 19568 | 15842 | 29484 | 163506 | 51721 | 636382 |
| 21. | Mayurbhanja | 554963 | 325247 | 16218 | 10172 | 163550 | 601587 | 81492 | 2193457 |
| 22. | Nawapara | 122164 | 86798 | 17804 | 14453 | 29798 | 87377 | 1298 | 230844 |
| 23. | Nawarangapur | 238932 | 145074 | 56765 | 21694 | 82689 | 98425 | 58818 | 696053 |
| 24. | Nayagarh | 148834 | 175720 | 33535 | 13516 | 33440 | 92660 | 111 | 139408 |

(Contd.)

TABLE 5.5(Contd.)

| Sl. No. | District | Cattle | | Buffalo | | Sheep | Goat | Pig | Poultry |
|---|---|---|---|---|---|---|---|---|---|
| | | Male | Female | Male | Female | | | | |
| 25. | Kandhamal | 193740 | 111424 | 32084 | 30164 | 5607 | 193424 | 41868 | 528810 |
| 26. | Puri | 189023 | 272996 | 5644 | 11446 | 75041 | 120128 | 2059 | 273264 |
| 27. | Rayagada | 201906 | 156766 | 57892 | 54.343 | 48093 | 158225 | 38976 | 498787 |
| 28. | Sambalpur | 308518 | 167039 | 16716 | 11787 | 18269 | 174957 | 17394 | 336420 |
| 29. | Subarnapur | 133898 | 107040 | 18311 | 10987 | 42028 | 87371 | 897 | 4716 |
| 30. | Sundargarh | 439583 | 280955 | 37896 | 17056 | 66584 | 439849 | 117815 | 1310533 |
| | | 7269676 | 6546572 | 748179 | 639845 | 1765288 | 5772114 | 601917 | 18434613 |

SOURCE: Livestock Census 2001, Directorate of Animal Husbandry and Veterinary Services (Provisional data).

TABLE 5.6: LOCATION OF BREEDING FARMS FOR DIFFERENT SPECIES IN ORISSA

| Sl. No. | Species | Location |
|---|---|---|
| 1. | Goat | 1. Bolangir 2. Keonjhar 3. Sambalpur 4. Sundargarh |
| 2. | Sheep | 1. Bolangir 2. Kalahandi 3. Sambalpur 4. Sundargarh |
| 3. | Pig | 1. Keonjhar 2. Sambalpur 3. Sundargarh |
| 4. | Poultry | 1. Bolangir 2. Cuttack 3. Angul 4. Ganjam. 5. Keonjhar 6. Koraput 7. Khurda 8. Sambalpur 9. Sundargarh |

SOURCE: State DAH & VS, District Profile, 1995-6.

TABLE 5.7: SLAUGHTER HOUSES IN ORISSA, 1998

| *Sl. No.* | *District* | *Location of Slaughterhouse* |
|---|---|---|
| A. | Balasore | 1. Nayabazar (Balasore) |
| | | 2. Motiganj (Balasore) |
| | | 3. Badakhua (Bhadrak) |
| B. | Bolangir | 1. Bolangir |
| | | 2. Tarva |
| | | 3. Titilagarh |
| | | 4. Sonepur |
| C. | Cuttack | 1. Kesharpur (Cuttack Town) |
| | | 2. Idiga (Cuttack Town) |
| | | 3. Jajpur |
| | | 4. Jajpur Road |
| | | 5. Choudwar |
| | | 6. Kendrapara Road |
| | | 7. Patapol |
| | | 8. Jagtpur |
| | | 9. Paradeep |
| D. | Dhenkanal | 1. Bhuban |
| | | 2. Dhenkanal |
| | | 3. Talcher |
| | | 4. Angul |
| | | 5. Kamakshya Nagar |
| | | 6. Pallahara |
| | | 7. Hindiol |
| | | 8. Athamallik I & I |
| | | 9. Handapa |
| | | 10. R.K. Nagar |
| | | 11. Thakurgarh |
| | | 12. Bamur |
| | | 13. Boinda |
| E. | Ganjam | 1. Berhampur |
| | | 2. Chattarpur |
| | | 3. Purusotampur |
| | | 4. Hinjili |
| | | 5. Rambha |
| | | 6. Kabisurya Nagar |
| | | 7. Polsara |
| | | 8. Khllikote |
| | | 9. Gopalpur |
| | | 10. Bhanjnagar |
| | | 11. Buguda |
| | | 12. Belguntha |
| | | 13. Aska |
| | | 14. Soroda |
| | | 15. Parlakhemundi |
| | | 16. Dgapahand |

| | | |
|---|---|---|
| F. | Kalahandi | 1. Bhawanipatna |
| | | 2. Kesinga (Regd.) |
| | | 3. Jubagarh |
| | | 4. Karihar Road |
| | | 5. Nuapada |
| | | 6. Dhramgarh |
| G. | Keonjhar | 1. Badbal |
| | | 2. Keonjhar |
| | | 3. Champua |
| | | 4. Anandpur |
| H. | Koraput | 1. Rayagada |
| | | 2. Koraput |
| | | 3. Jeypore |
| | | 4. Nawarangapur (Regd.) |
| | | 5. Malkangiri (Regd.) |
| | | 6. Similiguda |
| | | 7. Kotapad |
| | | 8. Umorakot |
| | | 9. Sunabeda |
| I. | Kandhamal | 1. Kandhamal |
| | | 2. Boudh |
| J. | Mayurbhanj | 1. Baripada |
| | | 2. Karinjia |
| | | 3. Rairangpur |
| | | 4. Udala |
| K. | Puri | 1. Kalpana (Bhubaneswar) |
| | | 2. Kalpana |
| | | 3. Khurda |
| | | 4. Nayagarh |
| L. | Sambalpur | 1. Barapalli |
| | | 2. Sambalpur (Regd.) |
| | | 3. Brajarajnagar |
| | | 4. Deogarh |
| | | 5. Hirakud |
| | | 6. Burla |
| | | 7. Jharsuguda |
| | | 8. Bamara |
| | | 9. Baragarh |
| | | 10. Kuchinda |
| M. | Sundargarh | 1. Rourkela |
| | | 2. Biramitrapur |
| | | 3. Rajganpur |
| | | 4. Sundargarh |
| | | 5. Norlukud |
| | | 6. Kuarmunda |
| | | 7. Bonai |
| | | 8. Lahunipada |
| | | 9. Koira |

SOURCE: DAH & VS, Orissa, Statistical Hand Book, 1994.

TABLE 6.1: SPECIES WISE POULTRY POPULATION IN THE STATE IN DIFFERENT CENSUS YEARS

| *Sl. No.* | *Year* | *Fowl* | *% Change* | *Ducks* | *% Change* | *Others* | *% Change* |
|---|---|---|---|---|---|---|---|
| 1. | 1961 | 6194102 | – | 183883 | – | 289667 | – |
| 2. | 1966 | 7342616 | (+) 18.55 | 161388 | (-) 12.23 | 194035 | (-) 33.01 |
| 3. | 1972 | 8022528 | (+) 9.26 | 325762 | (+) 101.85 | 103935 | (-) 46.40 |
| 4. | 1977 | 9221155 | (+) 14.94 | 212475 | (-) 3 4.77 | 56817 | (-) 45.33 |
| 5. | 1982 | 10231656 | (+) 10.9 | 320451 | (+) 50.11 | 123972 | (+) 118.19 |
| 6. | 1992(1987) | 11820972 | (+) 15.53 | 620899 | (+) 93.75 | 188897 | (+) 52.37 |
| 7. | 1995(1992) | 15191000 | (+) 28.50 | 719000 | (+) 15.79 | 98000 | (-) 48.11 |
| 8. | 2001 | 17663478 | (+) 10.62 | 647526 | (-) 9.94 | 223609 | (+) 128.17 |
| · | Overall Growth | | (+) 185.16 | | (+) 252.14 | | (-) 22.80 |

SOURCES: 1. Compiled from DAH & VS reports.
2. Livestock Census Orissa 2001 (Provisional data).

TABLE 6.2: DISTRICT WISE AVERAGE PRODUCTIVITY OF THE LAYER BIRDS AND RANKING ACCORDING TO EGG PRODUCTION PER LAYER BIRD

| *Sl. No.* | *District* | *Egg production per Layer per year* | | *Ranking according to the Productivity of Layer birds* | |
|---|---|---|---|---|---|
| | | *Desi Fowl* | *Improved Fowl* | *Desi Fowl* | *Improved Fowl* |
| 1. | Angul | 110 | 158 | 9 | 5 |
| 2. | Balasore | 127 | 156 | 3 | 7 |
| 3. | Bargarh | 113 | 153 | 7 | 12 |
| 4. | Bhadrak | 115 | 150 | 6 | 14 |
| 5. | Bolangir | 119 | 154 | 5 | 10 |
| 6. | Boudh | 92 | 165 | 24 | 3 |
| 7. | Cuttack | 123 | 191 | 4 | 1 |
| 8. | Deogarh | 99 | 0 | 16 | 28 |
| 9. | Dhenkanal | 104 | 138 | 12 | 21 |
| 10. | Gajapati | 99 | 166 | 17 | 2 |
| 11. | Ganjam | 92 | 125 | 25 | 26 |
| 12. | Jagatsinghpur | 133 | 156 | 1 | 8 |
| 13. | Jajpur | 95 | 138 | 21 | 22 |
| 14. | Jharsuguda | 103 | 140 | 13 | 20 |
| 15. | Kalahandi | 95 | 127 | 22 | 24 |
| 16. | Kendrapada | 129 | 156 | 2 | 9 |
| 17. | Keonjhar | 98 | 145 | 19 | 19 |
| 18. | Khurda | 105 | 159 | 10 | 4 |
| 19. | Koraput | 89 | 117 | 28 | 27 |
| 20. | Malkangiri | 96 | 0 | 20 | 29 |
| 21. | Mayurbhanj | 94 | 142 | 23 | 19 |
| 22. | Nawapara | 89 | 0 | 29 | 30 |
| 23. | Nawarangpur | 89 | 127 | 30 | 25 |
| 24. | Nayagarh | 99 | 151 | 18 | 13 |
| 25. | Kandhamal | 90 | 147 | 27 | 17 |
| 26. | Puri | 105 | 154 | 11 | 11 |
| 27. | Rayagada | 100 | 149 | 15 | 15 |
| 28. | Sambalpur | 112 | 149 | 8 | 16 |
| 29. | Subarnapur | 92 | 135 | 26 | 23 |
| 30. | Sundargarh | 102 | 157 | 14 | 6 |
| | State | 102 | 157 | | |

SOURCE: Compiled from the Integrated Sample Survey 1998–9, Directorate of Animal Husbandry and Veterinary Services.

TABLE 6.3: DISTRICT WISE POULTRY POPULATION AND EGG PRODUCTION

| *Sl. No.* | *District* | *Poultry Numbers* | *Ranking according to Population* | *Egg Production in mln.* | *Ranking according to Production* |
|---|---|---|---|---|---|
| 1. | Angul | 334445 | 22 | 9.572 | 23 |
| 2. | Balasore | 1078850 | 6 | 37.614 | 4 |
| 3. | Bargarh | 408660 | 17 | 13.420 | 17 |
| 4. | Bhadrak | 416229 | 16 | 17.814 | 12 |
| 5. | Bolangir | 848338 | 7 | 28.646 | 6 |
| 6. | Boudh | 149242 | 28 | 4.875 | 29 |
| 7. | Cuttack | 499901 | 14 | 23.152 | 8 |
| 8. | Deogarh | 175931 | 26 | 5.257 | 27 |
| 9. | Dhenkanal | 382193 | 18 | 11.126 | 21 |
| 10. | Gajpati | 369781 | 19 | 11.826 | 19 |
| 11. | Ganjam | 1437489 | 2 | 205.835 | 1 |
| 12. | Jagatsinghpur | 289949 | 23 | 9.715 | 22 |
| 13. | Jajpur | 543866 | 12 | 20.105 | 11 |
| 14. | Jharsuguda | 159762 | 27 | 4.360 | 30 |
| 15. | Kalahandi | 826130 | 8 | 21.343 | 10 |
| 16. | Kendarapara | 351681 | 20 | 11.540 | 20 |
| 17. | Keonjhar | 1121636 | 5 | 34.662 | 5 |
| 18. | Khurda | 1280999 | 4 | 74.596 | 2 |
| 19. | Koraput | 748039 | 9 | 22.040 | 9 |
| 20. | Malkangiri | 636382 | 11 | 13.895 | 16 |
| 21. | Mayurbhanja | 2193457 | 1 | 71.815 | 3 |
| 22. | Nawapara | 230844 | 25 | 6.212 | 25 |
| 23. | Nawarangapur | 696053 | 10 | 15.505 | 14 |
| 24. | Nayagarh | 139408 | 29 | 5.412 | 26 |
| 25. | Kandhamal | 528810 | 13 | 15.209 | 15 |
| 26. | Puri | 273264 | 24 | 8.853 | 24 |
| 27. | Rayagada | 498787 | 15 | 16.282 | 13 |
| 28. | Sambalpur | 336420 | 21 | 13.062 | 18 |
| 29. | Subarnapur | 4716 | 30 | 5.067 | 28 |
| 30. | Sundargarh | 1310533 | 3 | 23.981 | 7 |
| | | 18434613 | | 762.791 | |

NOTE: District ranks between first five numbers have been highlighted.

SOURCE: Integrated Sample Survey 1998-9, Directorate of Animal Husbandry and Veterinary Services

TABLE 6.4: ORGANISED POULTRY FARMS IN ORISSA, 1996

| *Sl. No.* | *District* | *Layer Farms* | *Broiler Farms* | *Duck Farms* | *Total Farms* |
|---|---|---|---|---|---|
| 1. | Balasore | 200 | 25 | 16 | 241 |
| 2. | Bolangir | 123 | 11 | 4 | 138 |
| 3. | Cuttack | 204 | 38 | 14 | 256 |
| 4. | Dhenkanal | 104 | 8 | 4 | 116 |
| 5. | Ganjam | 106 | 16 | 12 | 134 |
| 6. | Kalahandi | 53 | 6 | 10 | 69 |
| 7. | Keonjhar | 71 | 6 | 4 | 81 |
| 8. | Korqput | 85 | 13 | 6 | 104 |
| 9. | Mayurbhanj | 69 | 8 | 5 | 82 |
| 10. | Kandhamal | 24 | 5 | 2 | 31 |
| 11. | Puri | 196 | 16 | 18 | 230 |
| 12. | Sambalpur | 97 | 6 | 3 | 106 |
| 13. | Sundargarh | 53 | 6 | 3 | 62 |
| | Total | 1385 | 164 | 101 | 1650 |

SOURCE: DAH & VS Orissa.

TABLE 7.1: COMMON DISEASES ENCOUNTERED IN LIVESTOCK IN ORISSA

| *Species* | *Viral* | *Bacterial* | *Parasitic* | *Rickettesial* | *Miscellaneous* |
|---|---|---|---|---|---|
| Cattle & Buffalo | Rabies | Coli bacilliosis | Helminths | Anaplasrnosis | Toxicity |
| | Bovine Malignant Catarrh | Tuberculosis | Fasciollosis | | Nitrite poisoning |
| | Ethmodial Herpes Tumour | Jhone's disease | Schistosomosis | | Fluoride poisoning |
| | Ephemeral fever | Brucellosis | Amphistomosis | | Lantana poisoning |
| | Cow pox | Tetanus | Strongylosis | | Nutritonal Deficiency |
| | Papillomatosis | Pink Eye | Ascariasis | | Production Diseases |
| | | Mastitis | Monieziasis | | Ketosis |
| | | Malignant Oedema | Stephano filariasis | | Downer's Cow Syndrome |
| | | Pneumonia | Parafilarisis | | Hypocalcaemia |
| | | Actinobacillosis | Onchocercosis | | Hypomagnaesemia |
| | | H. Septicaemia | Protozoan | | |
| | | Black Quarter | Theileriosis | | |
| | | | Trichomoniasis | | |
| | | | Trypanosomosis | | |
| | | | Babesiosis | | |
| | | | Arthropod | | |
| | | | Ticks | | |
| | | | Lice | | |
| | | | Mange mites | | |
| Sheep & Goat | Rabies | Enterotoxaemia | Helminths | | Toxicity |
| | Chlamydiosis | Pasteurellosis | Fascioliosis | | Lantana poisoning |
| | Foot and Mouth Disease | Anthrax | Amphistomosis | | |
| | Sheep Pox | Mycoplasmosis | Strongylosis | | |
| | PPR | Foot rot | Schistosomosis | | |
| | Blue Tongue | Paratuberculosis | Oesophagostomosis | | |

(Contd.)

TABLE 7.1 (Contd.)

| *Species* | *Viral* | *Bacterial* | *Parasitic* | *Rickettesial* | *Miscellaneous* |
|---|---|---|---|---|---|
| | | Tetanus | Taeniasis | | |
| | | Pneumonia | Protozoan | | |
| | | Mastitis | Coccidiousis | | |
| | | | Anthropod | | |
| | | | Nasal bot | | |
| | | | Mange | | |
| Pig | Foot and Mouth disease | Anthrax | Helminths | | Nutrirional |
| | Rabies | Colibacilliosis | Ascariasis | | Piglet anaemia |
| | | Pasteurellosis | Stephaneuresis | | Ricket |
| | | Tuberculosis | Anthropod | | |
| | | Swine Eryseplas* | Mange | | |

NOTE: * Less Commonly seen; Chlamydiosis also form part of the list of diseases of bovine and sheep and goat, but cannot be classified under the categories falling in any of the columns.

SOURCE: Orissa LSR Report 1999.

TABLE 7.2: COMMON DISEASES ENCOUNTERED IN POULTRY IN ORISSA

| *Species* | *Viral* | *Bacterial* | *Parasitic* | *Rickettesial* | *Miscellaneous* |
|---|---|---|---|---|---|
| Poultry | Ranikhet Disease | Fowl Cholera | Helminthic | Psittacosis | Nutritional |
| | Fowl Pox | Salmonellosis | Ascaridiasis | | Deficiency diseases |
| | Mareks Disease | Chronic Respiratory Disease (CRD) | Taeniasis | | |
| | Gumboro Disease (IBD) | Infectious Coryza | Protozoan | | |
| | Infectious Bronchitis (IB) | Colibacillosis | Coccidiosis | | |
| | Infectious Laryngo tracheitis | Omphalitis | Mycotic | | |
| | Quail enteritis | Mycoplasmamosis | Aspergilliosis | | |
| | Avian Lecuosis Complex (ALC) | | | | |
| | Duck hepatitis | | | | |
| | Avian enceplomyelitis | | | | |
| | Egg drop syndrome | | | | |
| | Hydropericardium syndrome | | | | |

SOURCE: Orissa LSR Report, 1999.

TABLE 8.1: PRODUCTION OF FOOD GRAINS, PULSES, CROP RESIDUES AND BYPRODUCTS, ORISSA

| *Sl. No.* | *Crop* | *Grain Production '000 mt 1995-6* | *Straw / Stovers '000 mt* | *Grain to Crop Residues Ratio* |
|---|---|---|---|---|
| 1 | Straws | | | |
| 1.1 | Wheat | 36 | 36 | 1:1 |
| 1.2 | Rice paddy | 6226 | 8093.8 | 1:1.3 |
| 2 | Stovers | | | |
| 2.1 | Maize | 206 | 824 | 1:4 |
| 2.2 | Jowar | 14 | 56 | -do- |
| 2.3 | Bajra | 3 | 12 | -do- |
| 2.4 | Ragi | 213 | 852 | -do- |
| 2.5 | Small millets | 31 | 124 | -do- |
| 3 | Bhusa from pulse crops | | | |
| 3.1 | Green gram | 409 | 1636 | 1:4 |
| 3.2 | Black gram | 327 | 1308 | -do- |
| 3.3 | Horse gram | 189 | 756 | -do- |
| 3.4 | Cowpea | 15 | 60 | -do- |
| 3.5 | Arhar | 127 | 508 | -do- |
| 3.6 | Gram | 25 | 100 | -do- |
| 3.7 | Field pea | 13 | 52 | -do- |
| 3.8 | Other pulses | 89 | 356 | -do- |
| 4 | Sugar cane tops | 335 | 83.75 | 1:0.25 |
| 5 | Oil seeds | | | |
| 5.1 | Groundnut | 450 | 900 | 1:2 |
| 5.2 | Sesamum | 191 | 382 | -do- |
| 5.3 | Mustard | 81 | 162 | -do |
| 5.4 | Niger | 99 | 198 | -do- |
| | Total | 9079 | 16501.55 | |

NOTE: Estimates are for 1995-6, a normal year.
SOURCE: Orissa LSR Report, 1999.

TABLE 8.2: AVAILABILITY OF CONCENTRATE FEEDS GROWN IN ORISSA

| *Sl. No.* | *Concentrates Feed* | *Seed Yield '000 mt* | *Extraction Rate of By-products (%)* | *Meal Production '000 mt* |
|---|---|---|---|---|
| 1 | Oil Cakes | | | |
| 1.1 | Groundnut | 92 | 60 | 57.04 |
| 1.2 | Sesamum | 14 | 70 | 9.8 |
| 1.3 | Linseed | 15 | 70 | 10.5 |
| 1.4 | Mustard | 4 | 70 | 2.8 |
| 1.5 | Niger | 99 | 70 | 69.3 |
| 1.6 | Other oilseeds | 3 | 70 | 2.1 |
| | Cotton seed cake | 0.40 | | |
| | Total | 224 | | 151.94 |
| 2 | By-products | | | |
| 2.1 | Wheat bran | 23 | 8 | 1.84 |
| 2.2 | Rice bran | 4436 | 8 | 354.88 |
| 2.3 | Chunnies (pulses) | 569 | 3 | 17.07 |
| | Total | 5028 | | 373.79 |

NOTES: Cotton yield during 1995-6: 22000 bales, each bale is of 180 kg. Therefore total cotton output is 22000 x 180 = 3960000 kg. Cotton seed in 100 kg cotton is 35 kg. Therefore cotton seed in 22000 bales will be 1386000 kg. Cotton seed cake per 100 kg of cotton seed is 29.4 kg. Therefore total cotton seed output is 407484 kg.

SOURCE: Orissa LSR Report, 1999.

TABLE 8.3: AVAILABILITY OF FOOD GRAINS GROWN IN ORISSA, FOR LIVESTOCK FEEDING, 1995-6

| *Sl. No.* | *Crops* | *Grain Yield '000 mt* | *% Available for Animal Feed* | *Quantities available for Animal Feeds '000 mt* |
|---|---|---|---|---|
| 1. | Wheat | 31 | 2 | 0.62 |
| 2. | Rice | 6226 | 2 | 124.52 |
| 3. | Maize | 46 | 10 | 4.6 |
| 4. | Ragi | 44 | 5 | 2.20 |
| 5. | Bajara | 4 | 5 | 0.20 |
| 6. | Small millets | 31 | 10 | 3.1 |
| 7. | Jowar | 14 | 5 | 0.70 |
| | Total | 135.94 | | |

SOURCE: Orissa LSR Report, 1999.

TABLE 8.4: ANNUAL REQUIREMENT: CONCENTRATES, GREEN AND DRY FODDER FOR LIVESTOCK AND POULTRY

| *Sl. No.* | *Animal Category* | *Population '000* | *Concentrates '000 mt* | *Green Fodder '000 mt* | *Dry Fodder '000 mt* |
|---|---|---|---|---|---|
| 1. | Cattle | | | | |
| 1.1 | Crossbred Milch | 169 | 169.63 | 1542.12 | 308.42 |
| 1.2 | Indigenous Milch | 1713 | 1250.49 | 6252.45 | 3751.47 |
| 1.3 | Crossbred Young Stock | 321 | 117.16 | 410.07 | 878.75 |
| 1.4 | Others Including males over 3 yrs | 12563 | 6878.24 | 22927.47 | 34391.21 |
| 2 | Buffalo | | | | |
| 2.1 | Improved Milch | 8 | 4.38 | 43.80 | 23.36 |
| 2.2 | Others including males over 3 yrs | 1644 | 600.06 | 3000.30 | 2400.24 |
| 3 | Poultry | | | | |
| 3.1 | Improved Layers | 1209 | 48.54 | 8.82 | – |
| 3.2 | Improved Growing | 1597 | 34.94 | 4.00 | – |
| 4 | Sheep | | | | |
| 4.1 | Improved | 21 | 2.10 | 7.66 | – |
| 4.2 | Sheep others | 1843 | – | 1345.39 | – |
| 5 | Goat | 5412 | – | 3950.76 | – |
| 6 | Pig Improved | 11 | 10.03 | 4.01 | – |
| | Total | | 9115.57 | 39496.09 | 41753.21 |

SOURCE: Orissa LSR Report, 1999.

TABLE 8.5: AVAILABILITY OF ANIMAL FEED STUFFS IN ORISSA: COMPREHENSIVE SUMMARY 1996

| *Sl. No.* | *Fodder / Feed Category* | *Quantity '000 mt* | *Dry Matter %* | *Dry Matter '000 mt* |
|---|---|---|---|---|
| 1.0 | Dry Fodder: Straw / strovers | 16501.55 | 90 | 14851.39 |
| 2.0 | Green Fodder | | | |
| 2.1 | Cultivated | 461.45 | 25 | 115.36 |
| 2.2 | Grazing* | 25280.00 | 25 | 6320.13 |
| | Total | – | – | 21286.75 |
| 3.0 | Concentrates⁺ | | | |
| 3.1 | Meals / Bran / Oil Cakes | 1820.00 | 90 | 1638.00 |
| 3.2 | Cereals / Millets | 220.00 | 90 | 198.00 |
| 3.3 | Balanced commercial Feeds | 80.00 | 90 | 72.00 |
| | Total | 2120.00 | 90 | 1836.00 |
| | Grand Total | | | 22996.75 |

NOTES: * includes extra 9.00 mln mt green herbage available during the wet season and the imported concentrate materials.

⁺ Includes concentrate feed raw materials grown in the state as well as quantities imported into the state by the trade.

SOURCE: Orissa LSR Report, 1999.

TABLE 8.6: SUPPLY AND EFFECTIVE DEMAND BALANCE: FEED AND FODDER, QTY. MLN. MT/(PER CENT)

| *Sl. No.* | *Feed Stuff* | *Dry Fodder* | *Green Fodder* | *Concentrates* |
|---|---|---|---|---|
| 1.1 | Supply (Produced in the State) | 16.50 | 25.28 | 0.67 |
| 1.2 | Supply (Import through Trade Channels) | – | – | 1.45 |
| 2.1 | Effective Demand (LSR Estimate) | 21.59 | 30.00 | 2.12 |
| 2.2 | Nutritional Demand (Fd & Fdr. Team Estimate) | 41.75 | 39.50 | 9.12 |
| 3.1 | Deficit Qty / % Effective Demand | 5.09/(24) | 4.72/(16) | – |
| 3.2 | Deficit Qty / % Nutritional Demand | 25.25/(60) | 14.22/(36) | 84.53/(93) |

BASIS: Consumption Estimates, please see para 8.3 (d).
SOURCE: Orissa LSR Report, 1999.

TABLE 8.7: FEED MILLING PLANTS IN THE STATE

| *Sl. No.* | *Name of the Plant* | *Location* | *Capacity in mt* | *Date of Installation* |
|---|---|---|---|---|
| A. | *Government* | | | |
| 1. | Feed Mixing Centre | Bhanjnagar | 5 / day | – |
| 2. | Feed Mixing Centre | Koraput | 5 / day | – |
| 3. | Feed Mixing Centre | Remuna | 5 / day | – |
| 4. | Feed Mixing Centre | Sundargarh | 5 / day | – |
| B. | *Government Undertakings* | | | |
| 5. | Feed Processing Unit of OAIC | Berhampur | 10 / day | 28.7.1981 |
| 6. | Feed Processing Unit of OAIC | Bhubaneswar | 30 / day | 28.7.1981 |
| 7. | Feed Processing Unit of O.A.I.C | Sambalpur | 20 / day | 6.3.1984 |
| 8. | Feed Plant of OPOLFED | Bhubaneswar | 15 / day | – |
| 9. | Feed Plant of OPOLFED | Angul | 5 / day | – |
| 10. | Feed Plant of OMFED | Radhadamodarpur | 100 / day | 24.9.1986 |
| 11. | Feed Plant of Utkal Gomangal Samity | Patha Farm Cuttack | 8 / day | 1.10.1982 |
| C. | *Private Sector* | | | |
| 12. | M/s Animal Feed, Dairies & Chemicals Pvt. Ltd. | Jharpada, Bhubaneswar | 50 mt / year | 11.8.1980 |
| 13. | M/s Bhagyaluxmi Industries | Haripada, Phulbani | 20 hp | 12.11.1980 |
| 14. | M/s Arries Enterprise | Cuttack | 10 hp | 25.11.1980 |
| 15. | M/s Kamdhenu Cattle Feeds | Cuttack | 10 hp | 23. 1. 1981 |
| 16. | M/s Mamana Industries | Padampur, Cuttack | 5 hp | 25.5.1981 |
| 17. | M/s Jayadurga Animal Feeds | Cuttack | 15 hp | 25.5. 1981 |
| 18. | M/s Umar and Sons | Bhatapada, Cuttack | 15 hp | 29.5.1981 |
| 19. | M/s East Coast Nutrition & Chemicals | Cuttack | 30 hp | 1.6.1981 |
| 20. | M/s Sarojani Enterprise | Cuttack | 10 hp | 12.6.1981 |
| 21. | M/s Prestige Animals Feeds | Cuttack | 10 hp | 20.11.1981 |
| 22. | M/s East India Feed Industrise | Cuttack | 20 hp | 20.11.1981 |
| 23. | M/s Bhawani Enterprise | Nuapara | 10 hp | 22.12.1981 |
| 24. | M/s Durga Cattle Feed Industrise | Aska, Gangam | 7.5 hp | 1.1.1982 |
| 25. | M/s Kalahandi Cattle Feed Industries | Kalahandi | – | – |

(Contd.)

TABLE 8.7 (Contd.)

| *Sl. No.* | *Name of the Plant* | *Location* | *Capacity in mt* | *Date of Installation* |
|---|---|---|---|---|
| 26. | M/s Hind Rama Enterprise | Bhubaneswar | 20 hp | 17.4.1984 |
| 27. | M/s Jayagopal Cattle Feed | District Puri | 7.5 hp | 18.6.1984 |
| 28. | M/s Jagannath Feeds & Fodder | Ranital, Bhadrak | 17.5 hp | 16.2.1986 |
| 29. | M/s Maa Dakhina Kali Animal Feeds | Nayagarh | 22.5 hp | 4.2.1992 |
| 30. | M/s Sarba Mangala Industries | Nwarangpur | 10 hp | 10.3.1988 |
| 31. | M/s Jagadamba Animal Feeds Nutrition and Chemicals | Bhubaneswar | 15 hp | 20.2.1992 |
| 32. | M/s Handita Enterprise | Bhubaneswar | 500 mt / year | 23.3.1988 |
| 33. | M/s Mayar Feeds and Chemicals | Baripada | – | 23.5.1991 |
| 34. | M/s Utkal Feeds Pvt. Ltd. | Bhubaneswar | 30 kW | 14.11.1991 |
| 35. | M/s Tariani Feed Unit | Keonjhar | 7.5 hp | 10.3.1992 |
| 36. | M/s Bruders Pvt. Ltd. | Jatni | 70 hp | 28.3.1992 |
| 37. | M/s Honesty Cattle and Poultry | Cuttack | 140 mt/ month | 30.6.1992 |
| D. | *Feed Industries* | | | |
| 38. | M/s Pasupati Feeds Tangi | Cuttack | 1300/ year | 22.1.1993 |
| 39. | M/s Utkal Gomangal Samity C.F.P. | Sambalpur | 100 mt / day | 1994 |
| 40. | M/s Shree Ambica Fodder Industries | Cuttack | 10 mt / day | 3.8.1994 |
| 41 | M/s Shree Jagannath Supply Service Co-operative Society Ltd. | Cuttack | 12.5 hp | 7.9.1995 |
| 42. | M/s Fruit Crafts (India) Pvt. Ltd. | Cuttack | 21 hp | 23.5.1995 |
| 43. | M/s Nandni Feeds | Baripada | 15 hp | 21.9.1995 |
| 44. | M/s Sanjib Feeds | Jagatpur | 20 hp | 10.1996 |
| 45. | M/s Tarini Cattle Feeds | Rourkela | 13 mt / hour | 1997 |
| 46. | M/s Shree Nilachala Poultry Pvt. Ltd. | Puri | – | 1993 |
| 47. | M/s Jai Bharat Agro Ind. C.F.P. | Kalahandi | 10 mt / hour | 1998 |
| 48. | M/s Gokul Animal Feeds & Dairy Ltd. | Baijamunda | 2 mt/ hour | 1998 |

SOURCE: Orissa LSR Report, 1999.

TABLE 9.1 ORCHESTRATION OF THE BREEDING POLICY

| *Sl. No.* | *Name of the Districts* | *Breeding Policy* | *Remarks* |
|---|---|---|---|
| 1. | *Most Potential Districts Category 'A'* | | |
| | Cuttack, Puri, Ganjam, Khurda, Jagatsinghpur, Bargarh, Balasore Kendrapara, Jajpur, and Bhadrak | *Cattle:* 1. Cross breeding of local cattle with pure Holstein 2. Inter se mating of half breds with $F_1$ Holstein x Hariana half bred semen | 1. Grading up local cattle with Hariana semen as concurrent policy 2. Jersey and cross bred Jersey semen will be available to those who prefer Jersey |
| | | *Buffalo:* Grading up with pure Murrah semen | |
| 2. | *Potential Districts Category 'B'* | | |
| | Bolangir, Dhenekanal, Keonjhar, Angul, Sambalpur, Sundargarh, Mayurbhanj, Rayagada, Kalahandi, and Nayagarh | *Cattle:* 1. Continue cross breeding of local cattle with pure Jersey inter 2. Inter se mating of half breds with $F_1$ Jersey x Hariana cross bred semen | 1. Grading up with Hariana semen as concurrent policy 2. Holstein and cross bred Holstein semen will be available to those who prefer Holstein |
| | | *Buffalo:* Grading up with pure Murrah semen | |
| 3. | *Low Potential Districts: Category 'C'* | | |
| | Koraput, Gajapati, Jharsguda, Boudh, Phulbani, Nawapara, Deogarh, Nawarangpur, Malkangiri, and Subaranpur | *Cattle:* 1. Grading up local cattle with Hariana as basic policy | 1. Cross breeding with Jersey semen 2. Inter se mating of cross breds cattle with Jersey x Harians half bred semen as optional policy |
| | | *Buffalo:* Grading up with pure Murrah semen | |

NOTES: 1. Grading up of the local cattle with Hariana and Grading up of the local buffalo with Murrah, will be the 'policy universal' for the entire state in all areas. 2. Natural Service Bulls will be used to implement the breeding policy in areas where AI is not introduced.

TABLE 9.2: PROGRESS OF ARTIFICIAL INSEMINATION ACTIVITY IN ORISSA: CENTRES, TOTAL NUMBER OF AI, YEARLY AVERAGE AI PER CENTRE AND CALF BORN %

| *S. No.* | *Year* | *Numebr of AI Centres* | *Number of Inseminations* | *Yearly Average AI/ Centre* | *Calf Born Rate %* |
|---|---|---|---|---|---|
| 1. | 1985-6 | 1370 | 200313 | 146 | 37.04 |
| 2. | 1986-7 | 1456 | 194231 | 133 | 46.14 |
| 3. | 1987-8 | 1574 | 232537 | 147 | 41.70 |
| 4. | 1988-9 | 1569 | 253039 (1276) | 161 | 37.86 |
| 5. | 1989-90 | 1572 | 261561 (1509) | 166 | 43.16 |
| 6. | 1990-1 | 1626 | 271256 (2681) | 167 | 34.28 |
| 7. | 1991-2 | 1618 | 278198 (3363) | 172 | 39.21 |
| 8. | 1992-3 | 1623 | 321624 (3453) | 198 | 35.14 |
| 9. | 1993-4 | 1594 | 320463 (3460) | 201 | 40.04 |
| 10. | 1994-5 | 1721 | 409158 (4370) | 238 | 36.39 |
| 11. | 1995-6 | 1818 | 589406 (7959) | 324 | 30.40 |
| 12. | 1996-7 | 1971 | 633554 (8744) | 321 | 36.73 |
| 13. | 1997-8 | 2091 | 666246 (8829) | 319 | 32.22 |

NOTES: 1. Includes the centres and AI done by the co-operative organisations.
2. Figures in parenthesis are number of inseminations performed in Buffaloes.

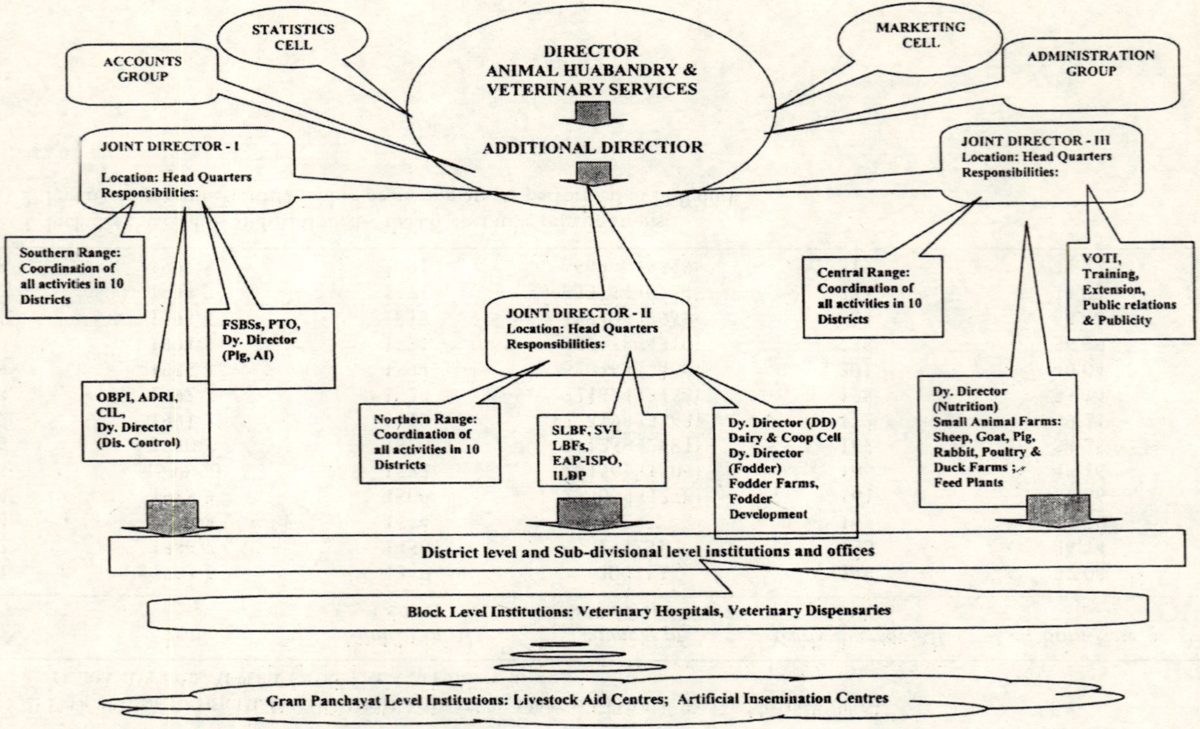


EXHIBIT 10.1: FUNCTIONAL ORGANOGRAM OF DAH &VS.

TABLE 10.2: INSTITUTIONAL NETWORK OF THE DEPARTMENT OF AHD

| *Sl. No.* | *Institution* | *Numbers and Location* | |
|---|---|---|---|
| 1. | Animal Disease Research Institute | 1 | Phulnakhara, Cuttack |
| 2. | Orissa Biological Product Institute | 2 | Bhubaneswar; Satelite OBPI, Berhampur |
| 3. | Frozen Semen Production Stations | 2 | Cuttack and Bahwanipatna |
| 4. | Externally Aided Projects | 2 | ISPO, Bhubaneswar, ILDP, Koraput |
| 5. | Orissa Veterinary Officers Training Institute | 1 | Laxmisagar, Bhubaneswar |
| 6. | Livestock Inspector Training Centres | 3 | Chiplima, Bhanjanagar, Bolangir, Cuttack, |
| 7. | AI Training Centres | | Bhawanipatna |
| 8. | Clinical Investigation Laboratories | 3 | Cuttack, Berhampore and Bhawanipatna |
| 9. | Special Livestock Breeding Project | 6 | |
| 10. | Special Livestock Development Project | 1 | |
| 11. | State Livestock Breeding Farm | 1 | Chipilima |
| 12. | Livestock Breeding Farms | 12 | |
| 13. | Poultry Breeding Farms | 9 | |
| 14. | Duck Breeding Farms | 2 | |
| 15. | Sheep Breeding Farms | 4 | |
| 16. | Goat Breeding Farms | 4 | |
| 17. | Pig Breeding Farms | 4 | |
| 18. | Rabbit Breeding Farms | 2 | |
| 19. | Fodder Farms | 12 | |
| 20. | Fodder Seed Production Farms | 6 | |
| 21. | Feed Mixing Centres | 5 | |
| 22. | Progeny Testing Unit | 1 | |
| 23. | Gosadan | 1 | |
| 24. | State Veterinary Laboratory | 1 | |
| 25. | Information Bureau | 1 | |
| 26. | Liquid Nitrogen Plants | 12 | |
| 27. | Rinder Pest Check Posts | 24 | |
| 28. | Rinder Pest Centres | 178 | |
| 29. | Intensive Cattle Development Projects | 4 | |
| 30. | ICD Zones | 16 | |
| 31. | ICD Centres | 335 | |
| 32. | Key Village Blocks | 23 | |
| 33. | Key Village Units | 238 | |
| 34. | Artificial Insemination Centres | 1468 | |
| 35. | Veterinary Hospitals | 58 | |
| 36. | Veterinary Dispensaries | 482 | |
| 37. | Livestock Aid Centres | 2939 | |

SOURCE: Orissa LSR Report, 1999.

TABLE 10.3: STATE & CENTRAL PLAN AND STATE NON-PLAN EXPENDITURE (RS. MLN)

| *Sl. No.* | *Five Year Plan* | *State Plan* | *Central Plan* | *State Non-plan* |
|---|---|---|---|---|
| 1. | First Plan | 4.70 | – | – |
| 2. | Second Plan | 15.21 | – | 25.64 |
| 3. | Third Plan | 40.02 | – | 32.37 |
| 4. | Fourth Plan | 42.83 | 0.05 | 62.24 |
| 5. | Fifth Plan | 42.50 | 6.70 | 71.56 |
| 6. | Sixth Plan | 100.00 | 21.18 | 134.80 |
| 7. | Seventh Plan | 285.20 | 31.67 | 495.07 |
| 8. | Eighth Plan | 524.00 | 208.35 | 1864.70 |
| 9. | Ninth Plan | 537.60 | 42.15 | 1060.00 |
| | Total | 1592.07 | 310.10 | 3746.37 |

SOURCE: Orissa LSR Report, 1999.
NOTE: Figures for only two years: 1997-8 and 1998-9.

TABLE 10.4: ANIMAL HUSBANDRY & VETERINARY SERVICES DEPARTMENT: BREEDING AND FODDER SEED FARMS

| *Sl. No.* | *Infrastructure* | *Numbers* | *Location / District* |
|---|---|---|---|
| 1. | State Livestock Breeding Farm | 1 | Chipilima |
| 2. | Cattle Breeding Farms and Fodder farms | 12<br>12 | Cuttack, Sundargarh, Bhanjanagar, Balasore, Mayurbhanj, Bhawanipatna, Kandhamal, Boudh, Bolangir, Keonjhar, Khurda, Koraput |
| 3. | Goat Breeding Farms | 4 | Keonjhar, Sambalpur, Bolangir, Sundargarh |
| 4. | Sheep Breeding Farms | 4 | Jirang, Chipilima, Deogaon, Kuanarmunda |
| 5. | Pig Breeding Farms | 2 | Bhanjanagar, Chiplima, Kuanarmunda, Matkambeda |
| 6. | Rabbit Breeding Farms | 2 | Chiplima, Koraput |
| 7. | Poultry Breeding Farms | 9 | Angul, Bhubaneswar, Bhanjnagar, Bolangir, Chiplima, Koraput, Keonjhar, Semiliguda and Sundargarh |
| 8. | Fodder Seed Farms | 12 | Balasore, Bolangir, Cuttack, Dhenkanal, Ganjam, Kalahandi, Keonjhar, Mayurbhanj, Phulbani (Kandhamal), Boudh, Sabalpur, Sundargarh |

SOURCE: District Profile, DAH & VS, 1995-6.

TABLE 10.5: INFRASTRUCTURE FOR ANIMAL HEALTH CARE: DEPARTMENT OF DAH & VS

| Sl. No. | Infrastructure | Numbers and Location | |
|---|---|---|---|
| 1. | Animal Disease Research Institute | 1 | Phulnakhara, Cuttack |
| 2. | Orissa Biological Product Institute | 2 | Bhubaneswar, Satellite OBPI, Berhampur |
| 3. | Clinical Investigation Laboratories | 3 | Cuttack, Berhampore and Bhawanipatna |
| 4. | State Veterinary Laboratory | 1 | Chipilima |
| 5. | Rinder Pest Check Posts | 24 | |
| 6. | Rinder Pest Centres | 178 | |
| 7. | Veterinary Hospitals | 58 | |
| 8. | Veterinary Dispensaries | 482 | |
| 9. | Livestock Aid Centres | 2929 | |
| 10. | Veterinary Dispensary (SPCA) | 1 | Cuttack |

SOURCE: Orissa LSR Report, 1999.

TABLE 10.6: INFRASTRUCTURE FOR PRODUCTION SUPPORT: DAH & VS, UGS AND OMFED

| Sl. No. | Infrastructure | Numbers and Location | |
|---|---|---|---|
| 1. | Frozen Semen Production Stations | 2 | Cuttack and Bahwanipatna |
| 2. | Externally Aided Livestock Development Projects | 2 | ISPO, Bhubaneswar, ILDP, Koraput |
| 3. | State Livestock Breeding Farm | 1 | Chipilima |
| 4. | Livestock Breeding Farms | 12 | |
| 5. | Poultry Breeding Farms | 9 | |
| 6. | Duck Breeding Farms | 2 | |
| 7. | Sheep Breeding Farms | 4 | |
| 8. | Goat Breeding Farms | 4 | |
| 9. | Pig Breeding Farms | 4 | |
| 10. | Rabbit Breeding Farms | 2 | |
| 11. | Fodder Farms | 12 | |
| 12. | Fodder Seed Production Farms | 6 | |
| 13. | Feed Milling Plants | 5 | |
| 14. | Progeny Testing Unit | 1 | |
| 15. | Gosadan | 1 | |
| 16. | Information Bureau | 1 | |
| 17. | Liquid Nitrogen Plants | 12 | |
| 18. | Intensive Cattle Development Projects | 4 | |
| 19. | ICD Zones | 16 | |
| 20. | ICD Centres | 335 | |
| 21. | Key Village Blocks | 24 | |

| | | | |
|---|---|---|---|
| 22. | Key Village Units | 263 | |
| 23. | Artificial Insemination Centres under UGS | 1796 | |
| 24. | Animal Feed Milling Plants, 100 mtpd & 20 mtpd | 2 | Chipilima & Patha |
| 25. | Stud Bull Stations for Natural Service | 163 | |
| 26. | Bull Calf Rearing Facilities under OMFED | 4 | |
| 27. | Animal Feed Milling Plant, 100 mtpd | 1 | Cuttack |
| 28. | Mobile Cluster AI Centres | 19 | |
| 29. | DCS based AI Centres | 284 | |

SOURCE: Orissa LSR Report, 1999.

TABLE 10.7: INFRASTRUCTURE FOR HUMAN RESOURCE DEVELOPMENT

| *Sl. No.* | *Infrastructure* | *Numbers and Location* |
|---|---|---|
| 1. | Orissa University of Agriculture and Technology | 1 Bhubaneswar |
| 2. | Veterinary College, OUAT | 1 Bhubaneswar |
| 3. | Orissa Veterinary Officers Training Institute | 1 Laxminagar, Bhubaneswar |
| 4. | Livestock Inspector Training Centres | 3 Balangir, Chiplima, Bhanjanagar |
| 5. | Frozen Semen Technology & AI Training Facility | 2 Cuttack and Bhawanipatna |
| 6. | OM TDC for Cooperative, AI & Vety. First Aid Training | 1 Kalyani |
| 7. | AI Training Centre, Puri Milk Union | 1 Puri |
| 8. | Training Centre (Donbosco - NGO) | 1 Kuarmunda |
| 9. | Poultry Training Institute | 2 |

SOURCE: Orissa LSR Report, 1999.

TABLE 10.8: INFRASTRUCTURE FOR DAIRY DEVELOPMENT

| *Sl. No.* | *Infrastructure* | *Number and Location* |
|---|---|---|
| 1. | State Co-operative Milk Producers' Federation | 1 Bhubaneswar |
| 2. | District Co-operative Milk Producers' Unions | 8 |
| 3. | Village Dairy Co-operative Societies | 656 (OMFED) |
| 4. | Village Dairy Co-operative Societies (All Women) | 330 (OMFED) |
| 5. | Village Dairy Co-operative Societies | 397 (DAH) |
| 6. | Dairy Plants (total cap. 150 ltpd) | 5 (OMFED) |
| 7. | Dairy Plants (total cap. 30 ltpd) | 5 (DAH) |
| 8. | Milk Chilling Plants (total cap. 75 ltpd) | 14 (OMFED) |
| 9. | Milk Chilling Plants (total cap. 70 ltpd) | 14 (DAH) |

SOURCE: Orissa LSR Report, 1999

TABLE 10.9: INFRASTRUCTURE FOR POULTRY DEVELOPMENT IN THE STATE

| *Sl. No.* | *Infrastructure* | *DAH / Public Sector* | *Private* | *Total* |
|---|---|---|---|---|
| 1. | Pure Line Breeding Farms | 3 | – | 3 |
| 2. | Parent / Grand Parent Multiplication Farm | 11 | 5 | 16 |
| 3. | Hatcheries | 11 | 15 | 26 |
| 4. | Feed mixing Units | 9 | 7 | 16 |
| 5. | Equipment Manufacturers | – | 7 | 7 |
| 6. | Biological Institute | 1 | – | 1 |
| 7. | Poultry Disease Diagnostic Laboratory | 6 | 1 | 7 |
| 8. | Poultry Co-operative Societies | – | 256 | 256 |
| 9. | Poultry Producer's Co-operative Union | – | 2 | 2 |
| 10. | Poultry Federation | | – | 1 |
| 11. | Poultry Training Institute | 2 | – | 2 |
| 12. | Special Poultry Projects | 4 | – | 4 |
| 13. | Feed Analytical Laboratory | 3 | – | 3 |

SOURCES: 1. Statistical Handbook, 1994, DAH & VS Department, Government of Orissa.
2. Poultry Industry Year Book, 1994.

TABLE 11.1: LIVESTOCK MARKETS IN ORISSA

| *Sl. No.* | *Name of the Market* | *Location* | *Market* | *Market Day* | *Name of Org. Society* |
|---|---|---|---|---|---|
| | *Cuttack District* | | | | |
| 1. | Gopinathpur | Gopinathpur / Kulalia | Athgarh | Monday | G.P,.Kulalia |
| 2. | Nauapatna | Nauapatna | Tigira | Friday | G.P. Nuapatna |
| 3. | Maniabandh | Maniabandh | Badamba | Friday | G.P. Maniabandh |
| 4. | Champeswar | Champeswar | – | Tuesday | G.P, Champeswar |
| 5. | Banki | Banki Town | Banki | Monday | N.A.C. (RMC) Banki |
| 6. | Tangi | Tangi / Katsani | Tangi Chowdar | Thursday | MMC Kendupatna |
| 7. | Nischintkoili | Nischintkoili | Nischantkoili | – | – |
| 8. | Salipur | Sauri | Salipur | Wednesday | – |
| | District Jagatsinghpur | | | | |
| 9. | Somanath Haat | Jagatsinghpur | Jagatsinghpur | Saturday | R.M.C. Jagatsinghpur |
| 10. | Kisannagar | Kisannagar | – | Saturday | R.M.C. Jagatsinghpur |
| 11. | Thakurani Haat | Kanakpur | Tirtol | Sunday | – |
| 12. | Bhagibarpacheri | Bhagibaripacheri | Kunjakati / Ersoma | Thursday | – |
| | District Jajpur | | | | |
| 13 | Baulang | Karikapada | – | Saturday | P.S. Market |
| 14. | Nanpur | Balichandpur | Badachana | Sunday | RMC Jajpur |
| 15. | Balamukhi | Kalayanpur | – | Friday | – |
| | *District Kendrapara* | | | | |
| 16 | Ichapur | Kendrapara | Kendrapara | Saturday | Municipality |
| 17. | Chhata | Chhata | Derabish | Monday | G.P. Derabish |
| 18. | Garadpur | Garadpur | Garadpur | Tuesday | G.P. Garadpur |
| 19 | Naganpur | Naganpur | Badapeta | Tuseday | N.A.C. Patamundei |
| 20 | Patamundei | Patamunedi | Patamunedi | Friday | N.A.C. Patamunedi |
| 21. | Chandola | Chandola | – | – | – |

| | | | | | |
|---|---|---|---|---|---|
| 22. | Rajakanika | Rajkanika | – | – | – |
| | District Nayagarh | | | | |
| 23. | Balugoan | Balugoan | Balugaoan | Monday | G.P. Balugoan |
| 24. | N.A.C. Nayagarh | – | Nayagarh | Monday | G.P. Nayagarh |
| 25. | Bahadajhola | Bahadajhola | Nuagoan | Thursday | R.M.C. Bahadajhola |
| | District Khurda | | | | |
| 26. | Begunia | Begunia | Begunia | Tues. / Sat. | G.P. Begunia |
| | District Puri | | | | |
| 27. | Sakhigopal | Sakhigopal | Sakhigopal | Tuesday | R.M.C. Sakhigopal |
| 28. | Kundehi | Kundehi | Kakatpur | Mon. / Fri. | G.P. Kakatpur |
| 29 | Nimapada | Nimapada | Nimapada | Sunday | N.A.C. Nimapada |
| | District Bargarh | | | | |
| 30. | Bhatli | – | – | – | – |
| 31. | Bargarh | Bargarh | Municipality | Fri. / Sat. | R.M.C. Municipality |
| 32. | Bhukta | – | – | Wednesday | – |
| 33. | Jaringi | Jaringi | Bijipur | Tuesday | O.S.M.B. |
| | *District Sambalpur* | | | | |
| 34. | Kuchinda | Kuchinda | N.A.C. Kuchinda | Friday | N.A.C. Kuchinda |
| 35. | Jaringi | Jaringi | Bijipur | Tuesday | R.M.C. Padampur |
| 36. | Kalla | Kalla | Barkote | Tuesday | G.P. Barkote |
| 37. | Ballma | Ballma | Barkote | Monday | G.P. Ballma |
| 38. | Reamal | Reamal | Reamal | Wednesday | G.P. Reamal |
| 39. | Kalibazar | – | – | – | – |
| | *District Bhadrak* | | | | |
| 40. | Angarpada | Purusandha | Banth | Tuesday | Private |
| 41. | Beteda | Beteda | Basudevpur | Monday | Private |
| 42. | Dhulasahi | Khulasahi | Tihidi | Friday | Private |

(Contd.)

Table 11.1 (Contd.)

| *Sl. No.* | *Name of the Market* | *Location* | *Market* | *Market Day* | *Name of Org. Society* |
|---|---|---|---|---|---|
| | *District Balasore* | | | | |
| 43. | Rameshwar hat / Rupsa | Patpurbazar | Balasore Sadar | Monday | – |
| 44. | Remuna | Sampad/ Remuna | Remuna | Sunday | – |
| 45. | Barikpur | Patharpentha | Bahanaga | Friday | G.P. Bahanaga |
| | *District Ganjam* | | | | |
| 46. | Hinjilikatu | N.A.C. Hinjilikatu | Hinjilikatu | Saturday | R.M.C. Hinjilikatu |
| 47. | Khalikot | Khalikot | Khalikot | Saturday | Private, Khalkot |
| 48. | Belaguntha | Belaguntha | Belaguntha | Monday | N.A.C. Belaguntha |
| 49. | Buguda | Buguda | Buguda | Saturday | N.A.C. Buguda |
| | *District Gajapati* | | | | |
| 50. | Parlakhemundi | Parlakhemundi | Parlakhemundi | Saturday | Municapal Market |
| 51. | Upalda | Upalda | Gosani | Sunday | G.P. Upalda |
| 52. | Chandiput | Chandiput | Mohana | Saturday | R.M.C. Chandiput |
| 53. | Raigad | Raigad | Raigad | Saturday | R.M.C. Raigad |
| | *Diatrict Angul* | | | | |
| 54. | Banarpal | Banarpal | Banarpal | Tuesday | R.M.C. Angul |
| 55. | Tukuda | Tukuda | Chandipada | Thursday | R.M.C. Angul |
| 56. | Baniabahal | Baniabahal | Angul | Sunday | R.M.C. Angul |
| 57. | Haida | Haida | Athamallik | Wed. / Sat. | G.P. Haida |
| 58. | Krutibaspur | Krutibaspur | Athamallik | Wednesday | G.P. Krutibaspur |
| 59. | Bijigoda | Bijigoda | Kaniha | Friday | G.P. Bijigoda |
| 60. | Seepur | Seepur | Kaniha | Sunday | G.P. Seepur |
| 61. | Talcher | Talcher | Talcher | Saturday | Talcher Municipality |
| 62. | Khamar | Khamar | Palalahara | Monday | G.P. Khamar |
| 63. | Maicharpur | – | Banarpal | Friday | R.M.C. Angul |
| 64. | Jarpada | – | Athamallik | Wednesday | G.P. Jarpada |

| | | | | | |
|---|---|---|---|---|---|
| | *District Dhenkanal* | | | | |
| 65. | Alsuahat | A lsuahat | Dhenkanal | Sunday | R.M.C. Dhenkanal |
| 66. | Pingua | Pingua | Gondia | Sunday | G.P. Pingua |
| 67. | Motanga | Motanga | Odapada | Wednesday | R.M.C. Dhenkanal |
| 68. | Alutoa | – | K. Nagar | Saturday | N.A.C. K. Nagar |
| 69. | Jirala | Jirala | Bhuban | Tuesday | Village Committee |
| 70. | Tipoli | – | Bhuban | Tuesday | G.P. S.P. Pur |
| 71. | Parajang | Parajang | — | Friday | G.P. Parajang |
| 72. | Dhalumunda | – | Parajang | Tuesday | Dhalumunda |
| 73. | Mahabir Road | – | K. Had | Sunday | Mahaibir Road |
| 74. | Ballav | Ballav | Gondia | Monday | G.P. Ballav |
| | *District Mayurbhanj* | | | | |
| 75. | Baliguda | Baliguda/Godiabandah | Badasahi | Saturday | R.M.C. Betanati |
| 76. | Kuliana | Kuliana | Kuliana | Sunday | R.M.C. Baripada |
| 77. | Saraskania | Saraskania | Saraskania | Saturday | R.M.C. Baripadaa |
| 78. | Hatabadra | Hatabadra | Kusumi | Wednesday | G.P. Hatabadra |
| 79. | Kundumundi | Kundumundi | Karanjia | Sunday | G.P. Patabil |
| 80. | Singda | Singda | Sukruli | Monday | Marketing Society |
| 81. | Jasipur | Jasipur | Jasipur | Tuesday | G.P. Jasipur |
| 82. | Angarpada | Angarpada | Raruan | Sunday | G.P. Angarpada |
| 83. | Bentkarpada | Bentkarpada | Takhurmunda | Saturday | G.P. Dikdar |
| 84. | Udala | Udala | Udala | Tue. / Fri. | N.A.C. Udala |
| | *District Keonjhar* | | | | |
| 85. | Harichandanpur | Harichandanpur | Harichandanpur | Friday | R.M.C. Keonjhar |
| 86. | Keonjhar | Keonjhar | Keonjhar | Sunday | Municipality |
| 87. | Banspal | Banspal | Banspal | Tuesday | R.M.C. Keonjhar |
| 88. | Champua | Champua | Champua | Friday | Dist. Marketing Soc. |
| 89. | Jhumpura | Jhumpura | Jhumpura | Wednesday | Dist. Marketing Soc. |

(Contd.)

TABLE 11.1 (Contd.)

| Sl. No. | Name of the Market | Location | Market | Market Day | Name of Org. Society |
|---|---|---|---|---|---|
| 90. | Salabani | Salabani | Anandapur | Wedensday | G.P. Salabani |
| | *District Nuapara* | | | | |
| 91. | Khariar | Khariar | Khariar | Friday | NA.C. Khariar |
| 92. | Khariar Road | Khariar Road | Khariar Road | Tuesday | R.M.C. Bhawanipatna |
| | *District Kalahandi* | | | | |
| 93. | Kutkela | Kutkela | Kutkela | Tuseday | G.P. Kutkela |
| 94. | Bhawanipatana | Bhawanipatana | Bhawanipatna | Tuesday | G.P. Kutkela |
| 95. | Balipada | Narla | Bhanpur / B.pada | Monday | – |
| 96. | Risida | Rarlamunda | Risida | Saturday | G.P. Risida |
| 97. | Dharmagarh | Dharmagarh | Dharmagarh | Friday | Marketing Society |
| 98. | Jardebra | Jardebra | Karlmunda | Saturday | R.M.C. Kesinga |
| 99. | Ranmal | Ranmal | Jaipatna | Sunday | H.I.M.S. Jiapatna |
| 100. | Tarsinga | Tarsinga | Karlamunda | Saturday | R.M.C. Kesinga |
| 101. | Parla | Behra | Dharmagarh | Sunday | R.M.C. Dharmagarh |
| 102. | Junagarh | Junagarh | Junagarh | Sunday | R.M.C. Junagarh |
| | *District kandhamal* | | | | |
| 103. | Baliguda | Baliguda | Baliguda | Saturday | R.M.C. Tikabali |
| 104. | Tikabali | Tikabali | Tikabali | Friday | R.M.C.Tikabali |
| 105. | Raikia | Raikia | Raikia | Monday | R.M.C. Tikabali |
| 106. | Tumudibandh | Tumudibandh | Tumudibandh | – | G.P. Tumudibandh |
| 107. | Palsaguda | Plasaguda | Kantamala | Saturday | G.P. Palsaguda |
| 108. | Dahya | Dahya | Boudh / Roxa | Saturday | G.P. Roxa |
| 109. | Naryaninagar | Naryaninagar | Telibandh/ Boudh | Tuesday | G.P. Telibandh |
| 110. | Tileswar | Tileswar | Harbhanga | – | G.P. Harbhanga |
| 111. | Bargoan | | -- | – | -- |

| | | | | | |
|---|---|---|---|---|---|
| | *District Koraput* | | | | |
| 112. | Pujariput | Pujariput | Nandpur | Thursday | R.M.C |
| 113. | Hatpada | Kunculli | Muliput/ Potangi | Friday | R.M.C. Kunduli |
| 114. | Kaswawalsa | Kaswawalsa | Naryanapatna | Thursday | R.M.C |
| 115. | Jeypore | Jeypore | Jeypore | Tuesday | R.M.C. |
| 116. | Kotpad | Kotpad | Kotpad | Tuesday | R.M.C. |
| 117. | Baligoan | Baligoan | Boipariguda | Saturday | R,M.C |
| 118. | Dasmanthpur | Dasmanthpur | Boipariguda | Wednesday | R.M.C. |
| 119. | Sonthaspur | Sonthaspur | Boriguma | Friday | R.M.C. |
| 120. | Kathargada | Kathargada | Boriguma | Tuesday | R.M.C. |
| | *District Malkangri* | | | | |
| 121. | Butapalli | Gidagida | Kosikorda | Friday | R.M.C |
| 122. | Bhaliguda | Bhaliguda | Melhies | Saturday | R.M.C. |
| 123. | Kalimela | Kalimela | Kalimela | Tuesday | R.M.C. |
| 124. | Jataguda | Sobranathpur | Kudumulugumma | Wednesday | R.M.C |
| 125. | Palam | Dosuguda | Kusukunda | Friday | R.M.C. |
| | *District Nowrangpur* | | | | |
| 126. | Katagumma | Katagumma | Kosachetra | Tuesday | R.M.C. |
| 127. | Dhadisahi | Dahadisahi | Chandalveli | Friday | R.M.C. Nowrangpur |
| 128. | Borigumma | Borigumma | Khatguma | Saturday | R.M.C. Nowrangpur |
| 129. | Nowrangpur | Nowrangpur | Nowrangpur | Monday | R.M.C. Nowrangpur |
| 130. | Umarkote | Umarkote | Umarkote | Sunday | R.M.C. Nowrangpur |
| | *District Bolangir* | | | | |
| 131. | Bolangir | Bolangir | Municipality | Sunday | R.M.C. Bolangir |
| 132. | Roth | Roth | Agalpur | Friday | G.P. Roth |
| 133. | Bhaliamunda | Badibhahal | Buisinga | Saturday | R.M.C. Bolangir |

NOTE: Markets closed during May to August.
SOURCE: DAH & VS Orissa.

TABLE 13.1: DAIRY CO-OPERATIVE SOCIETIES AND MILK PROCUREMENT IN ORISSA, 1999

| Sl. No. | Milk Union | Dairy Co-operative Societies (DCS) | | | Total Collection / Ave. per DCS lpd |
|---|---|---|---|---|---|
| | | Organised | Functional | Defunct | |
| A. | OMFED | | | | |
| 1. | Cuttack | 514 | 448 | 66 | 39505 / 88 |
| 2. | Puri | 342 | 273 | 69 | 12755 / 46 |
| 3. | Dhenknal | 148 | 90 | 58 | 3909 / 43 |
| 4. | Keonjhar | 116 | 24 | 92 | 1900 / 79 |
| 5. | Sambalpur | 219 | 219 | 00 | 13344 / 61 |
| | Total OMFED | 1339 | 1054 | 285 | 71413 / 68 |
| B. | ISPO | | | | |
| 6. | Ganjam | 128 | 83 | 45 | 5983 / 72 |
| C. | Dept. of AH | | | | |
| 7. | Balasore | 43 | 37 | 6 | 2553 / 69 |
| 8. | Bolangir | 83 | 23 | 60 | 1780 / 77 |
| 9. | Kalahandi | 74 | 28 | 46 | 863 / 31 |
| 10. | Nauapada | 41 | 22 | 19 | 1133 / 52 |
| 11. | Koraput | 42 | 16 | 26 | 1120 / 70 |
| 12. | Boudh | 42 | 18 | 24 | 582 / 32 |
| 13. | Sundargarh | 52 | 34 | 18 | 2838 / 83 |
| 14. | Mayurbhanj | 57 | 30 | 27 | 1437 / 48 |
| | Total AHD | 562 | 291 | 271 | 12306 / 42 |
| | Total Orissa | 1901 | 1345 | 556 | 89702 / 67 |

NOTES: 1. A: Unions affiliated to OMFED; B: Union promoted by ISPO; C: Unions Promoted by DAH & VS.

2. Average daily collection per DCS shown, presents the average for functional societies.

3. Many of the Milk Unions have collection areas spread over two or more districts and therefore Table 13.3 presents milk collection by the Organised Dairy Sector in the entire state.

TABLE 13.2: MILK PROCESSING / CHILLING PLANTS IN ORISSA, 1999 AND THEIR THROUGHPUT

| *Sl. No.* | *Milk Union* | *Dairy Plant* | *Capacity lpd* | *Chilling Plant* | *Capacity lpd* | **Average Throughout lpd* |
|---|---|---|---|---|---|---|
| 1. | Cuttack | No Dairy Plant | | 1. Tirtol | 20,000 | 39,505 |
| | | | | 2. Balikuda | 10,000 | |
| | | | | 3. Kendrapara | 4,000 | |
| | | | | 4. Banki | 1,800 | |
| | | | | 5. Adaspur | ** 4,000 | |
| | | | | 6. Athgad | ** 2,000 | |
| 2. | Dhenknal | Paikadahkora | 10,000 | 1. Angul | 2,000 | 3,909 |
| 3. | Keonjhar | Silisuan | 10,000 | 1. Anandpur | 4,000 | 1,900 |
| | | | | 2. Telkoi | **2000 | |
| 4. | Mayurbhanj | | | 1. Baripada | 2,000 | 1,437 |
| | | | | 2. Udala | 4,000 | |
| 5. | Koraput | | | 1. Ekamba | ** 2,000 | 1,120 |
| 6 | Samaleswari | Sambalpur | 10,000 | 1. Bargarh | 8,000 | 13,344 |
| | | | | 2. Buxma | 800 | |
| 7. | Ganjam Gajpati | Berhampur | 10,000 | 1. Aska | 4,000 | 5,983 |
| | | | | 2. Gajpati | 4,000 | |
| 8. | Puri | Bhubaneswar | 75,000 | 1. Nayagarh | 4,000 | 12,755 |
| | | | | 2. Tangi | 2,000 | |
| | | | | 3. Nimapara | 20,000 | |
| 9. | Balasore | Remuna | 4,000 | 1. Baliapal | 4,000 | 2,553 |
| 10. | Sundargarh | Rourkela Dairy | 30,000 | 1. Sundargarh | 2,000 | 2,838 |
| 11. | Kalahandi | Bhawanipatna | 4,000 | 1. Bhawanipatna | 10,000 | 863 |
| 12. | Boudh | | | 1. Charichak | 4,000 | 582 |
| 13. | Kandhamal | | | 1. Phulbani | 4,000 | Na |
| 14. | Bolangir | Bolangir | 4,000 | 1. Saintala | 4,000 | 1,780 |
| 15. | Rayagada | Rayagada | 4,000 | | | 1,120 |
| 16. | Nawarangpur | | | 1. Nawrangpur | 4,000 | Na |
| 17. | Jajpur | | NA | | NA | Na |
| 18. | Bhadrak | | NA | | 4,000 | Na |
| 19. | Malkangri | | NA | | NA | Na |
| 20. | Nawapara | | NA | | 4,000 | 1,133 |
| 21. | Subarnapur | | NA | | 4,000 | |
| | Total | | 1,61,000 | | 1,44,600 | 90,882 |

NOTES: * Throughput exhibited is the average for three years 1996-9 from their respective milk sheds.

** These plants are now defunct.

TABLE 13.3: MILK PROCUREMENT: SHARE OF THE ORGANISED SECTOR, 2008

| *Sl. No.* | *Reorganised Milk Sheds* | *Marketable supply lpd* | *Average Procurement lpd* | *Percent Milk Supply* |
|---|---|---|---|---|
| 1. | Cuttack | 267245 | | |
| | Jagatsinghpur | 172653 | | |
| | Kendrapara | 67499 | | |
| | | 507397 | 125000 | 24.63 |
| 2. | Puri | 256093 | | |
| | Khurda | 166309 | | |
| | Nayagargh | 45480 | | |
| | | 467882 | 60000 | 12.82 |
| 3. | Balasore | 157531 | | |
| | Bhadrak | 62772 | | |
| | Mayurbhanj | 89137 | | |
| | | 309440 | 20000 | 6.46 |
| 4. | Ganjam | 117457 | | |
| | Gajpati | 22004 | | |
| | | 139463 | 20000 | 14.34 |
| 5. | Sambalpur | 56487 | | |
| | Subranapur | 36540 | | |
| | Bargarh | 137756 | | |
| | | 230783 | 35000 | 15.16 |
| 6. | Kalahandi | 69763 | | |
| | Kandhamal | 34020 | | |
| | Bolangir | 85676 | | |
| | Boudh | 24962 | | |
| | Nauapara | 25143 | | |
| | | 239564 | 15000 | 6.26 |
| 7. | Dhenkanal | 81165 | | |
| | Angul | 88122 | | |
| | | 169237 | 15000 | 8.86 |
| 8. | Keonjhar | 102125 | | |
| | Jajpur | 57832 | | |
| | | 159957 | 10000 | 6.25 |
| 9. | Koraput | 46767 | | |
| | Nawrangpur | 40386 | | |
| | Rayagada | 49146 | | |
| | Malkangiri | 26026 | | |
| | | 162325 | 9000 | 6.1 |
| 10. | Sundargarh | 86425 | | |
| | Deogarh | 17045 | | |
| | Jharsugada | 25593 | | |
| | | 129063 | 15000 | 11.62 |
| | Total | 2502233 | 324000 | |

NOTE: Reorganisation of the milk sheds in Orissa is discussed later in this study, as a part of the supply management package recommended.

TABLE 13.4: INFRASTRUCTURE FOR MILK PROCESSING IN ORISSA BY 2008

| *Sl. No.* | *Reorganised Milk Shed* | *Marketable Supply lpd* | *Existing Processing Plants Capacity lpd* | | *Recommended Processing Plants Capacity lpd* | |
|---|---|---|---|---|---|---|
| | | | *Dairy* | *Chilling* | *Dairy* | *Chilling* |
| 1. | Cuttack | 267245 | | 24000 | 1,00,000 | |
| | Jagatsinghpur | 172653 | | 13800 | | |
| | Kendrapara | 67499 | | 4000 | | |
| | | 507397 | | 41800 | 1,00,000 | 110000 |
| 2. | Puri | 256093 | | | | |
| | Khurda | 166309 | 75,000 | | 1,00,000 | |
| | Nayagargh | 45480 | | | | |
| | | 467882 | 75000 | 26000 | 1,00,000 | 110000 |
| 3. | Balasore | 157531 | 4000 | 4000 | 30,000 | |
| | Bhadrak | 62772 | | 4000 | | |
| | Mayurbhanj | 89137 | | 6000 | | |
| | | 309440 | 4000 | 14000 | 30,000 | 33000 |
| 4. | Ganjam | 117457 | 10,000 | 4000 | 30,000 | |
| | Gajpati | 22004 | | 4000 | | |
| | | 139461 | 10000 | 8000 | 30,000 | 33000 |
| 5. | Sambalpur | 56487 | 10,000 | | 60,000 | |
| | Subranapur | 36540 | | 4000 | | |
| | Bargarh | 137756 | | 8000 | | |
| | | 230783 | 10000 | 12000 | 60,000 | 66000 |
| 6. | Kalahandi | 69763 | 4000 | 10000 | 20,000 | |
| | Kandhamal | 34020 | | 4000 | | |
| | Bolangir | 85676 | 4000 | 4000 | | |
| | Boudh | 24962 | | 4000 | | |
| | Nauapara | 25143 | | 4000 | | |
| | | 239564 | 8000 | 26000 | 20,000 | 26000 |
| 7. | Dhenkanal | 81165 | 10,000 | | 20,000 | |
| | Angul | 88122 | | | | |
| | | 169237 | 10000 | 2000 | 20,000 | 22000 |
| 8. | Keonjhar | 102125 | 10,000 | 6000 | 20,000 | |
| | Jajpur | 57832 | | | | |
| | | 159957 | 10000 | 6000 | 20,000 | 22000 |
| 9. | Koraput | 46767 | | 2000 | 10,000 | |
| | Nawrangpur | 40386 | | 4000 | | |
| | Rayagada | 49146 | 4000 | | | |
| | Malkangiri | 26026 | | | | |
| | | 162325 | 4000 | 6000 | 10,000 | 11000 |
| 10. | Sundargarh | 86425 | 30,000 | 2000 | 60,000 | |
| | Deogarh | 17045 | | | | |
| | Jharsugada | 25593 | | 800 | | |
| | | 129063 | 30000 | 2800 | 60,000 | 66000 |
| | | 2502233 | 161000 | 144600 | 4,50,000 | 502000 |

NOTES: 1. Locations of existing Dairy Plants and Chilling Plants are exhibited in Table 13.2.

2. Reorganisation of the milk sheds is proposed based on contiguity, supply volumes and supply logistics.

EXHIBIT G.1: STATE PROFILE

| *General Particulars 2001* | | *Livestock Population & Density 2001* | |
|---|---|---|---|
| Area (in '000 sq. km) | 155 | Livestock Population in millions | 23.33 |
| Sub Divisions | 58 | Poultry Population in millions | 18.43 |
| Tahsils | 171 | Density of Population per km$^2$ | |
| Blocks | 314 | Livestock | 150 |
| Cities & Towns | 138 | Cattle | 89 |
| *Gram Panchayats* | 5263 | Buffalo | 9 |
| Villages | 51349 | Sheep | 11 |
| % of Forest Area | 36.7 | Goat | 37 |
| % of Net Area Sown | 40.7 | Pig | 4 |
| % of Pasture | 4.09 | Poultry | 118 |
| Households Keeping Livestock & Poultry (in '000)* | | *Production and Yield 2001* | |
| Bovines | 3293 | Milk Production ('000 mt) | 847.78 |
| Sheep | 577 | Meat Production ('000 mt) | 43 |
| Goat | 1399 | Egg Production in millions | 822.10 |
| Pigs | 223 | Per capita availability of | |
| Poultry | 2241 | Milk per day in gms. | 62 |
| *Demographic Socio-Economic Particulars Census 2001* | | Per capital availability of Meat per annum in gms | 1157 |
| Population in millions | | Per capital availability of Eggs per annum in nos. | 22 |
| Total Population | 36.70 | Ave. Yield of Milk/day | |
| Population Male | 18.61 | in kg in Milk animals | |
| Population Female | 18.09 | Indigenous Cows | 0.505 |
| Population Rural | 31.21 | Crossbred | 3.925 |
| Population Urban | 5.49 | Buffalo | 1.845 |
| Decennial growth rate per cent | 15.91 | Ave. Yield of Eggs/annum | |
| Density of Population per km$^2$ | 236 | *Desi* Fowls | 102 |
| % of Cultivators | 44.31 | Improved Fowls | 157 |
| % Agricultural Labourers | 28.68 | Share in Meat prod. in per cent*** | |
| % of SC Population** | 16 | Bovines | 4 |
| % of ST Population** | 22 | Sheep | 23 |
| Overall Literacy per cent | 54.63 | Goat | 65 |
| Literacy Male per cent | 75.95 | Pig | 8 |
| Literacy Female per cent | 50.97 | | |
| *Veterinary Institutions 2001* | | | |
| Veterinary Hospitals & Dispensaries | 541 | | |
| Livestock Aid Centres | 2939 | | |
| Artificial Insemination Centres | 1510 | | |

NOTES: *Figure pertains to year 1995-6, **Census year 1991; and ***pertains to year 1998-9.

TABLE G.2: HUMAN AND LIVESTOCK POPULATION IN DIFFERENT YEARS IN ORISSA

| *Census Year* | *Human population million* | *Growth per cent* | *Density per km. number* | *Livestock Population million* | *Growth per cent* | *Density per km. number* | *Poultry population million* | *Growth per cent* | *Density per km. number* |
|---|---|---|---|---|---|---|---|---|---|
| 1951 | 14.6 | – | 94 | 12.12 | 78.00 | 4.99 | 32.00 | – | – |
| 1961 | 17.5 | 19.82 | 112 | 14.53 | 19.88 | 93.00 | 6.54 | 31.06 | 42 |
| 1971 | 21.9 | 25.05 | 141 | 17.56 | 20.85 | 113.00 | 8.49 | 29.81 | 55 |
| 1981 | 26.4 | 20.17 | 170 | 22.23 | 26.59 | 143.00 | 10.55 | 24.26 | 68 |
| 1991 | 31.7 | 20.06 | 204 | 22.98 | 3.37 | 148.00 | 16.01 | 51.75 | 103 |
| 2001 | 36.7 | 15.91 | 236 | 23.33 | 1.52 | 150.00 | 18.43 | 15.11 | 118 |

SOURCES: Census of India, Series 22, Orissa, Integrated Sample Survey, Directorate of Animal Resource Development,1995-6 and Livestock Census, 2001, Directorate of Animal Resource Development (Provisional data). Pertains to year 1956, 1972 and 1982 respectively.

TABLE G.3: ALL INDIA, ORISSA LIVESTOCK AND POULTRY POPULATION IN DIFFERENT CENSUS YEARS

| Sl. No. | Species | 1956 | 1961 | 1966 | 1972 | 1977 | 1982 | 1987 | 1992 | 2001 |
|---|---|---|---|---|---|---|---|---|---|---|
| | All India (no. in mln) | | | | | | | | | |
| 1. | Cattle | 156.7 | 175.7 | 176.2 | 178.3 | 180.8 | 192.45 | 199.69 | 204.53 | |
| 2. | Buffalo | 44.9 | 51.2 | 53.0 | 57.4 | 62.0 | 69.78 | 75.97 | 83.50 | |
| 3. | Sheep | 39.3 | 40.2 | 42.0 | 40.0 | 41.0 | 48.76 | 45.70 | 50.80 | |
| 4. | Goat | 55.4 | 60.9 | 64.6 | 67.5 | 75.6 | 95.25 | 110.21 | 115.28 | |
| 5. | Pig | 4.9 | 5.2 | 5.0 | 6.9 | 7.6 | 10.07 | 10.62 | 12.78 | |
| 6. | Total Livestock | 306.6 | 335.4 | 344.1 | 353.4 | 369.0 | 419.59 | 445.28 | 470.14 | |
| 7. | Poultry | 94.8 | 114.2 | 115.4 | 138.5 | 159.2 | 207.74 | 275.32 | 307.07 | |
| | Orissa (no. in '000) | | | | | | | | | |
| 1. | Cattle | 8220 | 9810 | 10629 | 11496 | 12121 | 12930 | 13577 | 14766 | 13810 |
| 2. | Buffalo | 888 | 1075 | 1269 | 1399 | 1350 | 1333 | 1509 | 1652 | 1388 |
| 3. | Sheep | 1117 | 994 | 1182 | 1369 | 1432 | 1990 | 1841 | 1865 | 1765 |
| 4. | Goat | 1695 | 2382 | 3082 | 2884 | 3416 | 4931 | 4804 | 5412 | 5772 |
| 5. | Pig | 129 | 217 | 180 | 387 | 295 | 410 | 590 | 572 | 601 |
| 6. | Total Livestock | 12128 | 14536 | 16122 | 17565 | 186266 | 22232 | 22986 | 25020 | 23336 |
| 7. | Poultry | 4991 | 6540 | 7698 | 8492 | 9490 | 10555 | 12601 | 16008 | 18434 |

SOURCES: 1. Integrated Sample Survey, 1995-6.
2. Livestock Census, 2001, Directorate of Animal Resource Development (Provisional data).

TABLE G.4: LIVESTOCK SECTOR OUTPUT VALUE 1999-2000 AT CURRENT PRICES

| Sl. No. | Output | Quantity | Unit Price in Rs. | Value Million Rs. | Per cent |
|---|---|---|---|---|---|
| 1. | Milk | 847.78 (000 mt) | 13.00 | 11021.14 | 47.13 |
| 2. | Meat | 43000 (000 mt) | 80.00 | 2925.60 | 12.51 |
| 3. | Work Output | 194.4 kwh | 3.00 | 582.00 | 2.49 |
| 4. | Eggs | 822.21 (mln) | 1.45 | 1192.20 | 5.10 |
| 5. | Poultry Meat | 24478.9 mt | 50.00 | 1468.80 | 6.28 |
| 6. | Hide & Skin | 3. 00 mln nos. | 500.00 large animal | 8.25 | 0.80 |
| | | | 60.00 for small animal | 179.01 | |
| 7. | Dung / Manure | 20.00 mln mt | 200.00 per mt | 4000.00 | 17.10 |
| 8. | Wool / Hair | 0.5 mln mt | 2500.00 mt | 5.00 | 0.00 |
| 9. | Bone Offal | 1000 mt | 2000.00 per mt | 2000. 00 | 8.55 |
| | Total | | | 23381.99 | 100 |

SOURCES: Steering Committee (LSR) Report 1999; Integrated Sample Survey, AHD, 1998-9; Economic Survey 2001-2.

TABLE G.5: LEVELS OF PRODUCTIVITY: CATTLE AND BUFFALO 1998-9 (PER DAY / PER YEAR)

| Sl. No. | Animal Category | Adult breedable female | Milk production per day | Total milk production / day & / year in kg / mt. |
|---|---|---|---|---|
| 1a. | Local Cattle | 3.82 million | 227 gm | 867140 / 316806.1 |
| 1b. | Local Cattle | 1.72 million in milk | 505 gm | 868600 / 317039.0 |
| 2a. | Crossbred Cattle | 0.32 million | 2.355 kg | 753600 / 275064.0 |
| 2b. | Crossbred Cattle | 0.20 million in milk | 3.925 kg | 785000 / 286525.0 |
| 3a. | Buffalo | 0.40 million | 960 gm | 384000 / 140160.0 |
| 3b. | Buffalo | 0.21 million in milk | 1.845 kg | 387450 / 139959.2 |

SOURCE: Integrated Sample Survey 1998–9, Directorate of Animal Resource Development.

TABLE G.6: DISTRICT WISE AVERAGE PRODUCTIVITY OF MILKING ANIMALS AND THE LAYER BIRDS

| *Sl. No.* | *District* | *Milk Production per day per animal in milk in kg.* | | | *Egg production per Layer per year* | |
|---|---|---|---|---|---|---|
| | | *Indigenous* | *Crossbred* | *Buffalo* | *Desi Fowl* | *Improved Fowl* |
| 1. | Angul | 0.486 | 3.006 | 1.977 | 110 | 158 |
| 2. | Balasore | 0.484 | 2.211 | 2.411 | 127 | 156 |
| 3. | Bargarh | 0.706 | 4.668 | 1.686 | 113 | 153 |
| 4. | Bhadrak | 0.478 | 2.917 | 1.41 | 115 | 150 |
| 5. | Bolangir | 0.454 | 2.395 | 1.529 | 119 | 154 |
| 6. | Boudh | 0.421 | 2.079 | 2.218 | 92 | 165 |
| 7. | Cuttack | 0.833 | 5.179 | 2.752 | 123 | 191 |
| 8. | Deogarh | 0.345 | 2.346 | 1.535 | 99 | 0 |
| 9. | Dhenkanal | 0.538 | 3.177 | 1.972 | 104 | 138 |
| 10. | Gajapati | 0.393 | 2.265 | 1.547 | 99 | 166 |
| 11. | Ganjam | 0.506 | 4.005 | 2.38 | 92 | 125 |
| 12. | Jagatsinghpur | 0.646 | 4.541 | 1.948 | 133 | 156 |
| 13. | Jajpur | 0.418 | 3.627 | 2.826 | 95 | 138 |
| 14. | Jharsuguda | 0.369 | 3.025 | 1.333 | 103 | 140 |
| 15. | Kalahandi | 0.408 | 2.316 | 1.446 | 95 | 127 |
| 16. | Kendrapada | 0.512 | 3.177 | 1.972 | 129 | 156 |
| 17. | Keonjhar | 0.465 | 3.058 | 1.553 | 98 | 145 |
| 18. | Khurda | 0.691 | 4.900 | 2.032 | 105 | 159 |
| 19. | Koraput | 0.408 | 2.138 | 1.501 | 89 | 117 |
| 20. | Malkangiri | 0.447 | 1.859 | 1.761 | 96 | 0 |
| 21. | Mayurbhanj | 0.466 | 2.240 | 1.933 | 94 | 142 |
| 22. | Nawapara | 0.363 | 1.804 | 1.757 | 89 | 0 |
| 23. | Nawarangpur | 0.365 | 2.138 | 1.372 | 89 | 127 |
| 24. | Nayagarh | 0.387 | 2.723 | 1.768 | 99 | 151 |
| 25. | Phulbani | 0.410 | 1.749 | 1.669 | 90 | 147 |
| 26. | Puri | 0.634 | 4.892 | 2.277 | 105 | 154 |
| 27. | Rayagada | 0.456 | 2.051 | 1.385 | 100 | 149 |
| 28. | Sambalpur | 0.669 | 4.356 | 1.869 | 112 | 149 |
| 29. | Subarnapur | 0.417 | 2.037 | 1.583 | 92 | 135 |
| 30. | Sundargarh | 0.454 | 3.329 | 3.063 | 102 | 157 |
| | State | 0.505 | 3.925 | 1.345 | 102 | 157 |

SOURCE: Complied from the Integrated Sample Survey, 1998–9, Directorate of Animal Husbandry & Veterinary Services.

TABLE G.7: DISTRICT WISE RANKING OF ANIMAL RESOURCES

| Sl. No. | District | According to Livestock Population | | | | | | According to Production | | |
|---|---|---|---|---|---|---|---|---|---|---|
| | | C | B | S | G | Pig | P | Milk | Meat | Egg |
| 1. | Angul | 8 | 10 | 12 | 8 | 23 | 22 | 11 | 15 | 23 |
| 2. | Balassore | 2 | 30 | 27 | 4 | 9 | 6 | 8 | 5 | 4 |
| 3. | Bargarh | 11 | 17 | 13 | 14 | 14 | 17 | 6 | 8 | 17 |
| 4. | Bhadrak | 9 | 26 | 28 | 13 | 19 | 16 | 19 | 11 | 12 |
| 5. | Bolangir | 10 | 4 | 5 | 7 | 24 | 7 | 10 | 14 | 6 |
| 6. | Boudh | 27 | 12 | 9 | 24 | 28 | 28 | 26 | 23 | 29 |
| 7. | Cuttack | 7 | 11 | 7 | 5 | 22 | 14 | 1 | 1 | 8 |
| 8. | Deogarh | 29 | 28 | 30 | 29 | 20 | 26 | 30 | 30 | 27 |
| 9. | Dhenkanal | 12 | 5 | 18 | 22 | 27 | 18 | 7 | 19 | 21 |
| 10. | Gajpati | 26 | 22 | 25 | 15 | 11 | 19 | 17 | 29 | 19 |
| 11. | Ganjam | 3 | 1 | 2 | 10 | 12 | 2 | 3 | 3 | 1 |
| 12. | Jagatsinghpur | 23 | 20 | 22 | 20 | 21 | 23 | 5 | 17 | 22 |
| 13. | Jajpur | 6 | 27 | 19 | 6 | 17 | 12 | 16 | 18 | 11 |
| 14. | Jharsuguda | 30 | 29 | 26 | 30 | 18 | 27 | 29 | 25 | 30 |
| 15. | Kalahandi | 13 | 6 | 6 | 9 | 15 | 8 | 13 | 16 | 10 |
| 16. | Kendarapara | 24 | 8 | 16 | 21 | 13 | 20 | 15 | 10 | 20 |
| 17. | Keonjhar | 5 | 13 | 3 | 3 | 8 | 5 | 12 | 7 | 5 |
| 18. | Khurda | 16 | 24 | 14 | 26 | 16 | 4 | 4 | 9 | 2 |
| 19. | Koraput | 14 | 2 | 4 | 12 | 5 | 9 | 20 | 12 | 9 |
| 20. | Malkangiri | 18 | 15 | 23 | 16 | 4 | 11 | 25 | 28 | 16 |
| 21. | Mayurbhanja | 1 | 25 | 1 | 1 | 2 | 1 | 14 | 4 | 3 |
| 22. | Nawapara | 28 | 16 | 21 | 27 | 26 | 25 | 24 | 26 | 25 |
| 23. | Nawarangapur | 19 | 9 | 8 | 23 | 3 | 10 | 23 | 20 | 14 |
| 24. | Nayagarh | 21 | 18 | 20 | 25 | 30 | 29 | 21 | 22 | 26 |

(Contd.)

TABLE G.7 (Contd.)

| Sl. No. | District | According to Livestock Population | | | | | | According to Production | | |
|---|---|---|---|---|---|---|---|---|---|---|
| | | *C* | *B* | *S* | *G* | *Pig* | *P* | *Milk* | *Meat* | *Egg* |
| 25. | Phulbani | 22 | 7 | 29 | 11 | 6 | 13 | 22 | 24 | 15 |
| 26. | Puri | 15 | 21 | 10 | 19 | 25 | 24 | 2 | 13 | 24 |
| 27. | Rayagada | 20 | 3 | 15 | 17 | 7 | 15 | 18 | 21 | 13 |
| 28. | Sambalpur | 17 | 19 | 24 | 15 | 10 | 21 | 17 | 6 | 18 |
| 29. | Subarnapur | 25 | 23 | 17 | 8 | 29 | 30 | 28 | 27 | 28 |
| 30. | Sundargarh | 4 | 14 | 11 | 2 | 1 | 3 | 9 | 2 | 7 |

NOTES: Ranks 1 to 5 have been highlighted.
C = Cattle, B = Buffalo, S = Sheep, G = Goat, P = Poultry.

SOURCE: Livestock Census Orissa, 2001, DAH & VS (Provisional data).

TABLE G.8: DETAILS OF CATTLE & BUFFALO ACCORDING TO CENSUS 2001

| Sl. No. | Species | Crossbred | Exotic | Indigenous |
|---|---|---|---|---|
| | *Cattle—Male* | | | |
| 1. | Under 1 year | 92388 | 3954 | 768428 |
| 2. | 1 to 2½ years (for indigenous up to 3 years) | 61987 | 2295 | 1020186 |
| 3. | For breeding only | 2949 | 256 | 54503 |
| 4. | For work only | 86111 | 4689 | 5089413 |
| 5. | For both breeding & work | 1057 | 238 | 62262 |
| 6. | Neither for breeding nor work | 778 | 25 | 22341 |
| | Total | 245270 | 11458 | 6997133 |
| | *Cattle—Female* | | | |
| 1. | Under 1 year | 135315 | 6607 | 998212 |
| 2. | 1 to 2½ years (for indigenous up to 3 years) | 126127 | 6967 | 1215191 |
| 3. | In milk | 223640 | 10417 | 1705325 |
| 4. | Dry | 113498 | 6281 | 1693411 |
| 5. | Not calved once | 22869 | 743 | 254991 |
| 6. | Others | 2896 | 77 | 14006 |
| | Total | 624345 | 31092 | 5881136 |
| | *Buffalo—Male* | *Improved* | | *Indigenous* |
| 1. | Under 1 year | 2107 | | 80736 |
| 2. | 1 to 3 years | 1302 | | 88415 |
| 3. | For breeding only | 519 | | 9308 |
| 4. | For work only | 2347 | | 541427 |
| 5. | For both breeding & work only | 191 | | 16186 |
| 6. | Neither for breeding nor work | 224 | | 5417 |
| | Total | 6690 | | 741489 |
| | *Buffalo—Female* | | | |
| 1. | Under 1 year | 4382 | | 113586 |
| 2. | 1 to 3 years | 4154 | | 132361 |
| 3. | In milk | 9757 | | 196274 |
| 4. | Dry | 5742 | | 143244 |
| 5. | Not calved even once | 519 | | 26281 |
| 6. | Others | 15 | | 3530 |
| | Total | 24569 | | 615376 |

SOURCE: Livestock Census, 2001, DAH & VS (Provisional data).

TABLE G.9: MEAT PRODUCTION IN ORISSA (MT)

| *Year* | *Sheep* | *Goat* | *Pig* | *Cattle & Buffalo* | *Total* |
|---|---|---|---|---|---|
| 1980-1 | 4750 | 6382 | 80 | 5630 | 16843 |
| 1981-2 | 5047 | 7395 | 79 | 6123 | 18645 |
| 1982-3 | 5327 | 7549 | 87 | 6681 | 19645 |
| 1983-4 | 6088 | 8409 | 94 | 7147 | 21882 |
| 1984-5 | 5700 | 6940 | 167 | 7932 | 20740 |
| 1985-6 | 4766 | 7674 | 250 | 8597 | 21286 |
| 1986-7 | 5561 | 7727 | 409 | 9627 | 23323 |
| 1987-8 | 5595 | 8097 | 465 | 7877 | 22033 |
| 1988-9 | 6018 | 8426 | 825 | 5955 | 21224 |
| 1989-90 | 6398 | 8622 | 1034 | 8664 | 24718 |
| | | | | **Cattle* | |
| 1990-1 | 6960 | 8848 | 1253 | 8991 | 26053 |
| 1991-2 | 9148 | 10611 | 2445 | 4792 | 27197 |
| 1992-3 | 10026 | 11479 | 2523 | 5400 | 29428 |
| 1993-4 | 11443 | 11763 | 2525 | 2305 | 28036 |
| 1994-5 | 12027 | 12361 | 2536 | 2294 | 29218 |
| 1995-6 | 12427 | 12840 | 2434 | 3867 | 31568 |
| 1998-9 | 8582 | 24654 | 3201 | 1691 | 38129 |

NOTE: * Slaughter of buffaloes was discontinued from 1989-90.

SOURCES: 1. Statistical Outline of Orissa 1997.
2. Statistical Hand Book 1994, DAH &VS, Orissa.

TABLE G.10: LIST OF SPECIALISTS INVOLVED IN THE LIVESTOCK SECTOR REVIEW, 1998–9

*Steering Committee of Livestock Sector Review*

| | |
|---|---|
| Sri. M.M. Mohanty | Ex-Principal Secretary, FARD - Chairman |
| Dr. S.K. Ray | Ex-Director, DAH & VS and Retd. Prof. Medicine, OVC-Member Convenor |
| Sri. S.C. Mohapatra | Managing Director, OMFED |
| Dr. S.C. Mishra | Dean, Orissa Veterinary College |
| Mr. Jan Morrenhof | Chief Project Adviser, ISPO |
| Dr. B. Bhuyan | Retd. Prof. & Head Agril. Economics, OUAT |
| Dr. M.P.G. Kurup | Former Board Member & Retd. Exe. Director NDDB - Coordinating Consultant - Livestock Sector Review |
| Dr. B.N. Mohanty | Retd. Dean, Orissa Veterinary College, Liaison Consultant LSR |

*Specialists consultants of study teams in situation analysis of Livestock Sector Review*

| | |
|---|---|
| Dr. B. Bhuyan<br>Retd. Prof. & Head Agril. Economics, OUAT | Micro-economics aspects of ruminant production |
| Dr. Trilochan Pathy<br>Retd. Jt. Director, Animal Husbandry Department | Institutional issues |
| Prof. B.N. Patro<br>Head ABG, OVC<br><br>Dr. G.K. Padhi<br>GM, MPI, OMFED<br><br>Dr. L.D. Mohanty<br>Retd. Addl. Director, AHD<br><br>Dr. P.C. Mishra<br>Retd. Deputy Director, AHD | Milk Group |
| Dr. J.B. Nayak<br>Retd. Prof. Head D. Animal Prod., OVC<br><br>Dr. A. Mohanty<br>Assoc. Prof. Animal Production, OVC<br><br>Dr. D. Naik<br>Director (PM&E), OUAT | Draught Animal |
| Dr. B.C. Patnaik<br>Retd. Director, Consultant Sheep and Wool Research Institution, Rajasthan<br><br>Dr. N.K. Parida<br>Retd. Addl. Director, AHD | Small ruminants production and Meat subsector in Orissa |

| Specialists | Area |
|---|---|
| Dr. G. Sahoo<br>Prof. & Head, Animal Production, OVC<br>Dr. P.K. Mohapatra<br>Retd. Project Director, ISPO | Pig and Swine Husbandry |
| Dr. S.C. Mohapatra<br>Retd. Director, Central Avian Research Institute, Izatnagar<br>Dr. S.C. Mishra<br>Senior Poultry Scientist, ICAR Poultry Project and Prof. & Head, Poultry Science | Poultry |
| Dr. M.P.G. Kurup<br>Former Board Member & Retd. Exe. Director, NDDB - Coordinating Consultant - Livestock Sector Review<br>Dr. S.P. Mittal<br>Former Sr. Executive, NDDB<br>Dr. P.K. Harichandan<br>Retd. Deputy Director, AHD<br>Dr. L.D. Mohanty<br>Retd. Addl. Director, AHD<br>Dr. B.C. Patnaik<br>Retd. Director, CSRI | Breeding of Livestock and Artificial Insemination |
| Dr. S.B. Tripathy<br>Retd. Prof. & Head Medicine OVC<br>Dr. D.N. Mohanty<br>Retd. Deputy Director, AHD | Animal Health |
| Dr. B.K. Sahu<br>Prof. & Head, Animal Nutrition, OVC<br>Sri. R.K. Nanda<br>Retd. Deputy Director, AHD | Animal Feed and Fodder |
| Dr. S.P. Mittal<br>Former Sr. Executive, NDDB<br>Dr. A.J. John<br>Livestock Consultant<br>Dr. P.K. Harichandan<br>Retd. Deputy Director, AHD<br>Dr. D.N. Mohanty<br>Retd. Deputy Director, AHD | Livestock Sector Review Field Study |
| Dr. (Ms) Sagari Ramdas, Anthra<br>Mr. Kurian Katticaran<br>Consultant, Andhra Pradesh<br>Dr. G.K. Tripathy<br>Lecturer, VOTI, Bhubaneswar | Gender Study, ISPO—Role of Women in Animal Husbandry in Orissa |

# Index